ALAN REDPATH

THE MAKING OF A MAN OF GOD

STUDIES IN THE LIFE OF DAVID

Fleming H. Revell
A Division of Baker Book House Co
Grand Rapids, Michigan 49516

Copyright © 1962 by Fleming H. Revell
a division of Baker Book House Company
P.O. Box 6287, Grand Rapids, MI 49516-6287

Library of Congress Catalog Card Number: 62-10731

ISBN 0-8007-5516-2

November 1993

Printed in the United States of America

Dedicated
to
the beloved President, Faculty and Student Body
of
Columbia Bible College, Columbia, South Carolina
whose fellowship in recent years has been such an
inspiration to me personally

The Alan Redpath Library

The Bible Speaks to Our Times
Blessings out of Buffetings
Faith for the Times
Law and Liberty
The Making of a Man of God
The Royal Route to Heaven
Victorious Christian Faith
Victorious Christian Living
Victorious Christian Service
Victorious Praying

FOREWORD

THE BIBLE NEVER flatters its heroes. It tells us the truth about each one of them in order that against the background of human breakdown and failure we may magnify the grace of God and recognize that it is the delight of the Spirit of God to work upon the platform of human impossibilities. As we consider the record of Bible characters, how often we find ourselves looking into a mirror. We are humiliated by the reminder of how many times we have failed. Great has been our stubbornness but greater still has been His faithfulness. Nowhere is this more true than in the story of the life of David, which is the subject of these chapters.

I can but testify to the fact that my own heart has been searched to its depths as I have been brought face to face with my own frailty and the abundant mercy of my Saviour. It is my earnest prayer that something of the impact which the Holy Spirit made upon my own life in the preparing of this book might be made upon yours in the reading of it.

The conversion of a soul is the miracle of a moment, the manufacture of a saint is the task of a lifetime. It is the matchless marvel of the Gospel of our Lord Jesus Christ to take a life from the dunghill and set it among princes—to replace the bias of degeneration by the bias of regeneration, and to cause a man who has sunk to the depths to cry to God, "Create in me a clean heart, O God; and renew a right spirit within me. . . . Then will I teach transgressors thy ways; and sinners shall be converted unto thee."

May the Lord be graciously pleased to use these pages, inadequate though they be, to help many into a deeper understanding of His making of a man of God.

I want to express my deepest appreciation to Miss Arline Harris for her skillful preparation of manuscript and to my wife for her patience in transcription.

ALAN REDPATH, Moody Church
Chicago, Illinois

CONTENTS

PART II   THE MAN OF GOD: LESSONS IN LEADERSHIP

PART I

The Man of God:

Tested in Training

And the Lord said unto Samuel, How long wilt thou mourn for Saul, seeing I have rejected him from reigning over Israel? fill thine horn with oil, and go, I will send thee to Jesse the Bethlehemite: for I have provided me a king among his sons.

And Samuel said, How can I go? if Saul hear it, he will kill me. And the Lord said, Take an heifer with thee, and say, I am come to sacrifice to the Lord. And call Jesse to the sacrifice, and I will shew thee what thou shalt do: and thou shalt anoint unto me him whom I name unto thee.

And Samuel did that which the Lord spake, and came to Bethlehem. . . . he looked on Eliab, and said, Surely the Lord's anointed is before him.

But the Lord said unto Samuel, Look not on his countenance, or on the height of his stature; because I have refused him: for the Lord seeth not as man seeth; for man looketh on the outward appearance, but the Lord looketh on the heart. . . .

Again, Jesse made seven of his sons to pass before Samuel. And Samuel said unto Jesse, the Lord hath not chosen these. . . . Are here all thy children? And he said, There remaineth yet the youngest, and, behold, he keepeth the sheep. . . .

Now he was ruddy, and withal of a beautiful countenance, and goodly to look to. And the Lord said, Arise, anoint him: for this is he. Then Samuel took the horn of oil, and anointed him in the midst of his brethren: and the Spirit of the Lord came upon David from that day forward. . . .

I SAMUEL 16:1-13

CHAPTER 1

THE BASIS OF GOD'S CHOICE

(I Samuel 16:1-13)

THESE ARE DAYS of immense significance to the Christian church. Any of us with discernment cannot but believe the truth of the Word of God, that the Lord Jesus Christ is coming back soon to take His people home and thereafter to establish His kingdom. Yet how few of us relate our lives to this significant truth!

The machinery of the church is put to very severe strain and is working overtime, but that which the machinery produces so often lacks evidence of heavenly reality. The mass production of modern industry —all kinds of goods which attract the eye but have little lasting quality —is too often evident in the Christian church. In days like these I believe that it is quality and not quantity that is going to count.

The Lord is still looking, as He did in David's time, for a man after His own heart. I believe it to be the priority responsibility of any ministry so to proclaim God's Word that such a quality of Christian man, by the grace of God and the power of the Spirit, may be the result. Not only is it such a life alone which can stand the fiery trials that are bound increasingly to attack our Christian faith and principles, but also through the life of a Spirit-filled man of God is the fastest and most effective method of evangelism.

We begin by considering the basis of God's choice of such a man. In the selection of everyone who enters the service of the King of kings there are always two sides: on the one hand there is the election of God in eternity, accompanied by His heavenly summons in the course of time to take up the cross and follow Him; on the other hand, there is the human response in commitment of life to Jesus Christ as Lord.

It is not my task or yours to guess who are among God's elect. This is a secret hidden in the heart of God from before the foundation of the world. Yet by the preaching of the Word of God there will be unmistakable marks revealed in the lives of a great multitude which give evidence that they belong to God's chosen people. We preach the gospel to every creature under heaven and say, "Look unto Jesus and be saved." That gospel is like a fan that drives away the chaff and leaves the wheat. It removes the worthless and reveals the precious. We discover before long the elect of God by their conduct and their conversation, which have been transformed by the convicting power of the Holy Spirit.

You and I become assured of our own election by the witness of the Holy Spirit with our spirit that we are indeed the children of God, and we discover within ourselves a new heart, a new creation in Christ, far from perfect and yet, by His grace, hungry for the Lord. Thus we know that our names are written in the Book of Life.

Concerning the principles of God's choice, I use the illustration of the anointing of David here to point out three basic truths. In the first place, God's choice of a man is contrary to human reason.

Nobody involved in the drama that day in Bethlehem would have guessed that David, of all the family of Jesse, would be God's chosen one. His brothers obviously despised him—you recall how scathingly Eliab greeted him when a little later he appeared to do battle against Goliath. To his family, he was only the lad who kept the sheep; the others pursued their business and pleasure in total disregard for the young stripling. They probably thought him very naïve, and quite moonstruck when he advised them to consider the heavens; they must have thought him an absolute fanatic when he meditated day and night upon the Lord.

Even David's father called him "the youngest" (I Samuel 16:11)— and the word used in this connection, I understand, suggests something other than mere youth. It meant he was the least in his father's estimation; so small was David in his father's esteem that it wasn't considered necessary to include him in the family when the prophet of God called them to sacrifice.

Samuel himself had no idea that David was God's chosen one. Samuel was ready to settle upon Eliab, thinking surely that this was the Lord's anointed, and he drew upon himself the rebuke of the Lord: ". . . man looketh on the outward appearance, but the Lord looketh on the heart" (I Samuel 16:7).

Incidentally, I always think it strange that Samuel should be ready to settle for another like Saul, after all his unhappy experience with that self-willed king. How often the prophet and the preacher have been

wrong in their judgment of people! In my own experience, I have seen
so many well-educated, intellectual, clever personalities who have
turned their heel on the simplicity of the gospel; it was not refined
enough for them. Sometimes we covet attractive and talented people for
the Lord's work, but they turn out to be heartaches because they are
not among God's chosen.

The basis of God's choice is contrary to all this—when He would
build a "man of God" He looks for different timber. As the Apostle
Paul expressed it in writing to the church at Corinth: "God hath
chosen the foolish things of the world to confound the wise . . . the
weak things of the world to confound the things which are mighty;
And base things . . . and things which are despised, hath God chosen,
yea, and things which are not, to bring to nought things that are: That
no flesh should glory in his presence" (I Corinthians 1:27-29).

Picture in your mind the seven sons of Jesse standing there: apparently they were magnificent specimens of humanity. In the Bible,
seven is always the number of perfection. These sons of Jesse seem to
me to picture the perfection of the flesh, but the perfection of the flesh
is always rejected in heaven. That is a hard lesson for us to learn, but
it is absolutely imperative that we understand it if we would be among
God's beloved. If you refuse that lesson, if you reject that principle,
you may still be quite a leader in Christian work—but not a God-
directed chosen one among His people, for that which is done in the
flesh is of no profit to God.

To educate and refine the flesh so that it may become profitable in
His service is never God's plan. He insists on the sentence of death
upon everything that you and I are in ourselves. All that we are apart
from what we are given by His grace at the moment of our regeneration is sentenced to God's judgment, no matter how intellectual or
proud or clever or good we may be. There is only one place for all that
is "self"—on Calvary.

You may not be intellectual or well thought of in your family circle;
you may be despised by others for your faith in Christ. Perhaps you
had only a little share in the love of your parents, as David did. But
remember that those who are rejected of men often become beloved of
the Lord. Your faith in the Lord Jesus may be very weak and you may
realize little of the dignity which Christ has purposed for you, but
the thought of God toward you began before He ever flung a star into
space. Then He wrote your name on His heart; it was graven in the
palms of His hand before the sky was stretched out in the heavens.

You may consider yourself very obscure and unknown, just a unit in the mass, a cog in the machine. Like David you might well say, "I was as a beast before thee" (Psalm 73:22), and "I am a worm, and no man" (Psalm 22:6). Yet in His abundant mercy God can stoop down from heaven's highest glory to lift a beggar from the dunghill and set him among princes.

Among the last words recorded in the Bible from the lips of our Lord Jesus are these: "I am the root and the offspring of David, and the bright and morning star" (Revelation 22:16). In other words, David's character was rooted in Him from before the foundation of the world, and at the moment of David's response to God's call and his utter abandonment to God's claim, the transformation that took place in David's life made it possible for Christ to be among his offspring. David became part of that magnificent divine plan which brought Jesus to birth at Bethlehem and revealed God's love to man.

In a measure what was true of David may also be true of you and me. Our lives are rooted in Jesus before the foundation of the world. That is God's side, and in response to the call that He makes for surrender, service, and sacrifice for Him—regardless of your intellectual capabilities, your talents, your training or lack of it—you also may be in His divine plan, because through your life the Lord Jesus may be revealed to others. Therefore, the basis of God's choice is altogether contrary to human reason.

Look again at this passage of Scripture and notice also that God's choice is conditioned upon heart response.

We would miss the whole meaning of this story in I Samuel 16 if we were to imagine that this was the first time God had spoken to David's heart. The public anointing was the outcome of what had taken place in private between David and God long before. David was anointed for his great service and his ministry as Israel's king because God, who discerns the hearts of all men, knew that David's heart was different from others. He had a prepared heart—but how?

Perhaps David owed much to the School of the Prophets which Samuel had founded. Or perhaps David met with God one night under the stars as he saw the heavens declaring the glory of God and the earth showing forth His handiwork. Perhaps the young shepherd drew near to the heart of God as he watched his flock on the mountainside. Whenever it was, there had been a moment when God found David long before Samuel came to Bethlehem and anointed him. There had been a moment of glad response from David to the call of God, a response which renewed his heart and caused him to write, even in his youthful days, such wonderful lines as the Shepherd Psalm.

God's call to any man and the anointing of the Spirit for service are conditioned upon that man's heart response. What kind of heart had David? Remember that lovely opening of his greatest Psalm: "The Lord is my shepherd; I shall not want" (Psalm 23:1). David had a believing heart; he knew his own sinfulness and his need of the grace and guidance of God to watch over him even as he protected the sheep in his charge. He said, "The Lord is *my* shepherd," casting himself upon God in believing faith.

"He maketh me to lie down in green pastures: he leadeth me beside the still waters" (Psalm 23:2). This young man's life was marked by quietness. He knew the joy of communion with the Lord; his was a meditative heart.

"He leadeth me in the paths of righteousness" (Psalm 23:3). Though by no means perfect, David's heart was set on holiness, and he longed for that attribute of God in his life above all else.

"Though I walk through the valley of the shadow of death, I will fear no evil" (Psalm 23:4). In the face of the worst enemy that could ever face him, David was confident; as he demonstrated later in his encounter with Goliath, he was brave, bold, and courageous.

"Thou preparest a table before me in the presence of mine enemies . . . my cup runneth over" (Psalm 23:5). David had a heart full of gratitude to the Lord for meeting his needs, for supplying him in things both spiritual and material, even with the devil looking on.

"Surely goodness and mercy shall follow me all the days of my life: and I will dwell in the house of the Lord for ever" (Psalm 23:6). David was no mere wistful follower, near to God on some days and some occasions but not on others: "My heart is fixed, O God, my heart is fixed," he wrote in Psalm 57:7. Such was David's heart—not fickle, but believing, meditative, set on holiness and righteousness, brave and courageous, grateful, and fixed upon God.

None of these things were David's by natural birth; he himself wrote, "I was shapen in iniquity; and in sin did my mother conceive me" (Psalm 51:5). But there had been a day when God had met this young man and had renewed his heart, so that the goodness of heart which was his qualification for the anointing of the Holy Spirit for power in God's service came from God Himself. The only qualification for heaven that any of us can ever have is such evidence of God's grace in our lives.

The choice of a "man of God" is based upon what God sees in a heart of response to His love. I would wish that some folk who are so positive of their salvation would condescend some time to examine themselves by the Scriptural qualifications. Of course, we must never doubt the Word of God or His promises, but the question is, "Is my confidence that I am God's own well founded? Is there any evidence of it in my life? What is my response to His love and grace?"

Are you afraid to go back to the foundation with David and say, "Search me, O God . . . And see if there be any wicked way in me, and lead me in the way everlasting" (Psalm 139:23-24)? If you go on through life blindly confident but never examining your own heart, that is a token of delusion—you are believing something that is not true.

Always I would preach the privilege we have of faith in a mighty God, in His promises and in His Word, the objective look at the cross as the basis of salvation, and the great fact of our security because He will never let us go. I would urge upon all to have full assurance of faith in that because He died and rose again, you are justified and saved. *But* I would beg that you be careful to distinguish between presumption and assurance. Preaching to a congregation privilege and not precept will produce dangerous lethargy in God's people. What many of us need today is a burning examination by the Holy Spirit, which may be bitter to the taste but which may awaken us to the disaster of imagining that we are Christians when there is no evidence in our lives of His grace.

God's choice of a man of God is conditioned upon heart response, not head response. I do not ask you if your heart is perfect, or if it never goes astray—God knows how prone we are to wandering and sin. But I ask you pointedly, praying that the Spirit may really challenge you with the question: Is your heart resting upon Jesus? Do you have a believing heart? Does it meditate upon God's Word and find comfort in the Scriptures? Does your heart desire and seek after holiness? Is it a grateful and humble heart, ever thankful to Him? Is it eternally fixed upon God, or is it a fickle heart, flirting with the things of this world?

That the Spirit may literally pull from under your feet any false basis of assurance in your salvation is my prayer for you. May He never let you rest until you have an assurance based upon what your heart has received of the grace and character of Jesus Christ, not simply upon what your heart believes. One who believes with the head only, without evidencing grace, love, gentleness, humility, or other token of the indwelling Christ, has no right to say he is a Christian. God's choice is contrary to all human reason, and is based upon the response of a man's heart.

In the third place, God's choice of a "man of God" is characterized by heavenly recognition. We may not know the heart of another, but there are certain evidences by which a man whom God has chosen becomes known, because heaven has bestowed upon him certain qualities which mark him out.

The first of these evidences in David's case took place when "Samuel took the horn of oil, and anointed him in the midst of his brethren: and the Spirit of the Lord came upon David from that day forward" (I Samuel 16:13).

It is doubtful whether anyone who witnessed that anointing understood what was happening. If David's father or brothers or the townspeople had known, someone would have run off immediately to tell Saul. I cannot imagine those seven brothers knowing the significance of what was taking place and standing there indifferently. They obviously didn't understand what Samuel was doing. But David knew, and although he never lifted a finger to get the throne for himself— in fact, he often spared the life of Saul even when that jealous king was attempting to kill him—David knew beyond all doubt that one day he would be king.

The oil Samuel poured out was the visible sign of the Spirit of God who from that day forward was upon David in mighty power. For our Lord Jesus there was not oil, but the appearance of a dove from heaven gently resting upon Him (Matthew 3:16). For the disciples on the day of Pentecost there was no oil but "cloven tongues like as of fire" (Acts 2:3) descending upon them from heaven.

Unfortunately, how often we meet professing Christian people today who have no power in witness, no radiance in their faces, no sweetness in their personalities, no reality in their spiritual lives. They are indwelt by the Spirit of God, but they are not anointed. The Holy Spirit is in them, but not *upon* them in power and reality.

Has the Spirit of God been searching your heart and convicting you of lack of grace, of love, of gentleness, of Christlikeness? Have you seen yourself as lacking in reality and joy, with no true evidence of His life in you? Does your heart cry out today for His cleansing as you confess before Him with a humble and broken spirit? Then to you I say, claim your anointing today, for God has promised that the fire of His Spirit and the glowing reality of His love will always descend upon that yielded life which places no confidence in the flesh but hungers for a God-renewed heart of holiness and righteousness. The recognition of heaven is the mark of your election, to all the world the revelation that you belong to Jesus. Is this anointing on you today? Is there the mark of reality in your spiritual life?

But that was not the only reward for David. His election was clear to everyone because the next thing that happened was that he came into collision with Saul. It is impossible for a man chosen of God to be at peace with the children of the devil. A man anointed of the Holy Spirit is immediately the target of Satan—the seed of the serpent and the seed of the woman will always be at enmity until Jesus comes.

It is possible that for a while you, like David, may be able to soothe your enemy and make him happy if you play your spiritual harp to him. But the moment the world discovers what you are, when the obvious evidence of heavenly reality rests upon you, they will begin to sling the javelins at you. Also, as in the case of David, you will discover that the place of rejection by others is the place of acceptance by God.

The greatest reward of all for David was when he was finally acclaimed king! He was crowned before all the people of Israel and received their homage. There is a crowning day coming for us, also. Our beloved Lord Jesus prayed for us: "Father, I will that they also, whom thou hast given me, be with me where I am" (John 17:24). And the Apostle Paul declared, "Henceforth there is laid up for me a crown of righteousness [the crown of a godly life], which the Lord . . . shall give me at that day; and not to me only, but unto all them also that love his appearing" (II Timothy 4:8).

I wonder what the effect of all this has been upon your heart. I trust that some have been greatly disturbed—if your life and character are destitute of the evidences of God's grace, if you have been going along without self-examination, simply believing with your head what you have read in the Bible but without its becoming part of your character.

I trust, also, that some of you have been greatly comforted. You may have thought you did not matter to anyone—your parents, your family, your friends—but now you realize that you matter immensely to God. Perhaps you have been made to cry out to Jesus with a hunger for Him you have never known before.

Are you among God's people, or are you believing a lie? Does your life bear examination? Is there evidence of the marks of His grace? If you are His, is the anointing of the Holy Spirit upon your testimony, or is your life cowardly, afraid, uncertain of itself, not knowing where you stand? God wants to meet with you, for He loves you and wants you to be a man after His own heart, one who is chosen, having the seal of the Spirit of God upon your life, the anointing of the Third Person of the Trinity.

And Eliab his eldest brother heard when he spake unto the men; and Eliab's anger was kindled against David, and he said, Why camest thou down hither? and with whom hast thou left those few sheep in the wilderness? I know thy pride, and the naughtiness of thine heart; for thou art come down that thou mightest see the battle. And David said, What have I now done? . . .

And David said to Saul, Let no man's heart fail because of him; thy servant will go and fight with this Philistine.

And Saul said to David, Thou are not able to go against this Philistine to fight with him: for thou art but a youth, and he a man of war from his youth.

And David said unto Saul, Thy servant kept his father's sheep, and there came a lion, and a bear, and took a lamb out of the flock: . . . Thy servant slew both the lion and the bear: and this uncircumcised Philistine shall be as one of them, seeing he hath defied the armies of the living God. . . .

Then said David to the Philistine, Thou comest to me with a sword, and with a spear, and with a shield: but I come to thee in the name of the Lord of hosts, the God of the armies of Israel, whom thou hast defied. . . . for the battle is the Lord's, and he will give you into our hands. . . .

And David put his hand in his bag, and took thence a stone, and slang it, and smote the Philistine in his forehead, that the stone sunk into his forehead; and he fell upon his face to the earth. So David prevailed over the Philistine with a sling and with a stone, and smote the Philistine, and slew him; but there was no sword in the hand of David . . .

And it came to pass, when he had made an end of speaking unto Saul, that the soul of Jonathan was knit with the soul of David, and Jonathan loved him as his own soul.

I SAMUEL 17:28—18:1

CHAPTER 2

VANQUISHING THE ENEMY

(I Samuel 17:28—18:4)

THE OLD TESTAMENT, as you know, is full of pictures of New Testament truth. It is not only a book of history, though it is that, revealing to us the great seed-plots of God's plan of redemption for the human race; it also illustrates many great truths later developed in the New Testament, setting them before us in pictorial language so that we may apply them in our hearts and daily lives.

There is one such truth of immense significance in this passage. I imagine this story has been familiar to most people from the earliest days of childhood—the story of David and Goliath. But I am not sure to what extent we have grasped its spiritual significance. Let us investigate some of the different aspects in this chapter, trusting that the Word of God may grip your heart, and the Spirit of God reveal to you some basic principles for your Christian life.

Notice first the magnificent giant that we find arrayed against Israel in the early verses of I Samuel 17—I cannot call him by any other name: he was a magnificent giant! You will find a description of him in verses 4-6, and it is a most impressive picture. His head, his shoulders, his chest, and his legs were all clothed in brass—he was just one scintillating mass of brass, glittering in the Palestinian sun. This Goliath, as he strutted up and down on one side of the valley, must have been very fascinating to look at, and very terrifying.

Not only so, but he seemed invulnerable; anyone might well quail before such an enemy: "And the staff of his spear was like a weaver's beam; and his spear's head weighed six hundred shekels of iron: and one bearing a shield went before him. And he stood and cried unto the armies of Israel, and said unto them, Why are ye come out to set your battle in array? . . . choose you a man for you, and let him come down to me" (I Samuel 17:7-8).

This giant in all his magnificence seemed absolutely beyond defeat. He was also irrepressible in his arrogance; for forty days he appeared, day by day uttering his challenge to battle and defiance to the people of God.

Notice that he was calling for a man; he was suggesting that instead of the two armies going into the fight, each one should have a representative. If the man the Israelites chose "be able to fight with me, and to kill me, then will we be your servants: but if I prevail against him, and kill him, then shall ye be our servants, and serve us" (I Samuel 17:9). In other words, he was prepared to be the representative of the Philistines, and all he asked was that the Israelites should select their representative and let an individual match decide the issue. What happened to Goliath would happen to his followers; what happened to the representative of the people of God would happen to them.

Here, then, we see this magnificent giant strutting to and fro in all his pride and arrogance, defying the armies of Saul. But if you look at the other side of the valley you see a pathetic picture, although this people belong to God and are in a covenant relationship with Him. Incidentally, the battle was lined up in a territory that belonged to Judah (I Samuel 17:1), and it was in this place that rightfully belonged to the people of God that Goliath was breathing out his defiance.

All that this helpless crowd of Israelites could do was to set the battle in array (I Samuel 17:2), which I take to mean that they were getting organized to fight. But when the enemy came in sight, how they quaked at the sight of that giant! "And all the men of Israel, when they saw the man, fled from him, and were sore afraid" (I Samuel 17:24). They were a people in covenant relationship with God, but actually in the bondage of fear before Goliath and all that he stood for!

Now it is impossible, surely, for any of us to escape the significance of that picture. On the one hand there is Goliath in all his impressiveness—there could scarcely be a more striking picture of Satan and his power. He may not strut around in armor like Goliath, but he is impressive and far too powerful for any human being to stand against.

In any city you will find a modern Satan who seems irresistible, arrayed in all kinds of fascinating garbs. He clothes himself in the philosophy of modern education, especially the theory that man is essentially good and needs only to be trained and educated to become civilized and perfect—a theory which denies the whole truth of the Bible that man is essentially sinful.

You will also find Satan arrayed in the attactive garb of modern literature, especially in the disgusting trash you can pick up in the bookstalls today which appeals to the flesh and to the carnal mind. You will find Satan, too, in the fascinating garb of liberty between the two sexes, in the slack standard of morals that exists today among young people: the carelessness of thought, the indulgence of the body. You will find Satan defying the people of God in all these things which are so alluring and tremendously powerful.

He is arrayed in modern civilization in so many ways that I scarcely need enumerate them: there he stands, a colossal giant, far too strong for any of us to attack. You may say you don't believe in him, but that is only another proof of his power; for the Bible tells us that the god of this world (the devil) "hath blinded the minds of them which believe not, lest the light of the glorious gospel of Christ, who is the image of God, should shine unto them" (II Corinthians 4:4). There are many people today who do believe he exists and who know something of his power, not only in the sense of controlling a nation or a city, but in their own souls. They recognize, in their combat with evil, that Satan is far too strong for them. A very fascinating, clever, intellectual, invulnerable giant is the devil of the 1960's.

On the other side of the valley, as Satan's only opponent today, what do we find? Here is the professing Christian church, a great company of people in covenant relationship with Almighty God by the blood of the cross, indwelt by the Third Person of the Trinity, belonging to the Lord Jesus Christ. Yet they, like the Israelites, are absolutely helpless to do anything about the powers of darkness arrayed against them.

We admit this to our shame; nevertheless, it is good for us to face facts as they really are. The church today is very largely well equipped and well organized: the battle is set in array, everything is planned, but when it comes to facing the enemy, we are fighting a losing battle.

It is interesting to note that the Israelites facing Goliath were led at that moment by a man who had forfeited through his disobedience the anointing of the Spirit of God. He had lost contact with his source of spiritual authority, and because he had, the people were helpless too and quaking with fear.

As we face the giants of our era in all their satanic power, the church seems so helpless to deal with the basic problems and sin of our day. Is it because we are bereft of spiritual authority? Perhaps our leadership, through disobedience and unbelief, has forfeited access to the source of spiritual power, and our only answer to the defiance of the devil is to try to set the battle in array, to organize and to plan. Surely we have never been better organized, but when we launch an attack in the name of the Lord, we lack the power that gives victory.

Here is our first picture: the present-day church is set in battle array against a strutting, arrogant, proud adversary. As Paul says in Ephesians 6:12, "We wrestle not against flesh and blood, but against principalities, against powers . . . against spiritual wickedness in high places." We see the enemy all around us gaining ground rapidly, and we find that we are without the power to deal with the main issues.

Let us look, however, at another aspect of the story, and see the mighty deliverance that was given the people of God that day. I remind you again of Goliath's suggestion that the whole issue should be settled by a representative: "Give me a man!" In other words, the issue will be settled by the representatives of each side.

Here we get a glimpse into the basic fact of the Bible, for the whole issue is not the devil arrayed against a multitude of Christian people— it is the devil against God! It is Satan versus Jesus! And the whole issue is basically settled, not only in the life of a church, but in the life of a Christian, by *our* Representative. What happens to the prince of the powers of darkness happens to all who follow him. What happens to our Lord, David's greater Son, happens to all who follow Him.

David here is a picture of the Lord Jesus Christ, who overcame Satan at Calvary, and also a picture of every child of God who is being made one with Him through faith and obedience. Christ is the Head and we are His body, and therefore if He has won the victory over Satan, so have we. How pointless would be any series of Bible studies unless we caught a fresh glimpse of the loveliness of our Lord Jesus Christ! Let us pick out some details here that direct our thoughts to Him.

David was, in the first place, sanctified by the Spirit. Before he took up this battle in the name of the living God, he had been anointed by the Spirit of God. After Samuel anointed him, we are told, "the Spirit of the Lord came upon David from that day forward" (I Samuel 16:13). There was also a day in the life of our Lord Jesus when, at His baptism, before He took up the battle on our behalf, He was anointed by the Spirit of God, who descended upon Him as a dove.

Then we read in I Samuel 17:17 that David was sent by his father to the battleground. He was sent from keeping the sheep, from the place of isolation, sent from his home out into public conflict. It is said of the Lord that "the Father sent the Son to be the Saviour of the world" (I John 4:14).

We find that when David arrived on the scene he was scorned by his brethren. Look at the language of his elder brother Eliab: "Why camest thou down hither? and with whom hast thou left those few sheep in the wilderness? I know thy pride, and the naughtiness of thine heart; for thou art come down that thou mightest see the battle" (I Samuel 17:28). See the battle? Why, there wasn't any battle, for nobody dared take up Goliath's challenge!

There never is a battle against the devil until the Lord Jesus takes it up on our behalf. You don't know anything about warfare until in the name of Christ you launch out into the attack. But that is just the nerve of the flesh to imagine that you are getting on with the battle, and all the other fellow is doing is to come and watch! David was scorned by his brethren, and it was said of our Lord that "He came unto his own, and his own received him not" (John 1:11). "He is despised and rejected of men; a man of sorrows, and acquainted with grief," wrote Isaiah (53:3).

Carrying the simile a bit further, we find that David was strengthened by his past experiences. When Saul challenged his credentials, saying that he could not go and fight against this Philistine "for thou art but a youth, and he a man of war from his youth" (I Samuel 17:33), David told him of experiences in his life when he kept his father's sheep. There came a lion and a bear, attacking as a lion and a bear do, taking a lamb out of the flock, and David killed them. "This will not be the first time I've met a powerful enemy," said David, in effect. "It will not be the first time I have proved the power of God to save me."

Before our Lord Jesus Christ went into the public arena of Calvary (if I may say it reverently) and fought there openly to save us from sin and hell, He had a private conflict face-to-face with the devil in the wilderness, and defeated him there.

David also was sustained by the Word of God. I like his defiance of Goliath when he said, "Thou comest to me with a sword, and with a spear, and with a shield: but I come to thee in the name of the Lord of hosts, the God of the armies of Israel, whom thou hast defied. . . . And all this assembly shall know that the Lord saveth not with sword and spear: for the battle is the Lord's, and he will give you into our hands" (I Samuel 17:45, 47).

Strengthened by experience and sustained by the Word of God, David went out to battle against the foe. The Lord Jesus went to Calvary outside the city wall and triumphed over Satan out of an empty tomb because alone in the wilderness He had repelled Satan's attacks by the strength of the Word of God. He had defeated him time and time again with the simple statement, "It is written."

One final simile, though there are many: David was successful in his conflict by faith, and faith alone. He prevailed over the Philistine with a sling and a stone, and there was no sword in David's hand. Saul offered him one; Saul's idea was to dress him up and make him as much like Goliath as he could. David, however, renounced the whole principle because he knew that the victory was "Not by might, nor by power, but by my spirit, saith the Lord of hosts" (Zechariah 4:6).

Of course, the most wonderful thing of all is this: that the victory of David was the victory of Israel. Every Israelite—mark this carefully, and may the Lord give you the thrill of it in your soul—became a conqueror that day because of David's triumph (I Samuel 17:51-52). They all shared in his victory.

Similarly, what happens to Christ happens to His people. The vanquishing of the enemy—not merely city-wide or nation-wide, but personally in the life—and all the temptation of his glittering fascinations which constantly hit at us, is entirely dependent upon our identification with David's greater Son, and our acceptance of the principles upon which He won the fight.

We are striking now at something that is absolutely fundamental. Here we expose, in the name of the Lord, the whole reason for the ineptitude of the Christian church really to tackle the social problems, the moral problems, the youth problems of our day. In spite of our correctness, in spite of our having set the battle in array, in spite of our organizations, in spite of our techniques and in spite of our head knowledge of truth, the whole reason for our failure to deal with modern problems is just here.

I speak to you as a fundamental believer in the Lord and in His Word in a position of truth which, God helping me, I shall never leave or forsake—but speaking as such I tell you I feel like hanging my head in shame! With all our boast of orthodoxy and correctness of organization and technique, what are we doing really to cope with the power of the devil in our cities today? Mighty little!

We see in David also a reflection of the one whose life is yielded to David's Lord. Here is the principle of victory: David had the anointing of God upon him because of faithfulness in the obscurity in his home life, because there he had passed the test. He was anointed by the Spirit of God alone in private before he came out into the public arena to stand in the name of the Lord.

What are you like at home? What about your conversation and behavior around the family table, your relationships with husband, wife, parents, or children? Is there the anointing of the Spirit of God upon your testimony in public because in private, in the humbleness of daily life, there has been a consistent and faithful testimony?

I said earlier that the whole army of the people of God stood bereft and helpless before the giant Goliath under the leadership of a man who had forfeited the anointing of God because of his disobedience. Today the Christian church is helpless. Behind the scenes and away from the public arena we are facing powers of darkness too strong for us because somewhere in our personal lives we have forfeited all right to the Spirit's anointing, His authority and His power. In His absence all we can do is to substitute planning and organization, schemes and techniques—and therefore we break down every time because the enemy is too powerful for us.

We are to be anointed by the Spirit and sent by the Lord. The only thing that gives a fellow or a girl courage to stand in their immediate circumstances (if they are in God's will) with all the pressures around them, is the knowledge that God has sent them there. The sovereignty of the Lord is behind them, though they may be scorned by others just as David was scorned by his brothers. Many can bear testimony to a day when, in the name of the Lord, they said to parents and loved ones, to a wife or family, "I am going to stand for Christ; I want to be God's best, and I am going to take up the battle in the name of the Lord." And the answer came, "You had better give up that idea! What can you do? Just a little nobody like you, you're just wasting your time!" You have borne the scorn and the curled lip of someone you love because you are dedicated to the Lord.

David was strengthened by experience: he could look back upon a day when he slew a lion and a bear. The confidence you may have as you go out in the name of the Lord today is that in the pages of your memory you can find days when you have faced a situation that was absolutely impossible, and the Lord stepped in and gave victory. It isn't the first time you have stood against a Goliath—you know what it is to be strengthened by experience and sustained by the Word of God.

So many Christians believe in the God of history and the God of prophecy; we believe all the great things He did in Wesley's day and in Moody's day. We believe in the great things He is going to do when He comes again. But how few of His people really believe that He is the God of today, that He is a present, living power in our hearts! In

Saul's mind, God was absent from the whole conflict; He didn't enter into it. But in David's mind, God was the greatest reality of all. Is God real to you like that today? Is He God not only of the yesterdays of your past, nor of the hopeful tomorrows of the future, but of death to self and absolute victory *today?*

David was strengthened and sustained by the Word of God, and by faith he was successful in the battle. He knew perfectly well it was no use imitating the enemy by dressing up like him and going out in Saul's armor—he saw the futility of that. Rather, he must put on the whole armor of God that he might stand his ground in that evil day.

To me, it is a pathetic thing to find so many Christians believing that the best way to bear witness for the Lord is to imitate the devil's methods, to try to resist Satan by the same kind of program and technique, ability and organization, which he himself has perfected. "We must not be thought too different," is the argument frequently used. But there is only one way to real victory, and David found it. You and I will only find it by the same principle of absolute faith in and reliance upon the power of the Lord Jesus.

In our concluding glimpse of this story, have you noticed that there was a spectator? His name was Jonathan, the son of Saul, who naturally watched the whole battle with great concern. He had been among those who had not dared launch out into the fight, but as he watched David go out and fight Goliath in the name of the Lord, his soul was knit to David's, and he loved him as he loved his own soul.

If only we could catch a glimpse again today of David's greater Son who went out into the battle for us at Calvary, who triumphed by all these principles, who proved to be more than Conqueror when God raised Him from the tomb! He shed His blood for our redemption and dealt with the power of sin in that battle on the cross. Surely our response to Him should be, "My Jesus, I love Thee! I know Thou art mine!" Doesn't your soul go out after Him who fought that battle, not for Himself, but on your behalf and mine?

Then Jonathan "stripped himself of the robe that was upon him, and gave it to David, and his garments, even to his sword, and to his bow, and to his girdle" (I Samuel 18:4). In other words, that day he saw the principle of victory, and he was identifying himself with that principle by which David had won. He was giving away all the carnal weapons of Saul's armor that he might cast himself in faith upon David.

This is the glorious note on which I conclude this message: what happened to David happened to his people; David's victory was their victory. What happened to the King of kings at the cross in His death, burial, and resurrection and ascension is something that happened to all those who come to Him. As Jonathan surrendered to David, he yielded to the same principle of life which governed David.

Although you may be in covenant relationship with God, have you learned that the weapons of our warfare are not carnal? Have you never realized that the Lord does not fight with sword or spear? Have you not discovered that you cannot match Satan with his weapons and with his armor? We have nothing except—and what a glorious exception—the Word of God, the power of His Spirit, the anointing of the Holy Ghost upon a life which has surrendered all confidence in the flesh.

Child of God, you may have victory yet, in spite of defeat, as you recognize the power of Goliath and his tremendous strength, if you, like Jonathan, love the Lord Jesus with all your soul and just put down at His feet every weapon, every confidence in technique and program, and recognize that the battle is won not by might, nor by power, but by the Spirit. If you come to Him in total submission, He will give you power from on high, because the Lord's victory is your victory. What happened to Christ is for all the members of His Body, and all God asks of you is an acceptance of that principle.

But the Spirit of the Lord departed from Saul, and an evil spirit from the Lord troubled him. And Saul's servants said unto him, Behold now, an evil spirit from God troubleth thee. Let our lord now command thy servants, which are before thee, to seek out a man, who is a cunning player on an harp. . . .

Then answered one of the servants, and said, Behold, I have seen a son of Jesse the Bethlehemite, that is cunning in playing. . . .

And David came to Saul, and stood before him: and he loved him greatly; and he became his armor-bearer. . . . And it came to pass, when the evil spirit from God was upon Saul, that David took an harp, and played with his hand: so Saul was refreshed, and was well, and the evil spirit departed from him.

I SAMUEL 16:14-23

And David went out whithersoever Saul sent him, and behaved himself wisely: and Saul set him over the men of war, and he was accepted in the sight of all the people, and also in the sight of Saul's servants.

And it came to pass . . . that the women came out of all cities of Israel, singing and dancing, to meet king Saul, with tabrets, with joy, and with instruments of music. And the women answered one another as they played, and said, Saul hath slain his thousands, and David his ten thousands.

And Saul was very wroth, and the saying displeased him; and he said, They have ascribed unto David ten thousands, and to me they have ascribed but thousands: and what can he have more but the kingdom? And Saul eyed David from that day and forward. . . . And Saul was afraid of David, because the Lord was with him, and was departed from Saul.

I SAMUEL 18:5-12

CHAPTER 3

SOULS IN CONFLICT

(I Samuel 16:14-23; 18:5-12)

As WE CONTINUE to study the making of a man of God from the life and character of David, it is a help to see such a person in contrast with other people who had the same opportunities and faced the same problems as he did.

Quite clearly, at this point of the story, the Holy Spirit brings to our attention David and Saul, setting them side by side for our careful, thoughtful meditation. Both of them were chosen for leadership and both of them were anointed by the Spirit. But with those two statements comparison ceases and contrast begins, for everything else in the life of Saul and David is in striking opposition. We see the sun begin to rise upon one life and to set upon the other. For one, there is steady growth in grace and in the knowledge of God; for the other there is tragic decline and disobedience to God: darkness, frustration, sin.

Yet Saul began so well, and he might have been all that David was. The two men are placed side by side for our examination, for our warning, and for our encouragement. The same loving God, the same heavenly resources are at the disposal of both, but we see one of them steadily rising and the other steadily sinking.

Let us examine the reason why one life should end in triumph and the other in tragedy. May God here speak to your heart concerning the direction of your own life in its spiritual progress. I would remind you it is not a snap decision that decides your eternal destiny. Unless that decision for Christ is followed by a life directed by the Spirit of Christ, it is not valid, because it is direction, trend, progress that evidence a man's destiny.

Some commentators suggest that the incident in I Samuel 16:14-23 is out of place, and should really appear at the conclusion of chapter 17, following the account of the battle between David and Goliath. The reason for such an argument is quite simple. When David returned from victory against the Philistines (I Samuel 17:55), Saul inquired of one of his captains who this young stripling was. If David had already been playing his harp to him, would not he have known?

That reasoning sounds very plausible, but it brings up one or two other problems. For instance, is it at all likely that Saul's servants, when they saw him under the possession of an evil spirit, would have brought him David as one who might be able to help him, when Saul was already eyeing David with jealousy (I Samuel 18:9)? Furthermore, would it have been necessary for Saul's servants to go into the detailed description of David in I Samuel 16:18 to introduce him to Saul? They would need only to say, "Here is the man who won the victory in the valley against the giant." No, I prefer to leave the passage where it is.

However, I would suggest that between the incident in the closing verses of chapter 16, when David soothed Saul's temper and disposition with his harp, and the moment when the young shepherd outmatched Goliath in the valley, David had been back home with his sheep. Maybe years had passed and the lad had grown to be a young man. At any rate, as he went home to his sheep, knowing that God's hand was upon him, he was perfectly prepared to await the time when God would speak again and call him out into the public arena. Here is a great example of patience in waiting upon God, and another evidence of David's progress in contrast to Saul's downfall.

We will now highlight some things that seem to clarify one man's advance and the other man's collapse, and may God speak to us about these things in our own lives, as they apply to us.

In the first place, there is what I would call the soul's decline. A spiritual decline is always obvious to everyone except the person involved. Sometimes he can go on hiding it for a while, at least in so far as his own conscience is concerned. But spiritual decline—backsliding, withdrawal from a walk and fellowship with God, a refusal to accept the principles of Christian living, a rejection of God's terms for spiritual vitality—soon makes itself evident in a man's character. The process is outlined here very clearly in Saul's jealousy of David.

"Saul has slain his thousands, and David his ten thousands" (I Samuel 18:7) was the shout of a great multitude acclaiming David in the hour of his victory. But Saul found it a bitter pill to swallow. He knew perfectly well that he had been rejected by God from the kingship because Samuel had told him so. Ever since that moment he had been looking around for any possible successor. As the crowd praised David, Saul must have had a premonition in his heart that this man was the one who was going to take his kingdom. In his anger he said, "They have ascribed unto David ten thousands, and to me they have ascribed but thousands: and what can he have more but the kingdom?" (I Samuel 18:8).

Jealousy got into Saul's soul, jealousy ripened until it became murderous intent. Saul had threatened David's life, as recorded in I Samuel 18: 10-12, and later he would spend years chasing him through the countryside in a fruitless attempt to slay him. Jealousy followed by attempted murder were sure signs that somewhere in Saul's life the darkness was setting in, as pointed up by the pathetic picture back in chapter 17. This one-time hero of Israel, facing the challenge of Goliath, slunk into his tent, afraid.

The whole army of Israel was waiting for a call to battle from their leader, but Saul was lurking in the darkness, afraid to face anyone. In earlier days, one trumpet blast from Saul would put the whole army on the move, but not now. He still had the formula of a faith in God: "The Lord be with thee," he said (I Samuel 17:37), as he tried to clothe the young man in his own armor, wishing him well as he went out to fight the giant. He had the formula, but he had lost the reality of God, and he dared not venture against the tremendous odds. He had lost his grip upon God, and therefore he had lost his grip upon his people. In his soul reigned frustration, darkness, jealousy, and murder.

By contrast, "David behaved himself wisely in all his ways; and the Lord was with him" (I Samuel 18:14). God was a living reality in the life of the young shepherd. How had that come about? That which marked the difference between these two men was what they did when they were alone. David worshiped God; he meditated upon his Lord day and night when he was alone with his sheep. Saul was self-indulgent. What a man does when he is alone with his thoughts will decide what he is when he is in public with other people. It is there that either by self-indulgence a man's character is wrecked, or by self-discipline a man's character is made.

Alone with God, David meditated and nourished his soul in the Lord. He learned how to bear quietly the sneers of his brothers as he came to do battle with Goliath (I Samuel 17:28). He was able to bear rebuke meekly, to take misrepresentation gently, to pass unruffled through the scathing criticism of those who should have known better. That was possible only because his heart was in tune with God; David learned that to be strong is to be gentle when provoked, and that the Lord would give him strength in the battle.

Do you see the contrast? On the one hand, sin, jealousy, bitterness, hatred, murder; on the other hand, gentleness and meekness. On the one hand, because of all the sin and hatred, there was powerlessness in the fight. On the other hand, the man with a gentle and meek spirit, who had meditated upon the laws of God, became mighty to conquer the powers of darkness.

Where do you fit into that picture so far? Are you a soul in declension, or a soul in growth? Is your life declining because it is self-indulgent, or are you growing because in the secret place your life has found its source deep in the Lord? What do you think about when you are alone? What does the devil do with your mind when you are by yourself? May the Spirit of God probe deep!

In the second place, we see also here a soul in desolation. "The Lord . . . was departed from Saul" (I Samuel 18:12). Allow that phrase to sink into your heart. The Lord was departed from him, and I cannot imagine anything more dreadful than a life from which God has been withdrawn. Picture Saul for forty days in his tent on one side of the valley while the giant Goliath struts up and down on the other. Saul's army waits in vain for a signal from him. Surely he had no appetite for food or for battle, or, in fact, for anything. He was desolate and empty, because the Lord had taken His hand off him.

Whenever God's presence is withdrawn from a soul, when His Holy Spirit is taken away in His convicting power, that man is left in hopeless revolt against everything around him. He becomes sour and bitter; he is afraid to meet people or talk to them; he is afraid to go anywhere, but shuts himself up alone, and he has no appetite for his Bible, for prayer, or for anything. Life has become absolutely meaningless; such a man often flings himself into the lake to end it all. God has departed!

But there is even worse: "the evil spirit from God came upon Saul" (I Samuel 18:10). An evil spirit from God—how can that be? God sends the Holy Spirit, we are told, to check and rebuke, to love and provide. Would God send an evil spirit? Yes, if a man stamps his foot and turns his back on the voice of the Omnipotent One, rejects the claim of God in Jesus Christ, revolts against the principles of heaven— at that moment God becomes his enemy.

There was a time, perhaps, when that man was in the stream of blessing, carried along in victory by the power of the Lord in his heart, rejoicing in his salvation and serving the Lord with gladness. But there came a moment when he turned his back upon God, when Satan tripped him up and he refused to repent and acknowledge his sin, so that he struggles against God, and his soul is in desperate peril.

The Scripture says that with the froward God shows Himself froward (Psalm 18:26). Against the rebellious life—the life that has turned its back upon Him—God matches all His heavenly power; the angels are arrayed against such a person. But if he goes eventually to a lost eternity, it will be only because he has trodden underfoot the blood of Jesus Christ; he has rejected the principle of the cross and of forgiveness.

God bars the road to hell at Calvary, but if a man stamps his foot and insists that he can work out his own passage, that he can somehow manage his own affairs with a bit of help from church and religion, then God sets unseen hosts across that man's path in heavenly array. Time and time again his conscience speaks to him, and the memory of a better life that he used to live haunts him. The fact that days have gone by that he can never recover and the conviction that, after all, he is fighting with God, deepen in his soul. All these things become his enemies. Such is the evil spirit sent from God to stop a man in his downward course to disaster.

To bring this to our level, if some of us are not careful we will find, as Judas found, that the very pleadings of Jesus Christ only begin to seal our doom. Oh, the desolation of a soul from which God has withdrawn! "My Spirit shall not always strive with man," He said (Genesis 6:3).

Isn't it strange that the one thing that helped Saul (I Samuel 16:23), which somehow brought rest into his fevered spirit and calmed his inner battle, was music? What a tremendous ministry is that of song and music! "Chords that are broken will vibrate once more," goes the old song we often sing, and how quickly do they begin to respond when they hear the lovely old songs of the faith. Many a man walking up and down skid row has heard such an old hymn and gone inside the mission hall to cast his wretched, debauched life at the feet of Jesus and to be delivered. How often a message in song has stirred our own hearts to think and to pray!

Why should that be? Because heaven is full of song and music; the Bible tells us so. It is an expression of the very life of heaven, and that is why the singing of a hymn can be used to speak to a heart that is desolate. Saul's poor, lonely soul responded to music when nothing else could touch him.

That is why the devil uses music, too, and he distorts it into modern jazz, a powerful weapon in his hands with which to capture the senses and stifle the soul. You see people going about the streets with transistor radios in their hands. They cannot be quiet; they are afraid to be without some noise, so they listen to the hypnotic throbbing of jazz. It dulls their conscience, drugs their senses, and stops their thinking. Why? Music, which has great power to influence a soul and draw him back to the reality of God and heaven, is a thing the devil has grasped and twisted and used to keep people blinded in his grip. Oh, the subtlety of the devil! Oh, the desolation of a life that is insensible to God!

By contrast we read that "David behaved himself wisely in all his ways; and the Lord was with him" (I Samuel 18:14). He lived and walked in fellowship with God. He knew what it was to abide under the shadow of the Almighty, to be hidden in the secret of God's pavilion. Therefore, in his heart there was no fear as he faced the enemy; in his hand there was no tremor as he went to do battle for the Lord. He was deadly in his aim, for he walked and talked with God. The harp he used was a symbol of the life he was living, the Lord Himself being the joy and melody it expressed. Because of his harmony with heaven, David had tremendous power and influence upon others.

That is always true. Let a man be right with God, reconciled through the blood of the cross, humbled at the foot of Calvary; let him be broken, coming to God guilty and hopeless and needy; and at that moment God takes hold of him and transforms and uses all his gifts and qualities, until that man becomes a mighty influence. But he has first to come down from his ladder of pride to the very foot of the cross.

Do you see the contrast? The Lord departed from Saul: the Lord was with David. We find a statement repeated in I Samuel 18:12 and 15: "Saul was afraid of David." Isn't that significant? If you are walking today at the very center of divine life, your heart singing with joy because it is right with God through the blood of Calvary—if you are saved and you know it, I tell you, unconverted people are a bit scared of you. They are not always too happy in your company. When I was an unsaved man, I remember how afraid I was in the presence of a man of God.

Observe the contrast: we have seen a soul in glorious progress and a soul in decline and desolation. We may ask why these things should be, for God has no favorites. Now I would draw aside the inmost veil and trace to the roots a soul's disobedience.

I commend to you the careful reading of I Samuel 15, where the prophet came and faced Saul with this accusation: "Because thou hast rejected the word of the Lord, he hath also rejected thee from being king" (15:23). Do you say it is tough of God to do that? Wait a minute—it was not just one act, it was an attitude of life. Disobedience began years before, when Samuel commanded Saul to wait for him before he offered the sacrifice, and Saul became impatient. Of course he did, for he did not know what to do with his idle moments, as David did. He became impatient with God as well as with Samuel, and offered the sacrifice himself. Then, later, he disobeyed God's Word and spared some of the Amalekites, as recorded in I Samuel 15. He repeatedly rejected the Word of the Lord and therefore his course was downward, irrevocably downward.

Do I speak to someone who has disobeyed the Word of the Lord? His Word came to you saying, "Believe on the Lord Jesus Christ, and thou shalt be saved" (Acts 16:31). But you said "No, it costs too much! I'm too proud. There are too many complications in my life."

The Word of the Lord came telling you to submit to the Lord Jesus and receive the Holy Ghost in His fullness, for He gives the Holy Spirit to them that obey Him. But you surveyed, on the other hand, some friendship, some iniquitous habit, and you said "No!" to the Lord. Oh, be careful! If a man rejects His Word, God will reject him. God withdraws His protection from the disobedient heart, and if that man be a child of God, though the Spirit of God will ever be in him, the protecting hand of God is taken off, His guiding power is removed, and he is delivered to the devil for the destruction of the flesh and the saving of the soul, as we are shown in I Corinthians 5:5.

As a result of his continued disobedience, Saul's heart became a prey to every evil, lurking thing. Here is the root of his jealousy; here is the source of his murderous thoughts. When he ignored God's command that he should slay the Amalekites, he never dreamed that his disobedience to God would end in attempted murder. He thought it didn't matter, that he could do it and get away with it.

The life which began with such promise ended with such folly. He became impatient with God's delays and disobeyed God's commands, and the darkness began to gather. This poor, desolate, lonely soul found himself encompassed by the thunderclouds of passion and madness and jealousy, all God's loving and protecting power withdrawn from him.

The last rays of the setting sun sink beyond the horizon and everything is dark. That is Saul!

By contrast, David went into battle shouting, "I come to thee in the name of the Lord of hosts!" (I Samuel 17:45). "In the character of God" is what he meant. To highlight this contrast, we find here a man whose only weapon—whose only strength for testimony, whose only power in ministry—was the name of the Lord. But that name is no magic "Open sesame"—if a man uses the name, it is because he is identified with the name.

To come in the name of the Lord Jesus, to stand with empty hands, without any other weapon at all—facing an unbeliever, facing a pagan tribe on the mission field, facing a company of godless business colleagues in the name of the Lord Jesus Christ—is to stand in a place of absolute authority. That is, provided as you stand in that name you are identified with Him, submitted altogether to the character and loveliness of Christ and to His sovereignty. Therefore, when you speak God speaks, and through your lips and life the Lord begins to work.

We have seen these two lives, and observed how David won that day because his motives were pure: "that all the earth may know that there is a God in Israel" (I Samuel 17:46). He was not concerned about his own glory, but he was concerned that people might know about his God. He put God in His proper place of authority, for he knew that he himself was only an instrument: "The battle is the Lord's." David could use God's name because the Lord was in His rightful place in his life. Contrast this man with Saul, and ponder the horror and the awful loneliness of a man who has rejected the word of God.

Which are you? Before God, are you in spiritual decline or in living faith? Is your religion only a formula, or is Christ real to you all the time? Are you desolate and bereft, or are you in fellowship with the Holy Spirit moment by moment? Are you living in disobedience to the Word of God, or are you following the Lamb of God wherever He may lead?

How much depends upon your answer! For the decline in your life can stop, the downward grade can cease immediately, the desolation of your heart can end, and Jesus can come with all His blessed grace to fill your life with His beauty and fragrance now, at this minute, *if* your disobedience ends right now.

> Make me a captive, Lord,
> And then I shall be free;

Force me to render up my sword,
    And I shall conqueror be.
I sink in life's alarms
    When by myself I stand;
Imprison me within Thine arms,
    And strong shall be my hand.

George Matheson

And David lamented with this lamentation over Saul and over Jonathan his son. . . .

The beauty of Israel is slain upon thy high places: how are the mighty fallen! Tell it not in Gath, publish it not in the streets of Askelon; lest the daughters of the Philistines rejoice, lest the daughters of the uncircumcised triumph.

Ye mountains of Gilboa, let there be no dew, neither let there be rain, upon you, nor fields of offerings: for there the shield of the mighty is vilely cast away, the shield of Saul, as though he had not been anointed with oil.

From the blood of the slain, from the fat of the mighty, the bow of Jonathan turned not back, and the sword of Saul returned not empty.

Saul and Jonathan were lovely and pleasant in their lives, and in their death they were not divided: they were swifter than eagles, they were stronger than lions.

Ye daughters of Israel, weep over Saul, who clothed you in scarlet, with other delights, who put on ornaments of gold upon your apparel.

How are the mighty fallen in the midst of the battle! O Jonathan, thou wast slain in thine high places.

I am distressed for thee, my brother Jonathan: very pleasant hast thou been unto me: thy love to me was wonderful, passing the love of women.

How are the mighty fallen, and the weapons of war perished!

II SAMUEL 1:17-27

CHAPTER 4

SOULS IN HARMONY

(II Samuel 1:17–27)

SOME INCIDENTS IN the life of David as recounted in the latter part of I Samuel are being passed over (but will be returned to later) in order to consider at this point the verses that comment upon the influence of Jonathan in the life of David.

We have noticed the decline of Saul in contrast to the steady rise of David, and Saul's great enmity toward David. Now we have an opposite influence: the strengthening hand of a God-given friend. What encouragement and help such a friend can bring to a man whom God is shaping and fashioning after His own likeness!

What does meditation on this passage reveal? The love of Jonathan for David is but a very pale reflection of the love of Christ for me—this must be the major chord of our study. But first, as we think about this familiar story of lovely Old Testament friendship, I want to gather from it some gems of inspiration and encouragement concerning the sanctifying power of godly friendships.

We see, in the first place, that the love of Jonathan for David was pure in its origin. It seems to have been a case of "love at first sight" (I Samuel 18:3-4). As Jonathan saw David come back from battle with the head of Goliath in his hand, he loved him as one brave soldier might love another.

Jonathan had already proved himself in battle. He and his armor-bearer had turned the tide of invasion not long before, and scattered the foe, gathering all the people of Israel around him in loyalty and affection. Then why did not Jonathan himself tackle Goliath? Think upon the story for a moment—what a tremendous sense of despair must have been in Jonathan's heart as he saw his father slipping back, disobeying God, losing his power of command, rejected from being king. What could the king's son possibly do to turn the tide in a situation like that?

But the moment that Jonathan saw David go out to battle, his heart went out to him in great affection and devotion. He "loved him," we read, "as he loved his own soul." Gladly would Jonathan have given his very life for David; "the soul of Jonathan was knit unto the soul of David," says the record. The qualities of character that Jonathan saw in David drew from him admiration and love.

I would pause to say that it is God's plan for souls to be knit together thus. Adam and Eve came into the world like that, knit together in a oneness which God had given to them. But sin, the great divider of human hearts as well as of men from God, soon did its deadly work and separated them one from the other with the result that ever since then each of us has started the solitary journey of life all alone. The human heart has cried out that it might be knit to another as Jonathan was knit to David, as Adam was knit to Eve. Therefore every true friendship, every real Christian courtship, every genuine oneness in marriage, is a re-establishment of this sacred union; it was God's purpose from before the foundation of the world.

Was your courtship pure in its origin? Did you fall in love at first sight perhaps because of something of Christ Himself that you saw in the qualities of the one you loved? Because you saw the loveliness of the Lord Jesus and the sweetness of His character, you loved for His sake, and you were knit together. Do your friendships start like that, or are you attracted to something that is lower? When a friendship, a courtship, a marriage, begins on that foundation, it will stand any test. If it starts on another foundation, it is built on sand.

In the second place, observe that Jonathan's love to David was disinterested in its action. How unselfish Jonathan was! You notice in these verses that, though the king's son and heir to the kingdom, he stripped himself of every symbol of his royalty in favor of the one who was his rival. It would have been only natural to be jealous. Instead, one day when David was hiding from Saul, Jonathan sought him out: "Jonathan Saul's son arose, and went to David into the wood, and strengthened his hand in God. And he said unto him, Fear not: for the hand of Saul my father shall not find thee; and thou shalt be king over Israel, and I shall be next unto thee; and that also Saul my father knoweth" (I Samuel 23:16-17).

David's faith was on the point of faltering. He might well have given up altogether. If he had, he would have ceased to be Jonathan's rival to the throne. But Jonathan went to him and strengthened his hand in God: he did the very thing that would put David above him. But Jonathan was happy to be in the background if only the one he loved could be exalted and put upon the throne. He was glad to step out of the picture if only the one whom he loved so dearly might have the place of prominence. Seldom does a friend put himself in the background for the sake of another like that.

Then, furthermore, Jonathan's love was steadfast in opposition. It is an amazing record that we have of Jonathan's intense loyalty to his father, a man rejected from the kingdom, a man who had turned his back upon God. Jonathan, all through the story, was loyal to Saul, so much so that David said in his lament over them, "Saul and Jonathan were lovely and pleasant in their lives, and in their death they were not divided" (II Samuel 1:23).

But Jonathan was consistently steadfast in his love for David, even in the face of opposition from his father, whose jealousy, hatred, and envy of David he knew. All the time Jonathan took David's side, comforting him; and yet he stood by in loyalty to his father, until one day he was killed in the battle alongside him. Jonathan did not allow his love for David to divert him from the path of duty. He remained true to what he believed to be his right course. Although he loved David as his own soul, he stood by his poor, desolate, helpless father, until they died together in the battle.

When I think of that story, my heart is stirred by a desire not only that I might have a Jonathan in my life—that is surely very wonderful, but very selfish—but also that I might find a David somewhere to whom I could be a Jonathan. Would you ask the Holy Spirit to make you a friend like that, to help you to cultivate in your life sanctifying disinterested, steadfast friendships?

Oh, that the Lord might let us play a part in shaping and fashioning another life in the image of Jesus Christ! Ask Him to make you a friend who will be to someone what Jonathan was, "a friend who sticketh closer than a brother." In such a friendship the great purpose of God in making us one in the body of Christ is fulfilled, for the Lord Jesus came "That they all may be one; as thou, Father, art in me, and I in thee, that they also may be one in us" (John 17:21). Let these thoughts be a challenge to us all, and perhaps a rebuke to some who are just no friends at all, but who stab in the back while they smile to the face. So many a human heart has been absolutely broken because of the betrayal of a false friend.

What sort of a friend are you? Are you trustworthy and steadfast in the midst of opposition and trouble? Is your friendship pure in its origin? Is it based upon right motives? Is your desire the welfare and blessing of another, even though it means that you are thrust into the background?

We come now to the major theme in this passage. I would repeat that though there is in Jonathan a reflection of the love of Jesus for my soul, I say it is only a very pale reflection, as I hope to show you.

"Thy love to me was wonderful," said David concerning Jonathan. But somehow I want to take those words and put them in your heart and on your lips. I can scarcely preach about them, but would bear testimony in the presence of the Lord Jesus Christ, and say to Him, "Lord, Thy love to me is wonderful!"

I have taken three thoughts concerning Jonathan's love to David. Let me apply the same to Christ's love for us, and begin by saying it was also pure in its origin. When did the Lord begin to love me? I don't know. Certainly it was long before the day when He said, "Let there be light!" It was long before there were any such creatures as human beings at all: for away back in eternity the Lord looked through the mirror of His fore-knowledge, and of His understanding, and of His omnipotence, and His love and delight were with the sons of man. His love had no beginning; there never was a time when He didn't love you and me. "I have loved thee with an everlasting love: therefore with lovingkindness have I drawn thee" (Jeremiah 31:3).

Did Jonathan love David in the first place because of what he saw of character and beauty and things to admire in David's life? Yes, he did. But oh, Lord Jesus, I can think of a thousand reasons why You should pass me by completely! For if that be the basis of God's love in Christ for my soul, I have not a hope in eternity. "But God commendeth his love toward us, in that, while we were yet sinners, Christ died for us" (Romans 5:8). He died for the ungodly, the just for the unjust, that He might bring us to God. There wasn't one lovely or good thing in any of us that could draw out love from the heart of a holy Saviour— there was everything to repel. Yet the infinite God, the altogether lovely One, whose ideal of love surely is far beyond anything we could ever imagine, whose capacity for love is beyond our understanding altogether, *He* loved us and gave Himself for us.

That is the miracle of miracles! That is far beyond our understanding. He could not rest in heaven without us, and heaven would not be complete unless you and I were there, that we should be His bride and He should be our Bridegroom. Oh, what love for an object that is so absolutely unworthy! God's love is so pure in its origin, without a single thing in us to attract, with no motive at all except for the great fact that God Himself is Love.

Furthermore, the love of God in Christ was also disinterested in its action. Did Jonathan strip himself of all the emblems of royalty and lay them at David's feet? Was he happy to suffer and to be in the background if only he could secure the promotion and honor of the one he loved? A greater than Jonathan is here today. He laid aside the glory which He had with the Father. He said of Himself, "The Son of man came not to be ministered unto, but to minister, and to give his life a ransom for many" (Matthew 20:28).

Let us sit down at the foot of the cross and just gaze at Him there. Mark that thorn-crowned brow; look at those hands and feet pierced with nails and see the blood. Look at that broken heart, the water and the blood, the gaping side. Think of it! This is the Lord of glory, dying amidst the scorn of the people He came to redeem. Think of Him in heaven with all authority in His hands and the angelic host around Him. Then look at Him hanging on a cross with the riff-raff of humanity sneering and gaping at him. When I realilze that there He took my sin, the pollution and filthiness of my life, as if it were His very own, and then poured it into oblivion as far as the east is from the west, I say, "Lord Jesus, Thy love to me was wonderful!"

Have you ever felt that your love for those who have gone on beyond would be like a great flood tide in its intensity if only they could come back? Suppose you found waiting in your own room the child you loved, the husband or wife, sitting there to welcome you—it just doesn't bear thinking about! But Jesus *did* come back! He rose again! He lives and loves us now as much as He ever did then!

A greater than Jonathan is here today, right now where you are. He is here to plan for you, to care for you. Is your lot hard to take? Is the going rough? Is there a cup of bitterness to drink somewhere? Are your friends of a totally different kind from Jonathan and have they hurt and grieved you? The Bible says that joy comes in the morning, for then we will see the King in His beauty with never a cloud between, and we will serve Him without any weariness or sin, and He shall present us faultless before the presence of God with exceeding joy. His love is so wonderful!

His love was so disinterested in action that He not merely stepped into the background, but He stepped right down to the cross. He came, not merely to comfort and strengthen our hands in God, but

Bearing shame and scoffing rude,
In our place condemned He stood.
Philip P. Bliss

In order that He might promote and honor those He loved, those who were so abased and sinful, so utterly unworthy, He stepped down and down until He was made sin itself that you and I might be exalted to the height of heaven. The love of Jesus is so wonderful!

His love remains steadfast in opposition. Did Jonathan endure the hatred of Saul for the sake of David? Did he strengthen David's hand in God in the face of all the enmity of his father? A greater than Jonathan is here, for not only did the Lord Jesus endure the hatred of His enemies, but think of the reception He had from me! Perhaps you can echo my testimony as I say in God's presence that there was a day when I refused the Lord, when I told Him I didn't want Him. I would not listen to the Lord because the devil was holding my heart and gripping my life. Yet Jesus came back again and again, through books and preachers, through testimonies and providences, through sufferings and troubles of every kind—He came back, and He would not take "no" for an answer.

Oh, the love of Jesus is so wonderful! Since that day when He captured my heart and brought me to Himself, there have been many times when I have been so cold, so worldly, so sinful. There have been times of being misunderstood and maligned, times of darkness and weariness, times of sorrow and pain. In all these experiences of life, His love would never let me go.

I wonder if it is too much to think that perhaps in heaven, through all eternity, I will be telling out that love, not to a handful of people, but to whole constellations throughout the universe, to millions of rational souls who have never heard of the love of a dying Saviour. I trust that my imagination is not running away with me—certainly my heart does! I believe that God's immense universe will need millions of redeemed people to go through all His creation everywhere in space to make known in limitless regions to countless intelligent beings who have never known what sin is, the story of what happened on this little planet called Earth—where God Himself lived and bled and died and rose again to bring salvation to unworthy men.

When I think about that, I am not very interested in present attempts to reach the moon and the planets. As a member of the ransomed throng, I expect to have part in telling redemption's story to all God's

created universe. That is space travel with an objective! Is it fantastic?
No, listen to Ephesians 3:10, "To the intent that now unto the principalities and powers in heavenly places might be known by the church
the manifold wisdom of God." I believe we have never begun to understand the tremendous scope of the redemption that is ours in Christ.

I would remind you "what is the exceeding greatness of his power
to us-ward who believe, according to the working of his mighty power,
Which he wrought in Christ, when he raised him from the dead, and
set him at his own right hand in the heavenly places, Far above all prin-
cipality, and power, and might, and dominion, and every name that is
named, not only in this world, but also in that which is to come: And
hath put all things under his feet, and gave him to be the head over
all things to the church, which is his body, the fulness of him that filleth
all in all" (Ephesians 1:19-23). Let that re-echo in your heart and mind
as you think of what heaven is going to be like. And to think that you
and I may have a part through all eternity in declaring the mystery
and the marvel of God's redemption in this little planet to countless
multitudes who have never heard or seen the love of God as we
know it!

Indeed, the love of the Lord Jesus is wonderful! Can you say that?

This example of human friendship, David and Jonathan, forms the
link in this message. If you can say, "Lord Jesus, Thy love to me is so
wonderful!" out of a heart full of gratitude and praise, as you have
accepted that love, then the amazing thing is that His love is shed
abroad in your heart by the Holy Spirit to make you a Jonathan. You
cannot claim to know the love of Christ if you are one thing to a man's
face and something else behind his back. The Lord tests the reality of
your response to His love, which He made known to you at Calvary
through the Lord Jesus Christ. How do you behave to your friends?
And also, how do you behave to your enemies? For when the love
of God—pure in its origin, disinterested in its action, steadfast amidst
all opposition—is shed abroad in your heart by the Holy Spirit, you
love like that, too.

As we are told in I Corinthians 13, love is forbearing and kind; love
knows no jealousy; love does not brag, is not conceited; love is not un-
mannerly, nor selfish, nor irritable, nor mindful of wrong. Love does
not rejoice in injustice, but joyfully sides with the truth; love can over-
look faults; love is full of trust, full of hope, full of endurance. Love
never fails!

Do you love like that?

And Saul sought to smite David even to the wall with the javelin; but he slipped away out of Saul's presence, and he smote the javelin into the wall: and David fled, and escaped that night. Saul also sent messengers unto David's house, to watch him, and to slay him in the morning: and Michal David's wife told him, saying, If thou save not thy life to night, to morrow thou shalt be slain. . . .

So David fled, and escaped, and came to Samuel to Ramah, and told him all that Saul had done to him.

I SAMUEL 19:10-11, 18

Deliver me from mine enemies, O my God: defend me from them that rise up against me.

Deliver me from the workers of iniquity, and save me from bloody men.

For lo, they lie in wait for my soul: the mighty are gathered against me; not for my transgression, nor for my sin, O Lord.

They run and prepare themselves without my fault: awake to help me, and behold.

Thou therefore, O Lord God of hosts, the God of Israel, awake to visit all the heathen: be not merciful to any wicked transgressors. . . .

But thou, O Lord, shalt laugh at them; thou shalt have all the heathen in derision.

Because of his strength will I wait upon thee: for God is my defence. . . .

Consume them in thy wrath, consume them, that they may not be: and let them know that God ruleth in Jacob unto the ends of the earth. . . .

But I will sing of thy power; yea, I will sing aloud of thy mercy in the morning: for thou hast been my defence and refuge in the day of my trouble.

Unto thee, O my strength, will I sing: for God is my defence, and the God of my mercy.

PSALM 59:1-17

CHAPTER 5

PERSECUTED BUT NOT FORSAKEN

(I Samuel 19:10–11, 18; Psalm 59:1–17)

STUDENTS OF SCRIPTURE have suggested quite a few alternatives for the date and context of the 59th Psalm. Some say that it was written in the time of Isaiah, and that the enemies referred to are the Syrian army. Others suggest that it was written in the time of Nehemiah, and therefore the enemies are Sanballat and Tobiah. But both the Hebrew text and the Septuagint (Greek) Version of the Old Testament give to this Psalm the title which appears at the head of it in the King James Version: "David prayeth to be delivered from his enemies when Saul sent, and they watched the house to kill him."

It is this context which I prefer to accept, and thus place the 59th Psalm at the point we have reached in our studies on David: "Saul also sent messengers unto David's house, to watch him, and to slay him in the morning" (I Samuel 19:11). This was the beginning of a very unhappy time in David's life, a dark and lonely experience which nevertheless played a tremendous part in the making of his character.

As we study Psalm 59 in this context, I suggest there is, in the first place, what I would call the presence of a gathering cloud in David's life. Its approach can be seen clearly from the record in I Samuel: "David came to Saul, and stood before him: and he loved him greatly; and he became his armourbearer" (16:21); "Saul hath slain his thousands, and David his ten thousands. And Saul was very wroth . . . And Saul eyed David from that day and forward" (18:7-9). "Saul was afraid of David, because the Lord was with him" (18:12). "Saul was yet the more afraid of David; and Saul became David's enemy continually" (18:29). At last, "Saul sought to smite David even to the wall with the javelin. . . . Saul also sent messengers to David's house, to watch him, and to slay him in the morning" (19:10-11).

Do you see the pressure growing, the gathering cloud relentlessly rising over the horizon until it reaches its bursting point? If only Saul had drowned that first fit of jealousy in a bath of prayer, what a different story we would have to tell! In the same way, if you and I had only drowned the first attack of something in our lives in a sea of prayer, what a different attitude perhaps would be ours today! But Saul didn't do it; he allowed jealousy to eat at him until nothing but murder would satisfy it.

You will recall how many attempts Saul had already made upon David's life. He made him a captain in his army (over a thousand men) in order to have him killed in battle. He demanded from him one hundred dead Philistines as the price of marrying his daughter, and David produced twice that many. Twice Saul hurled a javelin at David to pin him to the wall, and finally he sent messengers to his house to kill him. Only the warning of David's wife enabled him to escape through a window and run for his life.

Oh, what unhappy days those were! He was separated from his home by the pressure of Saul's hatred, and it was not David's fault, for he had done nothing to deserve it. He was not conscious of any sin in his life which might have brought this attack upon him: "The mighty are gathered against me; not for my transgression, nor for my sin, O Lord" (Psalm 59:3). Not that he would have claimed to be anything but a sinner, but on this particular occasion he knew he had not done one thing to deserve the pressure that threatened to crush him completely.

Before going further I would pause to ask if you are facing something like this. From one quarter or another the pressure on you is being applied until it has almost overwhelmed and broken you. As far as you know you are clear of guilt; you have done nothing to justify the attack that is being made upon you, yet this cloud has gathered. You saw it coming and tried to avoid it, but you could not; you find yourself in the middle of a cyclone, and there is no escape. How real is the pressure of a gathering cloud!

How true it is for those in Christian work: the pressure of criticism, the pressure of financial problems, the pressure of a thousand and one details, the gathering cloud that presses deeply upon you is very real.

It may be in your home life; it may be in terms of sorrow or hardship, suffering or persecution. All of us at one time or another know an experience of the gathering cloud which we cannot avoid. The horizon which recently was perfectly clear has darkened until it is black and ominous, and we find ourselves right in the path of a hurricane.

If you find yourself in that setting, I would have you learn a lesson from David's reaction, and how you may triun.ph in such a situation. Notice particularly, therefore, what I would call the prayer of a growing confidence. Watch how David reacts to this pressure—you may learn a lesson which will be a blessing to you the rest of your days. Indeed, it may help us to understand why God allows the cloud to come at all.

David commences this Psalm by casting himself upon God for deliverance. He prays himself out of his sense of helplessness into a quiet confidence, and then into a burst of victorious song, although the situation hasn't changed and the enemy is still there. He begins down in the depths, crying out to God that He would save him. Then he moves into a calm, quiet assurance that God is in control before finally bursting into a song of triumph. Traps and snares are laid for him all around, but he seems somehow or other to escape panic and find rest in the Lord.

"Thou therefore, O Lord God of hosts, the God of Israel, awake to visit all the heathen: be not merciful to any wicked transgressors" (Psalm 59:5). Notice what he calls God. As a matter of fact, he accumulates all the titles he can think of to call heaven to his aid in this crisis. "O Lord Jehovah, Elohim of Sabaoth, Lord God of hosts! Nothing less than all Thy resources are going to be adequate for me at this moment in my life. Lord, I need all there is of Thee, every attribute of Thy power and grace, faithfulness and strength. Lord, just at this moment—in the teeth of the wind that is now against me, in the thick of the clouds that are engulfing me—I need every bit of Thine omnipotence!"

That prayer is not at all presumptuous. David knew that in this particular situation he was innocent, and therefore he described his enemies as workers of iniquity, heathen, wicked transgressors. How was he sure that this was really an attack of the enemy upon him? Because he knew that Saul was fighting against God. Samuel had told Saul that he was rejected from the kingdom and David had been anointed king. Hence David knew that the pressure was coming from an enemy who was actually doing battle against the will of God. In his attempt to take David's life, Saul was deliberately seeking to frustrate God's purpose. Nor is he the last man who has stepped into the arena of life to defy God, nor the only one to be crushed in doing it.

"Thou, O Lord, shalt laugh at them; thou shalt have all the heathen in derision" (Psalm 59:8), is how David expresses his conviction that his enemies are God's enemies. Notice, he doesn't say only his immediate enemies, but "all the heathen." In other words, he is reasoning with himself and with God this way, "Lord, my deliverance in this situation is but a part of Thy great plan for the whole world to establish truth and righteousness."

The God who adds a little dewdrop upon a flower in the morning is the same God who put the stars in place and designed the path of every constellation in the heavens. And if Jehovah can care for all that, then surely He can care for me—that was David's argument.

I find it very refreshing to believe that here is your argument and mine with God whenever there is the pressure of a gathering cloud for which, before Him, you know you are not responsible. You are in that position in life, whatever it may be, because He has put you there. You know that you can lay hold of all His power to see you through, for your surrender to God in Jesus Christ means that He has guaranteed to deliver you from all your affliction, because that is only a small part of His great delivering purpose for His people. If God can care for the whole universe, He can care for you and your little need today.

May I say a word in passing to someone who may be putting the pressure upon a servant of God, who, humanly speaking, may be causing it by unkindness, or by spreading false rumors, or perhaps by gossip and criticism. Beware lest you are fighting against God as Saul was!

I look back to such a time in my life before my conversion. If you had known me then you would have said, "I couldn't imagine anyone in the world less likely to be saved than Alan Redpath!" Someone more careless, more indifferent, more ungodly, it would be hard to meet; but within three months I was saved. For at that time I was fighting against God, and I will tell you how I did it. I was putting the pressure upon a Christian and giving him hell on earth. I was mean and unkind and critical, spreading false stories about his character—doing everything I could to force that man away from the circle of my life. I wasn't fighting him; I was fighting the God who lived within him and shone through him.

Beware lest you are doing that today, for in your attacks upon an individual, whoever it may be, you are really attacking God. It may be a Sunday school teacher, a preacher, or a missionary. If you are criticizing or being unkind, ask yourself, "Is it the man I am attacking, or is it the Lord for whom he stands, the message that he proclaims, the witness he makes?"

In the midst of that cloud David brought his arguments to God, then he said, "But thou, O Lord, shalt laugh at them; thou shalt have all the heathen in derision" (Psalm 59:8). It is not a pleasant thing to be laughed at by anybody, but when God is doing the laughing—oh, the horror of being laughed at by God!

See also how David was assured that his enemies were God's enemies, and how he was strengthened to pray on with a wonderful sense of calm: "Because of his strength will I wait upon thee: for God is my defence" (Psalm 59:9). In the Authorized (King James) Version the words "because of" are added in order to preserve the sense of the sentence. But with the very slight change of one Hebrew letter, which might have been omitted in manuscripts, the translation of this text would read much more smoothly: "My strength, I will wait upon thee," instead of "his strength." I like the translation which puts it this way: "Upon thee, O my strength, will I wait; for God is my high tower," and then in verse 17, "Unto thee, O my strength, will I sing: for God is my high tower and my mercy."

Isn't that significant? Within the compass of these two verses David has prayed himself out of his panic (if he had any), out of fear or doubt into confidence and then into joyful song. There was no change in the circumstances that surrounded him, but his cry for deliverance became a calm waiting upon God and then a song of victory even with the enemy pressing him on all sides. How did such a thing happen to his soul?

First, see David's attitude: "I will wait upon thee." That word means "I will watch for Thee as the shepherd watches the sheep, as the sentry is on duty." "I will lift up my eyes unto the hills," David sang at another time, "from whence cometh my help? My help cometh from the Lord" (Psalm 121:1-2). Of course, I know that God watches over His people, but then I must also watch for the coming of His strength and His power. He looks down to care for me in the midst of the cloud, but I must watch for Him to pour out His blessing upon me in my need. My friend, if we fail to receive strength for the pressure of the cloud, it is usually because we are not looking for it.

To put it in a simple allegory, I wonder how many ships pass in the night with heavenly reinforcements of grace and patience, strength and courage, love and power, understanding and sympathy? They come with their heavenly cargo and dock at my wharf, but they go out again because I am not there to unload them.

We pray, but we don't wait. We ask, but we don't expect to receive. We know, but we depart from heaven's door before it is opened to us. If you are overwhelmed with the pressure of some cloud, it isn't God's fault. The fact may be that your hands are too full of other things to receive His strength and enabling.

"My soul waiteth for the Lord more than they that watch for the morning: I say, more than they that watch for the morning" (Psalm 130:6). Have you ever waited for the morning? You have a restless night, and you toss and turn and try every possible position; then you stand up and you lie down; you go to the window and you sigh, "Oh, when is it going to be light?" After a night of agony you have longed for the morning. "My soul, wait: watch for the dawn!" That is the language of David.

The help of God does not come to us when we are indifferent. It comes to the man who is depending on God in the thick of the fight. It comes to the one who tarries for the vision in faith. It comes to the one who believes that he who waits upon the Lord shalll never be confounded. It comes to the one who rests upon the promises of the Word. It comes to the one who believes that before he calls, God will answer. It comes to the man who lives by faith as if in the actual possession of the answer to his prayer, although the enemy is still around him. It is faith which turns distress into singing.

Then observe David's secure anchor. Who is this God to whom David went? How does he describe Him? "My strength and my high tower." "God my strength" means "God within me." "God my high tower" means "God all around me, protecting me." God-possessed and God-encompassed—such was David's anchor in the cloud. "What then have I to fear?" he asks. "I put God my Saviour between myself and all my enemies, and I lie down in peace."

He *is* my strength, not that I receive strength from Him, but rather that I take Him to be my strength in weakness. The name and character of the Lord is the strong tower, and the righteous run to it and are safe. This is the One upon whom we wait and for whom we watch eagerly; this is the One to whom we look through the cloud for His coming. In all the pressure of the storm which threatens to overwhelm us, we watch and wait:

> Hidden in the hollow
>   Of His blessed hand,
> Never foe can follow,
>   Never traitor stand;
> Not a surge of worry,
>   Not a shade of care,
> Not a blast of hurry
>   Touch the spirit there.
>   *Frances R. Havergal*

We have considered the pressure of a gathering cloud, the prayer of a growing confidence, and now, in the third place, let us look at the praise of a genuine conviction which is revealed in the last two verses of this Psalm. Notice that David is beyond simple calmness now, beyond just resting: he is joyfully praising the Lord. With the enemy still on the attack all around him, he is living in absolute victory in the middle of the cloud.

Many a hard-pressed child of God has learned to put the Lord Jesus between themselves and the enemy, and start singing! Have you learned that?

Do you notice that David has found yet another name for the Lord here? In the moment of calm waiting he said, "Thou art my defence; Thou art my high tower; Thou art my strength." But he says something else now: "Thou art my mercy." What a wonderful thought that is!

This Psalm reminds me of the building of a skyscraper. What confusion it is at the beginning! You look down into a deep cavity and see the men with great bulldozers pushing around mud which is indescribable. But when the building is completed, see its towering head up in the sunshine! What a marvel it is then! Somehow this Psalm begins down below ground as deep cries unto deep, but the climax is up in the sunshine of the presence of the Lord, where His glory fills the whole picture.

Here is a man under the pressure of a cloud, but his heart is right with God and therefore he is full of praise and joy. He is saying, in effect, "Lord, I called You my strength when I was so weak, and I meant it. I thought of You as my fortress when I was surrounded by my enemies, and I meant that, too. I know that You are still all those things to me, with my foes all around me and no relief from the pressure. You are still my strength and my high tower, but, Lord Jesus, You are something more: You are my mercy—the pressure of this gathering cloud has shown me Your tender pity. I never knew, Lord, how much You loved me, until You allowed this pressure to teach me to watch and wait on You."

Like David, you may have thought you were besieged by enemies who were crushing you to pieces. Instead, you find yourself in the grip of a loving, chastening, nail-pierced hand that is using the cloud to teach you God's way with His child. Long ago, in a covenant of mercy to His people and to the world, He said to Noah, "I will put my bow *in the clouds."* Never do you find it in the blue sky; you find the mercy of God in the very thick of the cloud.

The pressure of the gathering cloud that is upon your life today is in the hand of God and under His control. He knows when to say, "Thus far and no further." Let there be from your life the prayer of a growing confidence: My Lord, my strength, my defense! You are possessed by Him, because by His Spirit He lives within you; you are protected all around by Him from all your foes.

Therefore, while still under the cloud, do not be asleep when He calls at your dock with heavenly reinforcements. Do not be too busy about other things, with your hands so full attempting to meet the pressure in your own strength that when the ship comes with grace, patience, and love, you are not there. Wait and watch as a man watches for the morning; and so shall your waiting become the praise of a genuine conviction that this cloud is the mercy of God, and it has taken the pressure of it to drive you for shelter into the wounded side of a crucified Saviour.

> Ye fearful saints, fresh courage take;
> The clouds ye so much dread
> Are big with mercy, and shall break
> In blessings on your head.
> *William Cowper*

And Jonathan said unto David, Come, and let us go out into the field. . . .

Then Jonathan said to David, To morrow is the new moon: and thou shalt be missed, because thy seat will be empty. And when thou hast stayed three days, then thou shalt go down quickly . . . and shalt remain by the stone Ezel. And I will shoot three arrows on the side thereof, as though I shot at a mark. . . . But if I say thus unto the young man, Behold, the arrows are beyond thee; go thy way: for the Lord hath sent thee away. . . .

Saul said unto Jonathan his son, Wherefore cometh not the son of Jesse to meat, neither yesterday, nor to day? And Jonathan answered Saul, David earnestly asked leave of me to go to Bethlehem. . . .

Then Saul's anger was kindled against Jonathan and he said unto him . . . I know that thou hast chosen the son of Jesse to thine own confusion. . . . For as long as the son of Jesse liveth upon the ground, thou shalt not be established, nor thy kingdom. Wherefore now send and fetch him unto me, for he shall surely die.

And Jonathan answered Saul his father, and said unto him, Wherefore shall he be slain? what hath he done? And Saul cast a javelin at him to smite him: whereby Jonathan knew that it was determined of his father to slay David. . . .

And it came to pass in the morning, that Jonathan went out into the field at the time appointed with David, and a little lad with him. . . . And when the lad was come to the place of the arrow which Jonathan had shot, Jonathan cried after the lad, and said, Is not the arrow beyond thee? . . .

And Jonathan said to David, Go in peace, forasmuch as we have sworn both of us in the name of the Lord, saying, The Lord be between me and thee, and between my seed and thy seed for ever. And he arose and departed: and Jonathan went into the city.

I SAMUEL 20:11-42

CHAPTER 6

AN ARROW FROM HEAVEN

(I Samuel 20:11–42)

LET US NOT forget that we are considering the story of a man for whom God had an infinite purpose of blessing, whom He had already anointed with His Spirit in token of kingship. Yet at this particular point we find David going through a trial which tested his faith and endurance to the very limit. Indeed, every outward circumstance of David's life at this time seemed to give the lie to all the promises of God. Somehow that brings David very near, for the same kind of situation is experienced by many people even today.

God has an infinite purpose of blessing for each of His children, a purpose which is only beginning to be fulfilled as we come to Christ. But what Christian has not known what it is to have his faith in God's promises tested almost to the breaking point? This ancient story is recounted for us in the Word of God for our comfort and inspiration.

We will stay close to the narrative in I Samuel 20 as we notice some symptoms of David's despair. We heard him singing himself out of his problem by faith in the language of Psalm 59. But the mere fact that he rejoiced in God has not relieved the pressure at all—indeed, it seems to have intensified. I believe I can read between the lines of this story that David is now in a mood of great anxiety and almost of despair.

In the closing part of I Samuel 19 is the record of how David, having escaped from his home through the window when his wife gave him warning that Saul's messengers were coming to kill him, rushed to seek shelter with the prophet Samuel. Saul sent messengers to kill him there at Naioth in Ramah, and still more messengers, and eventually came himself in a desperate effort to finish David forever. The story closes by recounting how one after another the assassins sent by the king, and then King Saul himself, were held in the grip of the Spirit of God, spellbound and unable to touch David.

59

But David himself was not so conscious of God's protection as he was aware of his own panic and fear. Taking advantage of Saul's absence, he made a dash for Gibeah to ask his friend Jonathan a few pointed questions. These are found in I Samuel 20:1-9, and I would paraphrase this conversation so that you may catch the mood of this hunted and harassed servant of God.

David hurried into Jonathan's presence and said to him, "Jonathan, what have I done? What sin have I committed that your father should want to kill me? I am not to blame for this trouble. What is the matter with him?"

That was a reflection upon their trusted friendship, but Jonathan said to him quietly, "David, if my father was determined to kill you, don't you know I would have told you about it? If that was his intention, I am sure he would have said something to me—he keeps nothing from me."

"Oh, no," replied David, "he wouldn't tell you! Saul knows of our love the one for the other. Because of that he would never tell you he intended to kill me, because it would grieve you. As a matter of fact, Jonathan, I know there is only a step between me and death at this point."

"All right, David. What do you want me to do for you?"

"Tomorrow is a thanksgiving day, and I know that I ought to be in Saul's house sharing the feast, but I am going home to share it with my family in Bethlehem. My chair will be empty, and I will be missed. Now, if your father is angry about my absence, then you may be sure that he is set to kill me. If he is perfectly content that I should be away, then it will be all right. Remember, Jonathan, that you brought me into this covenant of friendship; deal kindly with me, won't you? If your father is determined to kill me—well, I would much rather you would kill me yourself than that I should fall into the hands of Saul."

"David, David, surely you can trust me enough to know that I would tell you if my father planned to kill you!"

Do you catch something of David's mood in that conversation? Can you blame him? Isn't it a comfort to think that even a man like that, under pressure, can come to a place where he doubts his friends and also doubts God? Should not David have known that because of the anointing of the Spirit of God upon his life Saul could not possibly kill him? Oh, yes, he should have known, but in the tremendous pressure of the situation the promises of God and His word somehow became unreal. It even made him doubt his friendship with Jonathan.

Are these symptoms to be found in your life today? Has the pressure of some situation, some circumstance, some trial, brought you to doubt the promise of God, and the Word of God, and His purpose for your life? Perhaps that day when you cried, in the words of Philip Doddridge,

'Tis done; the great transaction's done!
I am my Lord's, and He is mine;

is just a vague memory, and it doesn't seem relevant to the situation right now. The burden presses you down to the point where you have begun to doubt God, and even to doubt your friends. The one always follows the other; when a man begins to loosen his hold upon the promises of God he begins to lose his contact with spiritual friendships. A chill in our relationship with heaven is always followed by a chill in our relationships down here. Oh, how readily the sheer pressure of some situation that is absolutely overwhelming throws us completely off balance, until we learn the lesson that God has for us right in the middle of it.

What is the lesson that God has to teach us? Observe now the stone of David's destiny that is found in this chapter. In verse 10 David asked Jonathan how he was going to find out the truth about Saul's sentiments toward him. So Jonathan took him out into a field—it would not have been safe to continue their conversation in the palace. Out in the field, alone under God's heaven and solemnly before the Lord, Jonathan covenanted wtih David to tell him all that was in Saul's heart, whether it was good or evil.

It is apparent, you notice, that Jonathan showed greather faith in the promises of God than did David at this point. Jonathan asked him if he would remember him and his family, and show kindness to his house when the Lord had long since taken him to be with Himself. You will recall that David never forgot that, and later he showed kindness to Mephibosheth for Jonathan's sake. This agreement was the root of that act.

Then in verse 19 Jonathan said, "Now go, and after three days come back again. Come into this field and wait alongside the stone. I will come out from my father's house to shoot three arrows, and I will bring a boy with me (I have to do that to allay suspicion). Though we may not be able to talk to each other, I will shoot the arrows. If they land right by you, it will be safe for you to come back home with me; Saul is going to be kind. If, however, the arrows wing over your head and beyond you, go your way, for the Lord has sent you away. In other words, if that arrow goes beyond you, it is goodbye until we meet in heaven!"

What a fateful moment! Just a matter of a few yards was going to decide David's future. Either he would go back into Saul's house, to the comfort of Jonathan's friendship and the surroundings that were familiar to him, or he would have to go into exile as one cast upon the mercy of God with not a friend in the world to turn to. One or the other of these ways was to be God's path for David, the path that would lead him eventually to the throne of Israel.

There was no doubt in David's mind, I am sure, as to his preference. If he had been asked, he would have chosen to go back to Saul and to the comfort of Jonathan's love. That, surely, was to be preferred to the alternative of exile and the ruggedness of unknown mountains. The decision, however, was out of David's hands completely. All he had to do was to stand by the stone Ezel and wait for an arrow from heaven unerringly to hit the target—an arrow that would tell him either to go out into the wilderness or back into the palace of Saul.

I have called this place "the stone of David's destiny." The margin of verse 19 interprets it as "the stone that shapeth, or sheweth the way." The literal translation of the Hebrew word would suggest "the stone of departure." Driven by all the pressure of circumstances, David is brought to the place where he sees that the decision is not in his hands.

I wonder if this is the lesson the Lord is trying to teach some of us. For each of His children in every circumstance of life there is a stone of destiny. It is a stone, as Daniel tells us, "cut out without hands" (Daniel 2:34). It is a living stone, for it is the Lord of glory Himself. He is destined to have all power, to overthrow all our enemies and to set up His kingdom which will never be destroyed. If I truly belong to Him, if He has filled me with His Spirit and marked me as His, then whatever the pressure upon my life at this point, the issue is out of my hands altogether.

"Behold, I lay in Zion for a foundation a stone, a tried stone, a precious corner stone, a sure foundation" (Isaiah 28:16), declared God. Peter, in the maturity of his age and experience, wrote in his first epistle that we may come to Jesus Christ "as unto a living stone, disallowed indeed of men, but chosen of God, and precious" (I Peter 2:4), and we may become living stones to be built up a spiritual house, a holy priesthood.

Jesus Christ is our stone of destiny, rooted in a green hill outside

Jerusalem. The burden of the pressure of circumstances, whatever it is, may be rolled away as you bring it and leave it at His feet. What else can you do? You are in a predicament, unable to turn this way or that. It is a glorious position to be in: the government is upon His shoulder and your hands are right off the situation; only He can guide. All you can do is what David did, as he took his stand at his stone of destiny and waited.

It is a great thing to be in a position like that, when all you can do is to take your stand at Calvary, and wait. There are so many paths, and naturally some would seem far more attractive than others. Left to choose our way, what fools we would make of ourselves! There may be many alternatives that seem, humanly speaking, more reasonable and attractive than God's way. But there is only one way that leads to the throne, and that is God's plan for your life and mine.

Therefore I beg of you, my dear besieged fellow believer in Christ, out of my heart I say to you at this moment, "Stand still and see the salvation of God." Wait! The decision is beyond you; the battle is not yours but God's; let Him decide. "The stone which the builders disallowed, the same is made the head of the corner" (I Peter 2:7). The Lord Jesus Himself is a stone of destiny, and how precious to those who hide in His wounded side!

Returning to the narrative, let us notice also the symbol of David's departure. Jonathan now has no doubt that David was right concerning Saul's intentions: he "knew that it was determined of his father to slay David" (I Samuel 20:33). Indeed, you observe that in a fit of rage Saul almost took his son Jonathan's life. It was with a heavy heart that Jonathan picked himself up and, taking a lad with him, went outside the palace to shoot the arrows.

The arrows were not from Jonathan's hand alone, for he was but the instrument; he was to shoot the arrows from God right on the target, the arrows that went beyond David to say, "Goodbye, till we meet in glory." "Is not the arrow beyond thee?" shouted Jonathan (I Samuel 20:37).

Picture David standing by the stone Ezel, waiting. From a distance he sees his dear friend coming out, the man he loved with all his heart. He saw the boy with him also. Jonathan, as if he is at target practice, takes an arrow and shoots it. David tensely watches its flight as it arches over him, landing beyond him. I wonder what his feelings were then.

What was the message of that arrow to his heart? He knew it meant the Lord was sending him away. It wasn't mere chance that the arrow fell where it did. It had, in fact, come from the very hand of God. It was a symbol of the will of God, and behind its flight was the loving purpose of God for His harassed child. If David dared to linger now, after this word from heaven, he would lose his life, the crown, and everything that God had for him. This man's life was being emptied from vessel to vessel, like wine, in order to preserve its freshness and keep it from going musty. Every prop upon which he had leaned was taken away from him; now he must stand alone. Before him lay the rugged mountains and dark valleys, with no promise of relief from the pressure. Behind him was the comfort of friendship, of human love, of home, of perhaps a reconciliation with Saul and restoration to a position of honor. Now, nothing—but God!

Certainly the hardest thing of all was to lose the crutch of Jonathan's love. This was their goodbye, as far as they knew. "And Jonathan said to David, Go in peace, forasmuch as we have sworn both of us in the name of the Lord, saying, The Lord be between me and thee, and between my seed and thy seed for ever. And he arose and departed: and Jonathan went into the city" (I Samuel 20:42). They met only once more just before Jonathan died. Picture it, as David slowly departed up the mountain and Jonathan went back to his path of duty to live with a father who didn't understand him at all, who hadn't the slightest interest in his principles. Here are two friends cut asunder in the sovereignty of God.

This is not remote from us today. Let the Holy Spirit wing this word to your heart: "If any man will come after me, let him deny himself, and take up his cross daily, and follow me" (Luke 9:23). Listen again to the majestic words of the Saviour, "He that loveth father or mother more than me is not worthy of me: and he that loveth son or daughter more than me is not worthy of me" (Matthew 10:37). "Whosoever he be of you that forsaketh not all that he hath, he cannot be my disciple" (Luke 14:33).

Has the pressure of some trial thrown you into despair, causing you to doubt God's promises? The fact that you are the Lord's and He is yours seems to be almost irrelevant to the situation. But He has brought you to this place just to teach you what it is to take your stand at Calvary, at your stone of destiny, and to wait: to be still and know that He is God. In fact, that is all you *can* do. The decision is out of your control; you can only wait for Him to guide.

There is only one way to the throne, God's great destiny for you. There may be many alternative paths, but a false move at this point in your life could cause you to miss all His plan for you. If you take things into your own hands and try to run the situation yourself, the result will be disaster. You have to be still and wait, if God has shot His arrows beyond you. You have leaned upon Christian friends, seeking their counsel in prayer. You have agonized and wept and prayed. You have tried to hold on to the immediate circumstances, for your heart clings to the familiar, to the beloved, to the things around you with their promise of shelter and security. But the arrow has landed on target beyond you—perhaps because God has called you to some far distant surroundings, or it may be because He will leave you where you are. The message of the arrow beyond you is not primarily geographical, it is spiritual.

To all of us today the Lord Jesus is holding out nail-pierced hands and saying, "Come ye after me, and I will make you to become. . . ." And you know what is involved in going onward with Him, being poured from vessel to vessel until every prop is stripped from you and you have nothing and nobody upon whom you can depend, except God and His promises.

Trust not in the shelter of home and family ties. They will not last, no matter how precious they are. Live sacramentally like broken bread and poured-out wine. Let God empty you out that He may save you from becoming spiritually stale, and lead you ever onward. He is always calling us to pass beyond the thing we know into the unknown. A throne is God's purpose for you; a cross is God's path for you; faith is God's plan for you.

The arrow of God on the target may leave a scar on your heart. In the years to come you may look back upon this time and your eyes fill with tears as you remember the moment when the arrow went beyond. But the Saviour is alongside: He is reminding you that the blood which He shed for you, which takes you within the veil—to the place of constant access to His presence—is the blood that takes you outside the camp to the place of consecrated availability for His plan.

Have you fully understood the cross? It speaks of our access forever by the blood into His presence, but also of our availability, in the path of separation, for the plan and purpose of God to be fulfilled. He has brought you in and sealed you as His own, but now He has shot the arrow beyond you, and He is taking you out.

Then came David to Nob to Ahimelech the priest. . . . And David said . . . The king hath commanded me a business, and hath said unto me, Let no man know any thing of the business whereabout I send thee. . . .

Now a certain man of the servants of Saul was there that day, detained before the Lord; and his name was Doeg, an Edomite, the chiefest of the herdmen that belonged to Saul.

And David said unto Ahimelech, And is there not here under thine hand spear or sword? . . . And the priest said, The sword of Goliath the Philistine, whom thou slewest in the valley of Elah, behold, it is here wrapped in a cloth behind the ephod. . . .

And David arose, and fled that day for fear of Saul, and went to Achish the king of Gath. And the servants of Achish said unto him, Is not this David the king of the land? did they not sing one to another of him in dances, saying, Saul hath slain his thousands, and David his ten thousands?

And David laid up these words in his heart, and was sore afraid of Achish the king of Gath. And he changed his behaviour before them, and feigned himself mad in their hands, and scrabbled on the doors of the gate, and let his spittle fall down upon his beard.

I SAMUEL 21:1-13

Be merciful unto me, O God: for man would swallow me up; he fighting daily oppresseth me. . . .

Every day they wrest my words: all their thoughts are against me for evil.

They gather themselves together, they hide themselves, they mark my steps, when they wait for my soul. . . .

When I cry unto thee, then shall mine enemies turn back: this I know; for God is for me. . . .

For thou hast delivered my soul from death: wilt not thou deliver my feet from falling, that I may walk before God in the light of the living?

PSALM 56:1-13

CHAPTER 7

A GOOD MAN IN BAD COMPANY

(I Samuel 21:1–13; Psalm 56:1–13)

IN THE DEVELOPMENT of Christian character there sometimes come moments when darkness seems to fall, the sun seems to set, and to the man himself everything seems lost. Other people, observing his life, wonder if he is sinking beyond all hope of recovery. It is to such a moment in David's life that we now come.

I find it tremendously comforting that the Bible never flatters its heroes. It tells the truth about them no matter how unpleasant it may be, so that in considering what is taking place in the shaping of their character we have available all the facts clearly that we may study them.

Here was David, chosen to be king, destined to be master over great lands and wealth, but living in exile and begging bread. Anointed by the Spirit of God was David, but running for his life from his enemies and destitute of all his friends.

So often the providences of God seem to run completely counter to His promises, but only that He may test our faith, only that He may ultimately accomplish His purpose for our lives in a way that He could never do if the path were always smooth. It is when problems and difficulties seem to be overwhelming that the man of God learns some lessons that he could never learn otherwise. It isn't easy to walk with God, for the air at that height is somewhat rare. It is pure, but sometimes it is hard to breathe, and faith almost gives up in the attempt to keep pace with God's way with His child.

This is a strange story in David's experience, and yet perhaps not so strange, because it is so true to human experience. I am thankful that we can consider it in the presence of God and learn from it some of the things that I believe the Holy Spirit would teach us.

Let me highlight some lessons that we need to learn from this incident in the life of David. In the first place, notice the fear which drove

David into sin: he "fled . . . for fear of Saul" (I Samuel 21:10); he "was sore afraid of Achish the king of Gath" (21:12).

Fear is always the enemy of faith; this is the battleground of Christian experience. A man grows and triumphs as his faith overcomes his fear. To believe God, to rest in the Word of God, to enjoy the promises of God is to conquer our fear. But to doubt God and to question His motives causes our faith to shrink until literally we cease to be believers—we are believers in name, but not in practice or in action.

At this particular point in David's history, God had shot an arrow beyond him; he was going through this situation not because of any failure or sin that he had committed, but simply because of God's purpose in proving the reality of his love, his devotion, his faith. This crucible of testing was to prepare David for a throne for which already he had been chosen, and in token of which he had already received the anointing of the Spirit. I am underlining this because I want you to understand that what is happening to David at this point is all in the will of God to make of him a man of God. It takes but a moment to make a convert; it takes a lifetime to manufacture a saint.

David should not have feared, but he did. Neither should we fear, but we do. Sometimes (and let us be honest in the presence of God) the wind that is contrary, threatening to overturn the ship of our lives, is far more real to us than the presence of the Lord saying, "Be of good cheer; it is I; be not afraid" (Matthew 14:27).

It was not just at this point that David began to fear, however; the moment when, in obedience to the flight of the arrow at the command of God, he left his home, his friends, and the shelter of Jonathan's love and went out into the unknown, was not the time when he began to be afraid. He betrayed the fear of his heart, the growing uncertainty concerning the purpose and promises of God, when he said to Jonathan, "There is but a step between me and death" (I Samuel 20:3). The day when he had been anointed by the Spirit of God and received the assurance that he was chosen to occupy the throne had receded into the dim past.

David is now looking at God through the threatening clouds of opposition and trouble, instead of looking down at circumstances through the rainbow of God's love. It is very easy to lose 20-20 spiritual vision. It is easy to develop a spiritual squint, to see things in the wrong perspective, and to start to panic. But how does it all begin? How do you think it began in David's life?

I would apply New Testament truth to this Old Testament picture.

It is not enough to receive the anointing of the Spirit of God once; He must abide. "The anointing which ye have received of him abideth in you . . . abide in him; that, when he shall appear, we may have [not fear] confidence" (I John 2:27-28). When the Lord Jesus was baptized the Spirit descended and remained on Him, we read in John 1:33.

What was the cause of this man's panic when he was in the will of God, but surrounded by bewildering circumstances? Could it have been the same as ours is so often in similar surroundings, that we have relied too much on past experience? Have you neglected the daily renewal of God's grace and power in your life? When God thrusts us out into some uncertainty and problem to test our faith, do you think that is why faith is overcome by fear and begins to shrivel up? Do you ask Him daily with hunger of heart and soul for a new anointing of the Spirit for the needs of the day? Does the Lord look down and see you deeply in love with your heavenly Father, deeply concerned that day by day you might do His will, or are you relying upon the experience of bygone days?

Let me show you a very simple and practical test. Your Christianity is inadequate if it cannot stand down-to-earth examination in the simple details of life. Before you come to church on a Sunday morning, you spend time decorating your body. How long do you spend preparing your heart? You come to teach the children in Sunday school, or to preach the Word, and certainly to worship the living God. Do you preface it with an hour of dedication or an hour of decoration? Has God heard from you the cry of a hungry soul that recognizes its need for daily grace? Or are you teaching, preaching, witnessing, serving, and banking upon the experience of twenty years ago when you met God for the first time? Oh, what emptiness of heart there is today in so many Christians! No wonder fear comes in through the door and faith goes out through the window!

Turn again to the narrative and see what fear has done to David, as recorded in I Samuel 21. David made his way to the village of Nob, which belonged to the tribe of Benjamin. There the tabernacle was pitched at this time, and there in the sanctuary lived eighty-six priests (I Samuel 22:18-19). I doubt whether much disturbed their quietness except occasionally a visitor who came to perform his vows before God. They had no weapon of defense because they didn't need any; all they had was the sword of Goliath which was a memento of David's great victory.

To this secluded place David came seeking food and weapons,

and also guidance. He came alone, and immediately the priest suspected something was wrong: "David, why art thou alone, and no man with thee?" The priest Ahimelech seemed to have been unaware of the jealousy between Saul and David. He didn't know the situation and therefore he questioned why the king's son-in-law should be out alone without attendants.

The fact that David was not right with God was detected the moment he entered God's sanctuary. I would that the power of the Spirit of God might so be upon the congregation of His people that every time we come into the sanctuary He might say, "Why are you like this?"

David was found out, and he was afraid that Ahimelech would tell Saul. Thinking quickly, he told a deliberate lie: "Saul has sent me on an urgent mission and I am sworn to secrecy. Just around the corner my band of men is waiting for me to rejoin them. I have been away from home for three days and I must have some food."

Suddenly his heart missed a beat as he saw the dark countenance of the chief herdsman of Saul's cattle. Doeg had come there to pay his own vow to God, and was listening to it all. David knew at once that he would be betrayed, that Doeg would go back to Saul and tell him where David was. Seizing Goliath's sword, he ran for his life to be with Achish king of Gath.

See what happened: David lost confidence in God and in the fulfillment of God's purpose for his life which had been revealed to him. He went to God's house for comfort and help and guidance, but he was detected as being wrong in his soul. Instead of acknowledging the truth to the only one who could help him and confessing that he had been telling a lie, he ran for his life again.

You say, "Well, what of it? He got away with it, didn't he?"

Oh, no, he didn't! He learned one of the most bitter lessons of any man's experience. Turn to I Samuel 22:20-23. Just as David feared, Doeg told Saul of David's visit to the priest at Nob, but he glossed over the fact that Ahimelech did not know of Saul's enmity toward David and suggested that Ahimelech was taking sides with David against the king. Saul sent for all eighty-six of the priests, with their wives and families, and commanded Doeg to slay them. All of them died in this ruthless murder except one.

Then one day, as David was in the cave of Adullum with the others who had followed him into refuge there, he saw running toward him the one man who had escaped the slaughter. When he was told about it, David cried out in horror, with an awful sense of guilt upon his soul, "I have occasioned the death of all the persons of thy father's house!"

See what fear and doubting God's Word and His promises caused! David covered up before God instead of acknowledging his fears and doubts, and no man who covers his sin can prosper. David's sin led to tragedy.

Do you go to the house of God for comfort, and then realize that the Spirit has found you out, that the voice of the Lord is saying to you, "Why this? Why that?" Perhaps your spirit is sour, cold, indifferent, and God asks what is wrong. He knows why you are like that, but He wants you to tell Him. He wants you to confess that you have feared and panicked, that you have questioned His purpose and plan for your life. You have doubted His Word and His promises, and you have failed to renew before God every day the anointing of His Spirit, so that you have become spiritually stale.

God knows this, but instead of admitting it, you cover up and pretend all is well. You say, "The need is in the life of the unsaved sinner here. Why doesn't the preacher tackle the unconverted and leave me alone? Why does he try to meddle with my life like this?"

So you cover up, you lie to God, and you go away from His sanctuary holding on to your fears and your doubts. But beware—sin is expensive! God may forgive and restore you, but the consequences of your sin may involve not only you but others who are innocent. Perhaps its results may continue for years to come, or for eternity. Seeds may be scattered beyond your recovery. A bitter harvest may be reaped in the lives of other people because of your departure from a living faith and obedience.

Reliance upon past blessings is not enough. Coming to the house of God for comfort, without being willing to face up to doubts and fears and unbelief and admitting them to be sin, is not enough. If God has put you into some dark places and into some trials, it is not to drive you into sin, but to deliver you by your daily, repeated surrender and commitment to His will as you abide in Him. He wants to be your living Saviour today, not merely the God who met you years and years ago.

When you are living by faith through the darkness of circumstances, other people become aware of the radiance and sweetness of your life, and they are truly blessed. When you refuse to admit your failure, God cannot be revealed through you to others, and they may be lost for eternity. Oh, the sin of unbelief has desperate consequences, not only for yourself, but for others!

In the second place, notice the feints, the pretenses which dishonored David's God. In his panic, see where David has gone—to Achish king of Gath. Here is a good man in bad company! Why has a man of God gone to live with a Philistine and an unbeliever? I might suggest, perhaps with more truth than some of us would like to admit, that a persecuted Christian sometimes gets better treatment from the enemies of God's people than from his Christian friends. Was it not the king of Judah who imprisoned Jeremiah and the king of Babylon who let him loose? We glory in our wonderful gospel of love and mercy for the unsaved, but we usually act as if we have no gospel for the saint who has been tripped up by the devil!

Achish struck up quite a friendship with David. Perhaps David had conveniently relieved him of a very powerful rival for his kingdom in cutting off the head of Goliath, because this is where Goliath came from. Maybe Achish was glad to meet the man who had killed his adversary. But he could not control the feelings of his people who recognized David's presence as a menace: "And the servants of Achish said unto him, Is not this David the King of the land? did they not sing one to another of him in dances, saying, Saul has slain his thousands, and David his ten thousands?" (I Samuel 21:11).

Look at this man of God as he attempted to escape this desperate plight. He descended to the behavior of a madman: he banged his fists on the gate of the city, foamed at the mouth, and acted like a man who was out of his mind. Achish looked at him and at his followers and said, "For goodness' sake, send the man away! I have enough madmen around here without wanting another! Get rid of him!"

What a tragic picture! What an undignified moment in the life of a man who had been anointed by the Spirit of God! How utterly unworthy of his calling was his behavior! What dishonor to bring upon the name of his God!

But wait a minute before you condemn David: examine your own heart. Have you taken refuge from the dangers you found in the path of God's will in the company of His enemies? Have you, as David did, feigned your behavior in order to escape the consequences of your failure to walk with God? Then from heaven's standpoint, you are behaving like a madman. Watch a Christian who has panicked in God's will, who has allowed doubts and fears to overcome his faith, and is running away from God. Listen to his conversation, so utterly irrational. How empty is his talk, how hollow his laughter, how tense his manner, how strained his countenance!

However, there is another side to this picture of David. I am glad the Bible turns the key and opens the door to the inner shrine of this man's life. At this moment when he is so utterly down, we are shown exactly what is taking place in his heart. We can observe from the Psalms he wrote at this time the faith that delivered his soul.

What about a man of God who has become involved in such a mess? Judged from the human standpoint, he is hopeless; he has been tried in the balances and found wanting. God will have to discard such a man. When God thrust him out from home and friends to test the reality of his faith, he failed at the crucial point. Just another missionary casualty, you know! He certainly will not get back to the field, or into Christian work again—God has finished with him. Although we may think we have finished with him, God hasn't! How shallow is our judgment! The Bible tells the worst about its heroes, but it tells the best, too, praise the Lord!

Just at this point David wrote two Psalms. In Psalm 56 he is saying, "Lord, I have no respite from my enemy for one minute. There is not a step I take but they are watching me, hoping to trip me up. I wander from shelter to shelter, and my tears fall thick and fast. I am going through something I just can't take."

Then I see him, as it were, with trembling heart climbing out of the waves of the storm and putting his feet upon the rock: "What time I am afraid, I will trust in thee. . . . In God have I put my trust; I will not be afraid what man can do unto me. . . . For thou hast delivered my soul from death: wilt not thou deliver my feet from falling, that I may walk before God in the light of the living?" (Psalm 56:3, 11, 13).

David was walking on the edge of a precipice and carefully watching his footsteps. Then he slipped and precipitated himself into a situation that seemed irretrievable. But in that moment he lifted his hands to God crying, "Lord, I have nobody else! Here and now, dear Lord, I just trust Thee!" Then his step grew light, the burden was gone, and in the midst of the darkness he walked securely with his hand in God's.

He also wrote Psalm 34, the heading of which says, "when he changed his behaviour before Achish: who drove him away, and he departed." Notice the assurance in the words of this Psalm. Can a man in the wrong company, who has been doubting and fearing God, allowing faith to be crushed, behaving like a madman—can such a man really talk like that? Yes, he can. Other people cannot see it; all they

see is a backslider who is drifting away from God and behaving like a
fool. But in his heart he despises himself for it all, and from the depths
his soul cries out to heaven, "O God, in this I am going to trust you
forever!"

David changed his behavior, but in spite of it his heart was fixed
upon God. In the awful anguish of those hours that took him from
Gibeah to Nob, from Nob to Gath, from Gath to feigned insanity,
when he thought that the torch of his life was going out and the
purpose of God was frustrated forever, he just stretched out a feeble
hand and caught hold of the hand of his God. Here, in effect, is his
testimony, pleading to us out of the darkness of his own experience,
"I beg of you, from what I have proved, taste and see that the Lord is
good!" (Psalm 34:8).

Isn't the patience and mercy of God toward His people beyond our
understanding? If you have allowed fears and doubts to overcome
your faith because you have relied on past experience, then just lift up
the hands of faith to God. With a hungry heart look up to Him, for
if you cry to the Lord now, He will save you out of all your fears.

Most of God's blessings are conditional, and often He cannot do
what He wants to do for you because you will not do what you should.
Is the cause of your fear and doubting, which is resulting in spiritual
loss to yourself and to many others, simply that you have relied upon
the past? How long is it since God heard you cry for a new anointing,
for a fresh breath from heaven? How long is it since the Lord has seen
evidence in your heart that you really care as you ask? Let Him hear
that cry now and every day until Jesus comes; may the anointing abide
in you!

David therefore departed thence, and escaped to the cave Adullam: and when his brethren and all his father's house heard it, they went down thither to him. And every one that was in distress, and every one that was in debt, and every one that was discontented, gathered themselves unto him; and he became a captain over them: and there were with him about four hundred men. . . .

Abide thou with me, fear not: for he that seeketh my life seeketh thy life: but with me thou shalt be in safeguard.

I SAMUEL 22:1-2, 23

I will bless the Lord at all times: his praise shall continually be in my mouth.

My soul shall make her boast in the Lord: the humble shall hear thereof, and be glad.

O magnify the Lord with me, and let us exalt his name together. . . .

This poor man cried, and the Lord heard him, and saved him out of all his troubles.

The angel of the Lord encampeth round about them that fear him, and delivereth them.

O taste and see that the Lord is good: blessed is the man that trusteth in him.

O fear the Lord, ye his saints: for there is no want to them that fear him. . . .

The righteous cry, and the Lord heareth, and delivereth them out of all their troubles.

The Lord is nigh unto them that are of a broken heart; and saveth such as be of a contrite spirit.

Many are the afflictions of the righteous: but the Lord delivereth him out of them all. . . .

The Lord redeemeth the soul of his servants: and none of them that trust in him shall be desolate.

PSALM 34:1-22

CHAPTER 8

THE CAPTAIN AND HIS CREW

(I Samuel 22:1–23; Psalm 34:1–22)

AT THIS POINT in David's life there was a turning of the tide; he no longer sought refuge from the attacks of Saul among the enemies of God's people. After his sad experience of finding himself in the wrong company and feigning insanity, then being delivered by the mercy and goodness of God, David is now back in the territory of Judah.

About this time he wrote at least three Psalms—the 34th, 57th, and 142nd. To read them is to get an insight into what was passing through his heart. I quote just a portion from Psalm 142: "I looked on my right hand, and beheld, but there was no man that would know me: refuge failed me; no man cared for my soul. I cried unto thee, O Lord: I said, Thou art my refuge and my portion in the land of the living" (142:4-5).

So begins one of the most significant and interesting periods in the life of this exile. He is a king, anointed of God, but he is hiding in a cave, waiting for God's time until he should come to the throne. News of David's return spread around the country very rapidly, and soon there gathered to him a strange assortment of individuals: some were in distress, some were in debt, some were discontented. David became captain over them, training and disciplining them until he had formed the nucleus of the greatest army the Israelites ever had. They were destined to win the greatest victories that the people of God ever enjoyed in all their history.

Picture David at this time, awaiting God's moment when he should come from seclusion to the throne. See him gathering this motley group of men and speaking to them around their campfires in the language of Psalm 34:11, "Come, ye children, hearken unto me: I will teach you the fear of the Lord."

If we are going to understand what I believe God would say to us here, however, we must leave the narrative. Sometimes what is known as typology, the use of Old Testament persons to illustrate truth, can be a fanciful method of preaching, and often can be unscriptural, but somehow it seems inevitable at this point in David's life. Unquestionably the Holy Spirit, the Author of the whole Bible, is seeking to direct our attention to David as an illustration of God's great plan of deliverance for you and me.

Let us remind ourselves of the circumstances of David's life at this particular point. There was a king on the throne of Israel who had been disowned by God. Judgment had been pronounced, and its execution would soon take place. Saul had been rejected because of his disobedience and rebellion. God's anointed king, David, was in exile, and to him gathered all who recognized him to be God's chosen one. They were willing to be buried alive in a cave, metaphorically speaking, to await God's time when, having suffered with him, they would share the grandeur of his reign.

It seems to me that the analogy is obvious. What are the circumstances in which you and I live today? What is the spiritual significance behind the scenes, as it were, of world events today? What does the Bible say is behind the sin and suffering of this world? It tells us there is a king who has been rejected and disowned by God. Jesus Christ spoke of him as the "prince of this world"—Satan, the devil, the serpent, whatever you might like to call him. The whole world in which we live today is held in the grip of this evil being.

In the purpose of God from before the foundation of the world, Satan's destiny, as a member of God's heavenly hosts, was to be regent of this world, to govern this little planet on behalf of the King of all the universe. However, this great created being rebelled against the authority of the One who created him. In Isaiah 14:12 we are told that he exalted himself and sought to be as God, to sit upon the throne of the whole universe. Therefore he was rejected, disowned, and cast out of heaven. In order to replace him, to find another to supervise the affairs of this little planet on behalf of the Almighty, God made a man in His own likeness and image and, as the psalmist says in Psalm 8:4 and 6, "What is man, that thou art mindful of him? . . . Thou madest him to have dominion over the works of thy hands; thou hast put all things under his feet."

The prince of this world, however, persuaded the man whom God had made to share in his rebellion and to revolt against God's authority. The result was that this planet—though in orbit physically, in the material sense moving with the whole solar system in the universe—is spiritually out of orbit. From this little globe there goes up constantly to the throne of heaven a cry of suffering from the human race which, because of its rebellion and wrong allegiance, has become alienated from its Creator.

But God launched a dynamic counterattack in the person of Jesus Christ our Lord: He conducted a full-scale invasion, because our Lord became a man and lived as God intended men to live, in complete submission to His will. He lived a perfect life and died as a man in the place of all other men to pay the price of our rebellion and to uphold the justice of the throne of heaven. He rose again as a man into the place of all power and all authority, to enable the Holy Spirit to say in Hebrews 2:8-9, "But now we see not yet all things put under him. But we see Jesus . . . crowned with glory and honour."

The Captain of our salvation was rejected by men and crucified, but God lifted Him up from the grave, placed Him upon the throne, and crowned Him with glory and authority. Once again power is in the proper hands and we can begin to see the fulfillment of God's great purpose for the race that now, yielding to the prince of this world and the powers of darkness, remains in misery and suffering.

God launched a mighty counterattack in which Jesus, on behalf of us all, has conquered. One day He shall come out from His kingdom which, as it were, is yet invisible. He shall reign, and before Him every knee shall bow. What wonderful language is in Psalm 2:2 and 6, "The kings of the earth set themselves, and the rulers take counsel together, against the Lord, and against his anointed . . . Yet have I set my king upon my holy hill of Zion."

Do you see the truth of which this Old Testament story is so graphic a picture? Just as in David's day, there is a King in exile who is gathering around Him a company of people who are in distress, in debt, and discontented. He is training and preparing them for the day when He shall come to reign. Therefore the vital issue is, if you understand the spiritual significance of our day, in whose kingdom are you living? To which king are you giving your allegiance? Before whose authority are you bowing? Which master are you following every day?

With that question in mind, notice the men who came to David in his cave. First, there were those who were distressed. It must have been one thing to hear about David and to sympathize with him in his cause, but it was quite another to be driven to the cave out of sheer necessity and with utter distress of heart. Whatever the distress may have been—the record doesn't tell us, but distress under the reign of

Saul must have been pretty desperate—it was a blessed thing that drove this little group of men from the authority of one kingdom into the authority of the other, to seek refuge at the side of David.

No self-satisfied man would ever come to Christ, either. There is a church of which we read in Revelation 3 that they were rich and increased with goods, and had need of nothing. But at the door of that church stood the risen Christ saying, "Behold, I stand at the door and knock." He was outside that place where they were perfectly self-satisfied—no man who is in that condition will ever come to the Lord Jesus.

It was sheer distress that drove a prodigal son in a far country to cry, "I will arise and go to my father, and will say unto him, Father, I have sinned against heaven, and before thee, And am no more worthy to be called thy son" (Luke 15:18-19).

"This poor man cried, and the Lord heard him, and saved him out of all his troubles," is the testimony of David in Psalm 34:6. Notice repeatedly in this Psalm the language of distress and concern: "The righteous cry, and the Lord heareth, and delivereth them out of all their troubles. The Lord is nigh unto them that are of a broken heart; and saveth such as be of a contrite spirit" (17-18).

When a man recognizes that he has allied himself with one who is in rebellion against the King of kings, when he sees the significance of his position, he begins to cry out to God in his distress. It is the man who is distressed who is driven to the side of the Lord Jesus.

Observe also that there were some who were in debt. In fleeing to David these bankrupt, wretched people found a way of escape from every liability that was theirs under the rule of a king whom God had rejected.

So long as you remain in the enemy camp with the rejected ruler, there are ten commandments which thunder at you, and you find yourself condemned by God's law. That law is enforced in the language of the gospel which says, "He that believeth on him is not condemned: but he that believeth not is condemned already, because he hath not believed in the name of the only begotten Son of God" (John 3:18).

Heaven's justice and righteousness must be recognized and maintained. Apart from grace, you find yourself bankrupt and insolvent, desperately in debt and helpless to meet God's judgment. Therefore, your only hope is to fly to the wounded side of the Lord, who in His life kept God's law perfectly and in His death paid the price of your rebellion. "For what the law could not do, in that it was weak through the flesh, God sending his own Son in the likeness of sinful flesh, and for sin, condemned sin in the flesh: That the righteousness of the law might be fulfilled in us" (Romans 8:3-4).

I notice, too, that these men who came to David were discontented—embittered, disappointed, frustrated, restless. How many such there are today, and yet how few of them seek refuge in the Lord who alone can satisfy their hearts! So often multitudes of people gather around some broken cistern of this world, trying to satisfy their thirst for they know not what. They grumble about their troubles and complain about their lot, but how few of them run to the One who said, "If any man thirst, let him come unto me, and drink. He that believeth on me, as the scripture hath said, out of his belly shall flow rivers of living water" (John 7:37-38).

These are the kind of men who came to David: distressed, bankrupt, dissatisfied. These are the kind of people who come to Christ, and they are the only people who come to Him, for they have recognized their distress, their debt and bankruptcy, and are conscious that they are utterly discontented. The sheer pressure of these frustrations drives them to the refuge of the blood of Christ that was shed for them.

Notice one more thing here. What were the motives of these men who came to David? Why did they come? I suggest that they came because they believed David was God's anointed king and had a right to rule over them. They believed that Saul was a usurper who should have no authority over them. In other words, if you please, they were converted from Saul to David.

Have you believed in the Lord Jesus Christ and recognized that He is God's anointed King? Satan, who holds the whole world in his hands, has fooled the human race into taking sides with him against God. Have you seen that you are on the wrong side, and therefore you have believed in Jesus Christ? Then you have been converted from the devil to God.

May I suggest, too, that the men coming to David not only believed in his cause, but they decided for him. Belief led to action; they not only heard but obeyed. It is one thing to believe in the coming kingdom of Christ; it is another to take your stand for Him and to identify yourself with Him. "Whosoever heareth these sayings of mine," said the Lord Jesus, "and doeth them, I will liken him unto a wise man, which built his house upon a rock: And the rain descended, and the floods came, and the winds blew, and beat upon that house; and it fell not: for it was founded upon a rock" (Matthew 7:24-25).

In John 9 we have the story of a blind man whose eyes were opened, and when he was under fire because he dared to acknowledge Jesus, he said, "Whether he be a sinner or no, I know not: one thing I know, that, whereas I was blind, now I see" (9:25). It is one thing to believe that something is true, and another thing to make your stand openly for it. Faith must lead to action.

In deciding for David, please notice that these men passed from one kingdom into another. In the language of Hebrews 13:13, they went "forth therefore unto him without the camp, bearing his reproach." I must insist upon this teaching of the Word that decision for Christ, if it is valid, will always mean that you have acquired a new center of life in which Jesus Christ is now your Sovereign. Once you were in the kingdom of darkness; now you have moved out by faith and conviction—knowing you were in the wrong kingdom has caused you to take action and to submit to a new King and a new authority.

Decision for Christ means separation from the world. I am not speaking merely about giving up certain things and not doing certain things, which is all many professing Christians know about separation. It is a far deeper thing than that: it is the involvement of the whole personality leaving the service of the devil for the service of the King of kings.

These men believed on David, they decided for David, and they submitted to David. They yielded themselves to his leadership for the honor of his name and for the sake of his cause. They stood with him in exile and suffering so that one day they might share with him the kingdom. Similarly, none can claim to be a Christian unless he has taken these steps, unless his faith has led to this action of identification with Jesus Christ.

Finally, I ask you to notice the mastery these men found in David: he became a captain over them. As soon as they took their places as followers he immediately assumed his right to lead them.

I hope the significance of that has dawned upon your heart! From that moment they looked to David for everything. They looked to him for training. You recall that in I Chronicles 12:8 there is a description of these mighty men of David, who became "men of war fit for the battle, that could handle shield and buckler, whose faces were like the faces of lions, and were as swift as the roes upon the mountains."

Once they were in debt, discontented, in distress—a motley crew! They had nothing to commend them but their desperate need. But see what they became as David shaped them into a mighty army for his use. They looked to him for their training; and the immediate thing that happens the moment you step from one kingdom to another is that Jesus assumes His divine right to direct and govern your life.

The men in the cave of Adullam also looked to David for protection, because the moment they became David's followers they became Saul's enemies. They were open to all the persecution which came upon David; they had to share it. But he promised them protection: "Abide thou with me, fear not: for he that seeketh my life seeketh thy life: but with me thou shalt be in safeguard" (I Samuel 22:23).

In the same way, the moment you identify yourself with Jesus Christ you stir up the anger of the enemy of your soul. You become the target of the powers of darkness and therefore you must look to the Lord for safety. "Much more then, being now justified by his blood, we shall be saved from wrath through him. For if, when we were enemies, we were reconciled to God by the death of his Son, much more, being reconciled, we shall be saved by his life" (Romans 5:9-10). Moment by moment, day by day, under the banner of the King of kings, we look to Him for protection.

His followers in the cave also looked to David for reward. The cause of David was not a forlorn hope because it was the cause of God. Victory was absolutely sure; those who suffered with him one day would share his exaltation and the kingdom with him.

There is a day coming when the rejected Christ will be crowned Lord of all, and those who follow Him now will be abundantly rewarded when we enter into the joy of the Lord: "if so be that we suffer with him, that we may be also glorified together" (Romans 8:17).

I would ask you a very straightforward question: in which kingdom are you living? Which king are you serving? To whom are you yielding allegiance? If you are avowedly in the wrong camp, then I beg of you that you would quickly fly to the wounded side of Jesus.

There may be many who claim to be Christians, however, who are trying to be in both camps at the same time. You are vague in your testimony, uncertain in your purpose for life, indefinite in spiritual conviction, shallow in spiritual experience. You desire to be quite sure that one day you will share the Lord's reign, but you are not prepared to share in His rejection. You are not willing to leave the kingdom of the enemy and enter into the kingdom of God.

It is impossible to be in two camps at once, and I will tell you which camp you are really in! It is not the camp that your head takes you into! You may be at school, preparing for a future life of ministry or service, but so easily what you learn fails to get into your life and character. It does not seem to affect very much the way you live. You may know a lot of theology, but what about your relationship with the opposite sex? Does it make any difference in your behavior, in your ethics, in your purity of mind and thought and life? It is so easy for religion to be just a department of life, for church to be a habit for one day a week, but the rest of the time it can be flung off like an old coat. It just doesn't make much difference to the way you live at all.

My friend, you cannot be in both camps at once, and you are not on the side of your head, you are on the side of your heart. Your body brings you to church, but where does your heart take you? Where do your affections lead you, into what kind of predicaments? What about your desires, your thoughts, your ambitions? What about the real *you*? In spite of school and training and church membership, which camp are you living in today? In your heart, are you in the wrong camp? Or has there been a complete abandonment of the devil's sovereignty in favor of the Lord Jesus Christ?

That is the plain issue! If you are in heart distress, in debt to God's law, discontented and unhappy, then believe in Christ and submit to Him. He will train you, He will protect you, and one day He will reward you.

Then they told David, saying, Behold, the Philistines fight against Keilah, and they rob the threshingfloors. Therefore David enquired of the Lord, saying, Shall I go and smite these Philistines? And the Lord said unto David, Go, and smite the Philistines, and save Keilah. . . . So David saved the inhabitants of Keilah. . . .

Then said David, O Lord God of Israel, thy servant hath certainly heard that Saul seeketh to come to Keilah, to destroy the city for my sake. Will the men of Keilah deliver me up into his hand? . . . And the Lord said, He will come down. . . . And the Lord said, They will deliver thee up.

Then David and his men, which were about six hundred, arose and departed out of Keilah. . . . And David abode . . . in the wilderness of Ziph. . . .

And Jonathan Saul's son arose, and went to David into the wood, and strengthened his hand in God. And he said unto him, Fear not: for the hand of Saul my father shall not find thee; and thou shalt be king over Israel, and I shall be next unto thee; and that also Saul my father knoweth. . . .

Then came up the Ziphites to Saul to Gibeah, saying, Doth not David hide himself with us? . . . Saul and his men compassed David and his men round about to take them. But there came a messenger unto Saul, saying, Haste thee, and come; for the Philistines have invaded the land. Wherefore Saul returned from pursuing after David, and went against the Philistines. . . .

I SAMUEL 23:1-28

The Lord is my light and my salvation; whom shall I fear? the Lord is the strength of my life; of whom shall I be afraid? . . .

One thing have I desired of the Lord, that will I seek after; that I may dwell in the house of the Lord all the days of my life, to behold the beauty of the Lord, and to enquire in his temple. . . .

Wait on the Lord: be of good courage, and he shall strengthen thine heart: wait, I say, on the Lord.

PSALM 27:1-14

CHAPTER 9

LEARNING TO LOOK TO THE LORD

(I Samuel 23:1-28; Psalm 27:1-14)

AT THIS POINT in David's life his fortunes have just about reached their lowest ebb. Watching this man of God, we see him now in a moment of great adversity.

In I Samuel 22:5 we are told that, acting on the advice of the prophet Gad, who joined David in his exile and played a significant part in his life throughout the future, David left the shelter of the cave of Adullam. One can understand that a cave might be a dangerous place; he could find himself shut in it with the enemy surrounding him. So David forsook the cave for the desolation of the wilderness and the mountains. This was a wandering life; referring to it in one of his psalms, he spoke of himself as being chased "like a partridge on the mountain."

As we study the life of David, we have one great advantage because we can look at it in retrospect. We can see it all, especially how the purpose of God was so wonderfully fulfilled. At this particular time, David did not know anything of his glorious future except by faith. We can look back upon his experiences and learn some significant lessons that should be written forever upon the character and service of each of us.

We also live in days of adversity, but that is never any reason for discouragement. A man who faints in the day of trouble possesses very small strength. David was destined to reign as the king of Israel, but you and I are going to be sharing the throne of all the universe one day. This is our great period of preparation and training, and the Lord has many things to teach us.

In this study the narrative is purely incidental, the background against which to sketch in David's life and character. It is like a scaffolding around him which will come down completely; inside is his life, the building that is going up for the glory of God. It is from

87

studying David's inner life and his experiences with God that we draw strength and comfort and food for our souls, and we are not without ample material in the Word of God to help us.

At this point in his experience, David wrote at least three Psalms: the 27th, 31st, and 54th. Others may also have been written at this time, but these three sum up the spiritual conflict that was going on in his heart. They show what was shaping his life to make him a man of God.

To return to I Samuel 23: in the first few verses David is triumphing over his enemies; later he is facing the treachery of his friends. In both experiences, however, he is learning to look to the Lord. In fact, he is learning more and more what it is to trust in the Lord and to live by faith.

Tidings had come to David of a threatened attack by the Philistines on the border town of Keilah. The farmers there had just harvested their crops and the Philistines were coming in to plunder them. Saul, of course, was helpless to do anything about it. Neither did he care much, for he was too concerned at that point about the bitterness of his soul and his desire to get rid of David to bother about the Philistines.

But David and his men were within reach, so they responded to the S.O.S. from Keilah and defeated the enemy, recovering the stolen property. Then David and his men were welcomed by the men of Keilah to share with them in the life of the city as a reward.

Here was a little ray of sunshine for David. He was back in the fight once more, experiencing victory over his people's enemy, even though he was a hunted exile. That taste of victory from the shelter of the city of Keilah brought from him the song of Psalm 31:21, "Blessed be the Lord: for he hath shewed me his marvellous kindness in a strong city."

Yet as we read through this Psalm, we see he was not always on top; he wasn't always smiling. There is a significant change of mood; one moment he is on the crest of the wave, "I will be glad and rejoice in thy mercy: for thou hast considered my trouble; thou hast known my soul in adversities" (Psalm 31:7). Then he says, in verse 12, "I am forgotten as a dead man out of mind: I am like a broken vessel." But faith triumphs and is the dominant note here: "My times are in thy hand: deliver me from the hand of mine enemies, and from them that persecute me" (Psalm 31:15).

"My times are in thy hand," he says, and that means that in this moment of adversity and trial David knew that all the question marks of his life were in the hand of God. He knew it was impossible to be in God's hand and in the enemy's hand at the same time. The gloom begins to disappear and fear departs as faith emerges in glorious triumph. This man is rising out of his testing and adversity to learn to put his utter dependence on the Lord.

Therefore David breaks out into a song of confidence in verses 19 and 20: "Oh how great is thy goodness, which thou hast laid up for them that fear thee; which thou hast wrought for them that trust in thee before the sons of men! Thou shalt hide them in the secret of thy presence from the pride of man: thou shalt keep them secretly in a pavilion from the strife of tongues."

This man is capable of going up to the heights of joy and the next moment down into the depths of despair. He has gone through the dark tunnel of adversity in the wilderness, chased as a partridge upon the mountain, and now he is enjoying victory over the Philistines, and rejoicing over God's kindness in giving him the shelter of the city. He opens his heart to tell us, "You know, there was one time when I was so afraid that I was terrified to move. But somehow I just rested in God, and I knew the whole situation was in His hand."

As his doubts began to disappear and faith began to triumph, David made a confession in verse 22. He admits he was wrong and stupid to doubt God: "I said in my haste, I am cut off from before thine eyes." A better translation is, "I said in my agitation." You have to be very careful what you say to God when you are agitated, and what you say to other people, too. Don't trust yourself to pray and to be true to your prayer in a moment of agitation.

David was afraid and perplexed as to what to do next, with all the pressure upon him, but then he came triumphantly to say, "Lord, all the problems are in Thy hands, for Thou knowest best!" Thus he triumphed over his enemies, and the result is in the final word of counsel he gives to us in Psalm 31:24, "Be of good courage, and he shall strengthen your heart, all ye that hope in the Lord."

It is one thing to face an enemy and conquer him, but it is even more difficult to face the treachery of friends. David's stay in Keilah was not very long. As he sought God in prayer for guidance, he learned that Saul would attack the city. Not only would Saul attack, but the people of Keilah would betray him: "Will the men of Keilah deliver me up into his hand? will Saul come down, as thy servant hath heard? O Lord God of Israel, I beseech thee, tell thy servant. And the Lord said, He will come down" (I Samuel 23:11). Being warned of his danger, David left the city and departed again into the mountains and the wilderness. But now he has six hundred men under him; his army has increased by 50 per cent (I Samuel 23:13).

Saul was getting desperate, and at this point Jonathan came to David.

Notice how precious is verse 16: "Jonathan Saul's son arose, and went to David into the wood, and strengthened his hand in God." Thank heaven for a friend like that at such a moment! David never saw him again; the friends parted forever until they met in heaven.

Jonathan told David that Saul well knew that he would be king (I Samuel 23:17), but that did not alter Saul's determination to kill David. What a terrible state for a man to get into, knowing that he is fighting against God, but going on with it.

However, worse was to follow, from David's point of view, because the people who lived in the wilderness offered to betray him to Saul so that they might get back into the king's favor (I Samuel 23:19-20). Just as it seemed Saul had caught David in a trap, however, and was about to surround him, there came news of a fresh attack by the Philistines. Therefore, Saul left David at large in the wilderness and returned to defend the country from their powerful enemy.

Betrayed by the people of Keilah whom he had befriended, betrayed again by the inhabitants of the wilderness of Zith who thought it to their advantage to hand him over to Saul, David must have breathed a great sigh of relief at God's miraculous deliverance.

Turn to Psalm 54 to see what a man sings when those he has rescued betray him, when he has said goodbye to his dearest friend on earth whom he will never meet again, when he is facing tremendous persecution and adversity. First David speaks to God about his enemies: "Save me, O God, by thy name, and judge me by thy strength. Hear my prayer, O God; give ear to the words of my mouth. For strangers are risen up against me, and oppressors seek after my soul: they have not set God before them. Selah [think of that!]" (Psalm 54:1-3).

Then David talks to himself about God: "Behold, God is mine helper: the Lord is with them that uphold my soul" (54:4). Then at last he talks to God about himself: "I will freely sacrifice unto thee: I will praise thy name, O Lord; for it is good" (54:6).

May the Lord help you to understand and apply these lessons to your heart. Observe how David left the treachery of his supposed friends with the One who is sufficient to deal with them (54:7). He is now looking at God. First he was looking at his enemies and these supposed friends of his, but now he sees them through God. If you begin with God, your enemies grow small. If you begin with the enemy, you may never reach God. If you begin with Him, the problems begin to dwindle; if you begin with the problems, you never get through to God. "Selah"—think of that, and apply it to your life in your adversity and testing.

David is surrounded by those who would take his life, but this Psalm shows him stretching out a hand of faith. That is all he can do, and in conclusion he praises the Lord for the day when the enemy is going to be scattered: "For he hath delivered me out of all trouble" (54:7). He is beginning to praise God with the enemy still around him; he is beginning to trust the Lord enough that he can claim the victory, although he has no human hope. David is basing his confidence upon what he is learning of the character and will and purpose of God.

We turn now to the two little phrases which are repeated in I Samuel 23:2 and 4: "David enquired of the Lord." He was beginning to form a habit that became part of his life, something important which he could learn only in a dark hour like this. "Lord, I am in this situation because Thou hast put me here, and I am not going to take any action until I get clear direction from heaven."

David asked the Lord, and he did not take a step without a clear word of authority from God. This is made abundantly clear in the language of another Psalm he wrote. Often we have sung or read Psalm 27, but perhaps without realizing the circumstances under which it was written. In verse 14 he concludes from his experiences this exhortation: "Wait on the Lord: be of good courage, and he shall strengthen thine heart: wait, I say, on the Lord."

Have you ever looked at this Psalm in the light of what was happening in David's life? Did you think it was written when the sky was blue and everything was going well? No, it was sung in the darkest hour of his life. What a comfort it was that in dark days he could say, "The Lord is my light" (Psalm 27:1). These were dangerous days; therefore the Lord was also "my salvation." Wicked hosts were arrayed against him, but "my heart shall not fear: though war should rise against me, in this will I be confident. . . . For in the time of trouble he shall hide me in his pavilion" (27:3, 5).

Though he knew that his behavior when he had feigned himself to be mad would justify God's anger, yet he prayed, "Put not thy servant away in anger: thou hast been my help; leave me not, neither forsake me, O God of my salvation" (27:9). He asked God to lead him clearly and to deliver him from false witnesses that had risen up against him.

The great theme of this Psalm, the burden on David's heart, is his longing for an intimate fellowship with the Lord and a constant light upon his path. He desired to live so close that when he heard just a whisper from God to his heart saying, "Seek ye my face," immediately his heart would answer, "Thy face, Lord, will I seek." (27:8). He was learning something that only adversity can teach any of us; that is, to calm his fears, to steady his life, to stand still and watch for the salvation of God, to wait for a clear word of direction. He had discovered it would not be safe to move without heavenly guidance, so he waited upon God.

Perhaps the Lord also puts you and me through testings to teach us these same things. But how can we get guidance from heaven? How can we get the clear word from the Lord that David got? Can we know that there is light from heaven upon the next step? In the circumstances and confusion of life, in the pressure of adversity, can we know clearly, can we receive an authoritative word of direction from God? Yes, indeed!

There was a priest with David: Abiathar, the son of Ahimelech, the only one who escaped the murder of that whole household, had joined David in the cave of Adullam. On his priestly breastplate were the Urim and Thummim, bright and shining jewels that, as the priest went into the presence of God and prayed earnestly, grew dim if God's answer was "No." But if God's answer was "Yes," then the jewels shone all the more brightly. It was through the priest that David went to God, and from him that he heard whether the light was clear or dim. This was how David found unmistakable guidance. Later in the Old Testament times, God spoke to men through the prophets, until they, too, were silenced.

Have we no means of inquiry? Yes, we have. In Revelation 2:17 the Old Testament picture is brought into New Testament focus and into our experience. The risen Lord says to the church at Pergamos, "To him that overcometh will I give to eat of the hidden manna, and will give him a white stone, and in the stone a new name written, which no man knoweth saving he that receiveth it." To the overcomer Christ will give a brilliant, shining stone. It is believed that this is a New Testament allusion to the Old Testament method of guidance by the Urim and Thummim, the stones that shone in the breastplate of the high priest.

Where do you go when you are in a jam? We have always with us the great High Priest, who ever lives to make intercession for His people. He will send that flashing light from heaven into the soul of the man who longs to know His will, and He will give it unmistakably, for in Him each of us has a personal Urim and Thummim. To whom is it given? It is given to the overcomer, the man whose heart has been washed in the blood and whose life has been filled with the Holy Spirit. To the overcomer is the word from heaven, "This is the way, walk ye in it."

On the other hand, against the man whose life is stained with sin, to the Christian whose life is worldly and carnal, the doors of heaven remain closed until he repents and turns to God. Only where the blood has been sprinkled is the Word of God made known. The cross marks the path that leads us right into the very presence of God, as desperately and urgently we need a word from heaven for our present testimony and ministry. Equally urgently and eagerly God waits to tell us what we should do at this time, but He is only going to give His word to the overcomer.

God will not give His power or show His purpose to a worldly, compromising, defeated Christian who couldn't care less about His will, who gives himself over to the gods of material gain and amusements, who revels in the lust of the flesh and unholy desires. How much His church needs the blood of Christ applied to every part of its life, that the will of God might be made known!

Are you in doubt? One voice may say to you, "Come this way." Prudence may suggest to you one thing, faith another. Worldly wisdom says *this* path, but the voice of the Spirit says *that* path. If you are not sure, get alone somewhere with God until every other voice is silent and all human opinions are shut out, and learn to look to the Lord.

But remember, the stone of brilliant splendor, the flashing, clear revelation from heaven that enables us to say with assurance, "This is the way," is given only to the overcomer. If you want guidance, therefore, are you prepared to pay the price for it? A guided life is dependent upon a cleansed heart. There is no victory without a fight, and there is no battle without wounds. Those inflicted by the treachery of friends hurt David most of all, but there are no wounds that cannot be healed by the Great Physician. All these things David learned in adversity, and in the battle with his enemies he overcame fear by faith.

If you want guidance and direction, if you want the light from heaven on your path, are you honestly prepared to pay the price and live as an overcoming Christian?

> Hast thou no scars, no hidden scar on foot or side or hand?
> I hear thee sung as mighty in the land,
> I hear them hail thee, bright, ascendant star.
> Hast thou no scar?
> No wound, no scar, yet as the Master shall the servant be,
> And pierced are the feet that follow thee,
> But thine are whole.
> Can he have followed far who has nor wound nor scar?
>
> *Amy Carmichael*

And it came to pass, when Saul was returned from following the Philistines, that it was told him, saying, Behold, David is in the wilderness of Engedi. Then Saul took three thousand chosen men out of all Israel. . . . And he came to the sheepcotes by the way, where was a cave; and Saul went in to cover his feet: and David and his men remained in the sides of the cave. . . . Then David arose, and cut off the skirt of Saul's robe privily.

And it came to pass afterward, that David's heart smote him, because he had cut off Saul's skirt. And he said unto his men, The Lord forbid that I should . . . stretch forth mine hand against him, seeing he is the anointed of the Lord. . . .

But Saul rose up out of the cave, and went on his way. David also arose afterward, and went out of the cave, and cried after Saul, saying, My lord the king. And when Saul looked behind him, David stooped with his face to the earth, and bowed himself. And David said to Saul, Wherefore hearest thou men's words, saying, Behold David seeketh thy hurt? Behold, this day thine eyes have seen how that the Lord had delivered thee to day into mine hand in the cave: and some bade me kill thee. . . . Moreover, my father, see . . . I cut off the skirt of thy robe, and killed thee not . . . and I have not sinned against thee; yet thou huntest my soul to take it. The Lord judge between me and thee, and the Lord avenge me of thee: but mine hand shall not be upon thee. . . .

Saul said, Is this thy voice, my son David? And Saul lifted up his voice, and wept. And he said to David, Thou are more righteous than I: for thou hast rewarded me good, whereas I have rewarded thee evil. . . . Swear now therefore unto me by the Lord, that thou wilt not cut off my seed after me, and that thou wilt not destroy my name out of my father's house.

And David sware unto Saul. And Saul went home. . . .

I SAMUEL 24:1-22

CHAPTER 10

LOVING YOUR ENEMIES

(I Samuel 24:1-22)

GOD HAD A GREAT purpose of blessing, a great destiny for David, but at this point he was being put through the crucible of testing to determine his fitness for what God had planned for him. Therefore, in a very real sense we are studying the life story of each of us as Christians.

It is not the will of our Father in heaven that anyone should perish. It is His concern that each of us should come to know Him whom to know is life eternal, and that we should become heirs of God and joint-heirs with Christ. This is the great destiny that God has for us, and only in the realization of it can we find real peace and happiness. But in order that it might be fulfilled, God often uses the flame, as Peter said, "That the trial of your faith, being much more precious than of gold that perisheth, though it be tried with fire, might be found unto praise and honour and glory at the appearing of Jesus Christ" (I Peter 1:7).

David was now at a point of greater danger than any he had hitherto experienced. It is always God's way to use each victory that we have won by grace as the background for the next phase of testing at a deeper level. That is part of the making of a man of God. Here then, in I Samuel 24 and 27, we find David presented with two golden opportunities to rid himself of his enemy, Saul, to shorten the day of suffering, and to make a grab for the throne which God had promised him.

David, with his six hundred men, had taken refuge at a place called Engedi, which means "the haunt of a wild goat." This was a very mountainous area southwest of the Dead Sea in which were many caves and great rocks, and there David was sheltered. One day Saul, with his three thousand picked men, hunted for David through this rocky country where it would be very difficult to find anyone.

David and his men were hiding in a cave, pressed around the sides of it as they watched Saul's men march by, then Saul himself turned suddenly and came inside to get a little shelter from the heat. As he entered the darkness from the brilliance of the sunshine, he could see nothing inside; he was completely unaware of the presence of David and his men. Then he decided to take a nap in the coolness.

What a chance for David! Breathlessly his men waited; perhaps they whispered some advice to him, saying in effect, "Here is your opportunity! God has brought your enemy right within your reach and you can destroy him easily. You can end all our hardship and suffering and sit on the throne today!" (I Samuel 24:4).

You can imagine with what intensity they watched their leader slip stealthily through the dimness with a dagger in his hand—they expected to see it driven into Saul's back. Imagine their amazement when David just cut a little bit off the end of Saul's robe and quietly returned to his hiding place in the darkness. They had thought David brave, but he must have seemed to them a coward at that moment. What a fool he was to miss such a chance to get rid of his powerful enemy!

Notice David's words; he was ashamed that he had done even the little he had to Saul: "The Lord forbid that I should do this thing unto my master, the Lord's anointed, to stretch forth mine hand against him, seeing he is the anointed of the Lord" (I Samuel 24:6). David controlled himself, and what is even more remarkable, he also controlled the six hundred men who were with him; he "stayed his servants with these words, and suffered them not to rise against Saul."

When Saul eventually left the cave, David ran after him into the open and confronted him with the evidence of his mercy, proving to him that he had no intention of harming him. David asked Saul whom he thought he was chasing: saying in effect "After whom is the king of Israel come out? I am as helpless as a dead dog and as hard to catch as a flea. Why don't you leave me alone?" (I Samuel 24:14).

On another occasion, recorded in chapter 26, Saul was again on the chase with his three thousand men, and David found him at night, in his camp asleep. Apparently without putting a sentry on duty, Saul, with Abner his captain and the whole army, made camp and went to sleep while David and his men watched them.

David took with him a trusted friend, Abishai, and together they went down into the valley, stealthily creeping into the midst of the camp until they came to where Saul was asleep, and Abner; and once again there was made to David the same whispered suggestion. Abishai used words like these, "God has delivered your enemy into your hand again. If you are squeamish about killing him yourself, let me do it for you. I will smite him with a spear right through the heart into the earth beneath him—one stroke and that will be the finish, I won't need to repeat it" (I Samuel 26:8).

Once again from David came the same reply: "Destroy him not, for who can stretch forth his hand against the Lord's anointed, and be guiltless?" Then they withdrew, taking Saul's spear and his water bottle. Safely away from Saul's camp, to relieve the tension of that tremendous moment, they shouted back across the valley at the sleeping army, waking them all up and taunting Abner with being asleep on duty.

David had missed another opportunity of getting rid of his enemy, of ending his suffering. Surely, when a chance to get even with someone who has done you wrong presents itself, you should take it. When the opportunity comes to escape from a tight corner, you ought to take the initiative. Or should you?

What do we learn from the narrative in these chapters to bless our own hearts? First of all, see the principle which David has learned. Though Saul was rejected by the Lord, yet the man was still the Lord's anointed. Others insisted you have to love your friends and hate your enemies, but somehow David had learned what the Lord Jesus came to teach us, "Love your enemies, bless them that curse you, do good to them that hate you, and pray for them which despitefully use you" (Matthew 5:44).

If David had slain Saul he would have been taking things out of God's hands, and to seize the initiative himself could have been disastrous. It was far better for David to await God's time than to attempt to help Him to do something merely because circumstances were uncongenial.

When a moment like this comes in life, we need to beware of it. How easy it is to take the initiative, how hard to wait for God! How painful perhaps are the circumstances, but how much more painful are the consequences of action outside God's will! How hard it is to learn the lesson which our Lord practiced, "Who, when he was reviled, reviled not again . . . but committed himself to him that judgeth righteously" (I Peter 2:23). How difficult it is to wait for the slowly unfolding purpose of God; how much easier to take things into our own hands and make a dash for it! Always it is hard to "stand still, and see the salvation of the Lord" (Exodus 14:13).

To Saul, David said, "The Lord judge between me and thee, and the Lord avenge me of thee: but mine hand shall not be upon thee" (I Samuel 24:12). In other words, David knew that God had put him into that situation for a purpose that He knew best, because He had a great destiny for David's life. Because God had put him there, David trusted Him to get him out without his having to lift one little finger to help, neither would he allow anyone with whom he was connected to do anything about it.

No matter what the situation may be, God's child needs to learn to wait and watch for the Lord, who has put him there to prove the kind of stuff he is made of. "My soul, wait thou only upon God." Because David had learned that principle, he refused to take the initiative and act out of God's will.

When a man learns that lesson he is getting somewhere spiritually, and he is about to see liberated through his life a new measure of power. See what happened because David took this line. Think of the effect, for instance, upon himself. Just suppose he had given way and had killed his enemy. That would have ended the song in his heart; it would have silenced his music and put an end to the Psalms that he wrote. He would have gone through life with a bad conscience and a shadow from the past.

Much later, David had a very sad experience and had to live again for a while in exile. His son Absalom had rebelled against him, and as David was about to return to Jerusalem, a man named Shimei came to curse him. He tried to tell David that this rejection by his people had happened because the Lord was rewarding him for his shameful treatment of Saul (II Samuel 16:8). David knew the accusation was not true, but if he had acted out of God's will here it would have been true. He knew that he had not done anything to bring about Saul's death, and therefore God delivered him from the curse of Shimei.

What would have been the effect on his six hundred men? There are many evidences that the gentleness of David and his love for Saul influenced his men and showed up as part of their character in the days that lay ahead. If David had acted wrongly it would have affected his whole army, and much of his godly influence would have been lost.

Most of all, what about Saul himself? "And it came to pass, when David had made an end of speaking these words unto Saul, that Saul said, Is this thy voice, my son David? And Saul lifted up his voice, and wept" (I Samuel 24:16). "Then said Saul, I have sinned: return, my son David: for I will no more do thee harm, because my soul was precious in thine eyes this day: behold, I have played the fool, and have erred exceedingly. . . . Then Saul said to David, Blessed be thou, my son David: thou shalt both do great things, and also shalt still prevail. So David went on his way and Saul returned to his place" (I Samuel 26:21, 25).

This poor wretched man, who spent his days battling against God, had suddenly come face to face with the love and patience of God shining out through another man's life, and for a moment it melted Saul. There is a pathetic remembrance of days when things were different between them: "My son David," he reminded himself of that sweet family relationship. There was a confession of sin, "I have played the fool, and have erred exceedingly." It would seem that just for a moment, like a flash of lightning, this man was melted by the power of love and saw his stupidity and folly. But alas, he had been so held in the grip of passion that he no longer had power to shake off his madness.

It is only the love of God shed abroad by the Holy Spirit that can cause effective repentance and cleansing—not simply Christian work or service, but the shining sweetness and fragrance of the love of Jesus Christ. It is this which touches a life that is out of adjustment to the will of God. It is this which makes a man realize he has been a fool and that he has sinned. It is love that melts coldness of heart and brings conviction. That is why Calvary has such magnificence; that is why at Jesus' cry, "Father, forgive them, for they know not what they do," thousands of hearts have been melted by the love of God revealed to them there.

That is why the practice of love in your life liberates spiritual power as nothing else can. It is not simply the distributing of a tract; it is not the preaching of a sermon or the teaching of a Sunday school class. It is something far deeper: a life saturated with love, a life that has learned the principle that David learned, to love not merely your friends, but also your enemies; and a life that has learned, also, to wait upon God.

But what a miserable picture Saul is! This man let passion and sin drive him right over the precipice until he seems almost beyond hope. What is the use of saying, "I have played the fool," if he goes on playing the fool? What use are his tears and confession before David if he doesn't act upon his remorse?

We sometimes see people streaming down the aisle in an evangelistic meeting with tear-stained faces, but what difference does emotion make if it does not lead to obedience? What profit is it that a heart has been stirred, unless from that moment the man lives in submission to the will of God? Indeed, it does make a difference, for if a man is emotionally upset, as Saul was, and awakens to his condition, but only weeps about it and still doesn't obey God, his second state is a thousand times worse than the first. Emotion that does not lead to action only leads deeper into sin and rebellion.

I am fearful for the man who is not far from the kingdom of God, who has often wept under the sound of the preaching of the gospel, who has often seen the reality of the love of God in Jesus Christ at the cross, who has often recognized his own sinful ways and said, "I have played the fool," but five minutes after the message is over he is outside the church, all conviction forgotten. He has silenced the holy emotion and has gone out to live in disobedience again, in spite of the stirring of the Holy Spirit in his heart.

Remember that Saul was anointed of God; he had been given the same privileges and opportunities that David had. The one accepted His anointing with godly fear, submission, and yieldedness. The other refused the principle of obedience and faith, and became an outcast.

Eternity is decided by a series of choices which each of us makes in the course of life. How near repentence did Saul come when he felt the impact of David's love? It was the love of God in David's life that awakened him, even though he went back into his stubborn ways. What made David behave like that? How did he learn this principle of love? Why didn't he take advantage of Saul? We have often wanted to behave like that, but we have failed to do it. How did David succeed?

As a matter of fact, the answer is very simple. In these studies we have not only narrative, but we have heart experience. The narrative is in the books of Samuel; the experience is in the book of the Psalms. David opened his heart to show what was going on in it. At this time he wrote Psalm 57, where we find out how he learned love and graciousness. Here is how David learned not to hurry God, but to stand still and see the salvation of the Lord.

In Psalm 57:4, he spoke about his enemies: "My soul is among lions: and I lie even among them that are set on fire, even the sons of men, whose teeth are spears and arrows, and their tongue a sharp sword." Have you ever been in a position like that? David recognized his enemies, who were there all along.

But he prayed and talked with God alone in the secret place with the door shut. The greatest fact of all was not his enemies, but God; and the fear of the enemy was overcome by faith in his God. Listen to the opening verses: "Be merciful unto me, O God, be merciful unto me: for my soul trusteth in thee; yea, in the shadow of thy wings will I make my refuge, until these calamities be overpast." Like a mother bird under whose warm and protecting wing a little chick is secure, so David's Lord is his place of refuge.

With the enemy all around him, and with the hatred of Saul getting more intense day by day, this is what David said: "I will cry unto God most high; unto God that performeth all things for me. [He does the performing; I do the waiting.] He shall send from heaven, and save me from the reproach of him that would swallow me up. Selah [just think of that!]. God shall send forth his mercy and his truth" (Psalm 57:2-3). So David lies down to rest on the promises of God, and puts himself under the protection of His wings, although the enemy is still around him.

It is a wonderful Old Testament picture, and there is a New Testament story to match it. In Acts 12 we read that Simon Peter was put in prison and was to be beheaded the next morning. Prayer was held for him that night in the city—every believer in Jerusalem was wide awake praying for Peter. But he was fast asleep, probably the only Christian asleep there that night. How could he sleep?

Only a few weeks previously in a personal interview the Lord Jesus had said to him, "Simon, when thou wast young, thou girdedst thyself, and walkedst whither thou wouldest: but when thou shalt be old ... another shall gird thee" (John 21:18). That night in jail, with his head due to come off the next morning, Simon reflected upon the promise of the Lord and said to himself, "Well, my Lord said that I would be old, and that was only a few weeks ago, so no matter what Herod may try, he can't touch me. I am going to sleep." So he lay down on the promises of God.

Charles Wesley reflects this faith in his beautiful hymn:

> Jesus, Lover of my soul,
>   Let me to Thy bosom fly,
> While the nearer waters roll,
>   While the tempest still is high:
> Hide me, O my Saviour, hide,
>   Till the storm of life is past;
> Safe into the haven guide;
>   Oh receive my soul at last!

The soul of David, among deadly enemies, overcame all its fears by faith in the promises of God. He left all the issues of the day in the

Almighty Hands, and out of his life of intimate fellowship with God there arose the power that could keep six hundred ruffians in subjection to his rule and bring conviction to the heart of an ungodly man like Saul.

For David had learned his lesson in this desperate moment of his experience: he must refuse to take the initiative and he must lean upon the living God. David, who was under the authority of the Lord, became the one in authority over all the others. But Saul, proud and arrogant, rebelled against the sovereignty of God and became a pathetic, tragic figure: a slave to himself, his passion and his sin, only a puppet king of a decaying kingdom.

See those two pictures plainly before you: into which could you step and say it is true of you? Basically, you are in one or the other of these situations. You may be walking with God in the light of His Word, having come to a saving knowledge of Jesus Christ and having submitted gladly to His rule in all things, though you may be often tested until it is almost beyond your endurance. Many times you may have been tempted to get your own back or to take a step out of God's will, but you have refused and have instead waited upon God. You are hiding under the shadow of His wings in absolute peace, and you are watching God work through your life in power.

Or you have said "No" at some point in your life to the authority of the Lord Jesus Christ. Though anointed by the same Spirit and given the same privileges and opportunities, you are moving out of God's will, out of the stream of blessing, out of the place of power and victory, out of the place of authority—one day (as Paul feared concerning himself), having proclaimed the rules to others, to be yourself cast away.

Which is it with you? It is never too late to begin again, to come to Calvary and submit to the authority of our crucified, risen Saviour: you may do that right now.

And David heard in the wilderness that Nabal did shear his sheep. And David sent out ten young men, and David said unto the young men, Get you up to Carmel, and go to Nabal, and greet him in my name: And thus shall ye say to him that liveth in prosperity . . . give, I pray thee, whatsoever cometh to thine hand unto thy servants, and to thy son David. . . .

And Nabal answered David's servants, and said, Who is David? and who is the son of Jesse? there be many servants now a days that break away every man from his master. . . . And David said unto his men, Gird ye on every man his sword . . . and there went up after David about four hundred men; and two hundred abode by the stuff.

But one of the young men told Abigail, Nabal's wife, saying . . . evil is determined against our master, and against all his household: for he is such a son of Belial, that a man cannot speak to him. . . .

And when Abigail saw David, she . . . fell at his feet, and said . . . Let not my lord, I pray thee, regard this man of Belial, even Nabal . . . seeing the Lord hath withholden thee from coming to shed blood, and from avenging thyself with thine own hand, now let thine enemies, and they that seek evil to my lord, be as Nabal. . . . Yet a man is risen to pursue thee, and to seek thy soul: but the soul of my lord shall be bound in the bundle of life with the Lord thy God; and the souls of thine enemies, them shall he sling out, as out of the middle of a sling. . . .

And David said to Abigail, Blessed be the Lord God of Israel, which sent thee this day to meet me. . . . So David received of her hand that which she had brought him, and said unto her, Go up in peace to thine house; see, I have hearkened to thy voice, and have accepted thy person.
I SAMUEL 25:4-35

CHAPTER 11

HANDLING THE HIGHHANDED

(I Samuel 25:4-35)

As YOU HAVE studied your Bible I am sure you have been impressed many times with the faithfulness of the Holy Spirit in recording facts about people. To present the best side of the picture for David, one would gloss over the story in I Samuel 25. It seems no advertisement for the Lord's cause to recount such a sad lack in the life of a man of God as we find related here.

But no, the Spirit of God is the Spirit of truth, and He is not afraid to reveal what is in our hearts. He always delights to work against the background of absolute hopelessness. Even a man after God's own heart, who already has shown many spiritual qualities and much evidence of spiritual growth, is capable of losing his temper and taking vengeance into his own hands. We find David rushing to commit a terrible sin from which he is mercifully delivered by the providential interference of the Lord. This is a very heart-searching, and yet wonderfully comforting, revelation.

Let me ask you, therefore, as we turn to this narrative, to look at the provocation to sin with which David is faced here.

Because of Saul's continuing enmity, David had taken refuge in the southernmost part of the land of Judah, in the wilderness of Paran. His presence in these borderlands of Judah had been a real help to the farmers and shepherds and all the people who lived in those areas, because David protected them time and time again from the attacks of the Philistines. One of Nabal's servants bore witness to this when he said, "The men were very good unto us, and we were not hurt, neither missed we any thing, as long as we were conversant with them, when we were in the fields: They were a wall unto us both by night and day, all the while we were with them keeping the sheep" (I Samuel 25:15-16).

Therefore it seemed only right to David, when he heard that one of the wealthiest of the farmers was shearing his sheep (a man called Nabal, who owed a good deal of his riches and fortunes to David's protecting hand), that he should send a few of his men to ask Nabal for a little recognition of his services: "Give, I pray thee, whatsoever cometh to thine hand unto thy servants, and to thy son David" (I Samuel 25:8).

The character of this man Nabal is vividly pictured for us in a few strokes of the pen as the Holy Spirit records it. Notice the comment of his servant in the second part of verse 17: "He is such a son of Belial, that the man cannot speak to him." We have also the comment of his wife—after all, she should know: "Let not my lord, I pray thee, regard this man of Belial, even Nabal: for as his name is, so is he; Nabal is his name, and folly is with him" (I Samuel 25:25).

Nabal certainly gave a very churlish reply to David's servants: "Who is David? and who is the son of Jesse? there be many servants now a days that break away every man from his master. Shall I then take my bread, and my water, and my flesh that I have killed for my shearers, and give it unto men, whom I know not whence they be?" (I Samuel 25:10-11).

It is always an unpleasant shock to meet a man like that, but they are everywhere—overbearing, contemptuous, hardhearted. Nabal knew perfectly well who David was, and why David was forced into this vagabond life, yet he insinuated that David was in fact being disloyal to Saul, and he covered his refusal to help him under a very pious show of regard for law and order. He told David's men that he would rather give his riches to the people who had worked for them than to idlers like themselves.

That got under David's skin, of course! It was a great provocation; his kindness was being repaid with insolence. His generous protection of Nabal had been unrecognized, his own motives and circumstances completely misrepresented.

Have you and I ever thought like that? Your kindness has been met by harshness, your service has been unrecognized, and your motives have been misrepresented. Indeed, even today your patience may be exhausted!

Let us not minimize the provocation, or how intolerable the situation was, or how unkind Nabal was to David. One would have every excuse to retaliate in such a situation.

Notice also that here is a passion to which David is succumbing. I am not surprised at Nabal, but I would be staggered at David's reaction, except that I know my own heart. Look at verse 13: "And David said unto his men, Gird ye on every man his sword. And they girded on every man his sword; and David also girded on his sword: and there went up after David about four hundred men; and two hundred abode by the stuff" (I Samuel 25:13).

Can you picture that? David, in a blazing temper, set out with four hundred men not only to murder Nabal, but also every male relative. He was muttering to himself, "Surely in vain have I kept all that this fellow hath in the wilderness, so that nothing was missed of all that pertaineth unto him: and he hath requited me evil for good" (I Samuel 25:21).

David! David! What is wrong with you? Why, one of the most wonderful things we have learned about you recently is your patience with Saul. You learned to wait upon the Lord, you refused to lift your hand to touch the Lord's anointed, although he had been your enemy for so many years. But now, look at you! Your self-restraint has gone to pieces and a few insulting words from a fool of a man like Nabal has made you see red! David, what's the matter?

"I am justified in doing this," David would reply. "There is no reason why Nabal should treat me as he has. He has repaid all my kindness with insults. I will show him he can't trifle with me. It is one thing to take it from Saul, who is my superior at this point, but this sort of man —this highhanded individual must be taught a lesson!"

Has that ever been your reaction? Doesn't it expose something that ought to make us cringe in the presence of God? For here is the inveterate sinfulness of the human heart, even when renewed by grace. Does it not show beyond all possible doubt that I cannot stand against the enemy of my soul unless the Lord upholds me moment by moment? This story tells me that however long I may have been on the Christian path, however often I may have overcome one temptation or another, however many times I have defeated sin in one area, it can strike in another and crush me in a moment. I may have overcome great temptation by the grace of the Lord; I may have stood my ground against the fierce onslaught of the enemy in one way or another and yet be tripped up by the smallest pin prick that gets under my skin.

The victories which I win—by the grace of God and through the power of the blood of Jesus—cannot impart strength to me for the future. No spiritual triumph in my life can give me power to resist the devil the next time he comes. There is nothing so sinful but that I may fall to it at any time, unless moment by moment I am being kept in His love. To show restraint in dealing with one person who has been unkind, highhanded, hateful, is no guarantee that an unguarded moment may not come when I will say, "I am going to wreak my vengeance on this person," especially if it is someone to whom I think I am superior.

How tragic it is that after years of Christian experience, men and women saved by God's grace, redeemed by Jesus' blood, indwelt by the Holy Spirit, fall into a silly little trap like that and ruin their testimony! That trap is the temptation to hit back, the passion to pay off the highhanded individual in his own coin. Even though for years we have shown restraint in one area, on one level, on that very same thing—when we have been attacked by somebody else—we may suddenly find that a pin prick has caused us to explode.

We find David here on the very verge of committing a sin which would have cast a dark shadow upon his whole life: murder, no less! Of course, you say you would never do that. No, perhaps you wouldn't, but you don't murder people simply by shooting them, you can also do it by hating them. The Lord is not interested only in knocking the gun out of your hand; He is concerned about taking the poison from your heart and making you love your enemies. Notice with me now, not only the provocation and the passion, but also the principle that will save us from them.

Nabal's servant, hearing of the effect of his message on David, immediately informed Abigail, Nabal's wife, and bore testimony to David's kindness to them. Abigail was a very interesting and remarkable woman: "she was a woman of good understanding, and of a beautiful countenance" (I Samuel 25:3). Those two things don't always go together. There is beauty that is only skin-deep, or applied from the outside, which often accompanies an empty head and a shallow life. But whenever you find true Christian character in the heart, then somehow the loveliness of it shines out even in the plainest of countenances.

But, I ask myself, why did such a woman as Abigail get involved with a man like Nabal? I suppose in the custom of her day and time she may not have had anything to do with it; probably her marriage was planned by her parents when she was a child. But why do you think that modern Abigails get involved with modern Nabals, when they have everything to do with it? How often a Christian girl, or a Christian man for that matter, with high ideals and Christian principles, has been deceived by flattery or enticed by money and has entered into an alliance with someone who has no principles at all, except during the time of their engagement in order to "catch" the fish! The result is absolute misery for the rest of their lives.

May I say to you lovingly, but firmly, if such a circumstance has befallen you, that is no reason for you to invoke the law of the country to get out of the entanglement. Perhaps God knew that you needed the fiery trial to humble you and to make you a testimony to your partner. The Bible says you must stay as you are. Maybe there will come to you one day, as there came to Abigail, a new opportunity; but until then, it is for you to prove the grace and power of the Lord in your heart to strengthen you and to keep you pure.

I would say this, too, if I should happen to be speaking to some young person who is tempted to sell out to the lure of money or position, irrespective of the Christian character or lack of it in the other person involved: such a marriage, contrary to the will of God, always ends in one way—disaster. You never raise that other person to your level, you sink down to his—I have seen that happen so often.

Returning again to the narrative, we find that Abigail hastened to prepare a liberal gift for David and set out to meet him (I Samuel 25:18-20). To listen to the pleading of this woman with David is like listening to the pleading of the Holy Spirit with us when we face a similar provocation. See how this wonderful woman of such fine character and lovely countenance approached David and pleaded with him that he would not soil the page of his life needlessly.

You notice that she agreed Nabal was entirely wrong, but she suggested that he was not worthy of one moment's notice by David: "Let not my lord, I pray thee, regard this man of Belial, even Nabal [and the word means "fool"]: for as his name, so is he" (I Samuel 25:25). In other words, she admitted that David was right and Nabal was wrong, but she advised David not to waste his attention on a man who was not worth it.

Then she expressed her thankfulness that David had been spared so far from avenging himself and pleaded with him not to stoop to that level now. In a very sweet and lovely way she appreciated his true desire to fight the Lord's battles and to keep a character that was unstained. She reminded him of a coming day when all the purposes of God for his life would be fulfilled as she said, in effect, "David, how wonderful it will be on that day not to have to look back on a black shadow cast by murder."

The master stroke of the whole argument, however, is in the words of verse 29. In effect she said, "David, your soul is wrapped up in a bundle of life in the Lord your God, and the strength of that bundle lies in the identity of God with all that goes on inside it. He is there with you! Therefore, the life of a man after God's own heart is safe in

God's keeping, and what can the churlishness of Nabal do against you? Why should you stoop to his level?" Then she added a very lovely touch by reminding him that he was taking four hundred men, with two hundred behind looking after the stuff, to do what God could do as easily as throwing a pebble out of a sling! I wonder if David held his head a little lower at that point and remembered a day in his youth —in all the ardor of his love and affection and commitment to the Lord, and the fragrance of that fresh anointing of the Spirit—when he took one stone out of a sling and killed a giant. When the issues are left in God's hand, it is as easy as that. But taking them out of His hand, and getting hot under the collar with everything bursting inside you until you get your own back, is not the way for a man of God.

Isn't this a lesson to all of us who would seek to get alongside others in need and help them nearer to the Lord? Abigail's argument was so gracious and tender, without a word of harshness or rebuke. When you are on the point of letting somebody "have it," if only you would stop and kneel in the presence of the Lord, then the Holy Spirit would speak to you just as Abigail spoke to David.

How David melted under her pleading! "Blessed be the Lord God of Israel, which sent thee this day to meet me: And blessed be thy advice, and blessed be thou, which hast kept me this day from coming to shed blood, and from avenging myself with mine own hand" (I Samuel 25:32-33). How thankful he was, not simply for her gift—evidently he had forgotten all about that, for he said nothing about it—but for her intervention in his life at that moment to deliver him from an act that would have left a stain upon his life forever.

I don't know about human stories, but God's love stories always have a happy ending, and this is no exception. Soon afterwards, Nabal drank himself to death—that wasn't a very happy ending! But then David sent a message to the woman of lovely countenance and good understanding to say, "I want to marry you," and Abigail became his wife. What a happy ending to something that could have been a desperate tragedy!

Does the Holy Spirit draw near to you now and say, "My child, of course you are right, for that person should never have treated you like that. Even though he has been very highhanded, it is not worthy of one moment of your attention. Remember who you are and remember the great purpose I have for your life. Remember your high calling, that you are a child of God, a joint-heir with Christ, destined to share My kingdom." You must not meet the Lord Jesus with soiled hands or a life stained by something that could ruin you after so many years of Christian experience.

"Listen, my child," says the Lord to us today, "I know that you have no stock of grace at your command. The strength that I gave you yesterday is not enough for today. The grace you have already received will not enable you to stand right now. Depend upon Me again for what you need at this moment." We have to learn that the Christian life is a succession of holy moments in which we count on His grace and strength to see us through.

"Oh, but I can't live like that!" you may object.

Then let this be the climax of the Lord's appeal to your heart: your life is bound up in the bundle of life with the Lord your God. He has identified Himself with you in Jesus Christ who died for you on Calvary. Now identify yourself with Him.

What do I mean? I will tell you. Abigail is just a picture; the Lord is the great Reality, and He wants you to marry Him today, to become identified with Him, to find indeed that your life is bound up in a bundle of life with Himself. Then all these complicated situations that drive you to the point of distraction He will deal with as simply as throwing a stone out of a sling. Trust Him right now in whatever situation you may find yourself so that you may rest in Him and in His power.

*And David said in his heart, I shall now perish one day by the hand
of Saul: there is nothing better for me than that I should speedily escape
into the land of the Philistines; and Saul shall despair of me, to seek
me any more in any coast of Israel: so shall I escape out of his hand.
And David arose, and he passed over with the six hundred men that
were with him. . . . And David dwelt with Achish at Gath, he and his
men, every man with his household. . . . And it was told Saul that David
was fled to Gath: and he sought no more again for him.*

*And David said unto Achish, if I have now found grace in thine eyes,
let them give me a place in some town in the country, that I may dwell
there: for why should thy servant dwell in the royal city with thee?
Then Achish gave him Ziklag that day: wherefore Ziklag pertaineth
unto the kings of Judah unto this day. And the time that David dwelt
in the country of the Philistines was a full year and four months.*

*And David and his men went up, and invaded the Geshurites, and
the Gezrites, and the Amalekites . . . and left neither man nor woman
alive, and took away the sheep, and the oxen, and the asses, and the
camels, and the apparel, and returned, and came to Achish.*

*And Achish said, Whither have ye made a road [raid] to day? And
David said, Against the south of Judah, and against the south of the
Jerahmeelites, and against the south of the Kenites. And David saved
neither man nor woman alive, to bring tidings to Gath, saying, Lest
they should tell on us, saying, So did David, and so will be his manner
all the while he dwelleth in the country of the Philistines. And Achish
believed David, saying, He hath made his people Israel utterly to abhor
him; therefore he shall be my servant for ever.*

I SAMUEL 27:1-12

CHAPTER 12

A FIT OF DEPRESSION

(I Samuel 27:1-12)

AT ONE MOMENT we find David facing circumstances calculated to tempt him to blazing anger and immediate retaliation. At the next moment, he is surrounded by such constant and overwhelming attacks from his lifelong enemy that he is discouraged and almost ready to give up. Here is the anvil upon which the character of a man of God is hammered out, the fiery furnace through which he is melted and poured as steel for the glory of his Lord. Thus the iron gets into a man's soul.

The language of David at this point in his life is in the minor key of depression and sadness, as we hear in extracts from psalms which he wrote at this period. "Why standest thou afar off, O Lord? Why hidest thou thyself in times of trouble?" (Psalm 10:1). "How long wilt thou forget me, O Lord? for ever? how long wilt thou hide thy face from me?" (Psalm 13:1). "My God, my God, why hast thou forsaken me? why art thou so far from helping me, and from the words of my roaring?" (Psalm 22:1).

A man who talks like that is at the breaking point. Is the recurrence of moods of depression your problem? Do you come to the task to which God has called you each day with despair and frustration until you feel like throwing the whole thing over and maybe even yourself out the window? Come with me, my harassed brother or sister in Christ, into the treasury of God's Word, into the quietness of God's purpose, and let us look at the reason for depressions, the results of giving in to them, and the wonderful remedy for all of them.

I never like to meet a gloomy Christian—he is a miserable specimen! So are people who go around with faces a mile long, looking as if they were carrying the whole world on their shoulders! They have moods, and they give way to depression and despair at the least little excuse. What is the reason for that?

It would seem, on the surface anyway, that David had ample reason to feel as he did. Saul's hatred was deeply rooted; jealousy was eating up his heart and he resorted to every possible expedient to capture and kill David. Furthermore, Saul had traitors like Doeg at his disposal, ready to betray David into his hands. Perhaps the most graphic statement concerning the situation is in I Samuel 23:14 where we read these enlightening words, "Saul sought him every day." The pressure was absolutely relentless. Even checks imposed upon Saul's conscience by David's kindness (when on at least two occasions he had him at his mercy and spared him) made no difference, because Saul was determined on nothing less than murder.

Despite all that, David had six hundred men with their wives and children (and I Samuel 30:3 and 6 suggest this comprised a large number of people) under his care, in addition to two wives of his own. How was he to feed such a crowd? How was he to protect them in such a wild country? How was he to avoid capture by the three thousand trained men of Saul's army who were constantly after him and who knew every inch of this territory? These problems produced grounds for fear; David had every excuse to say in his heart, "I shall now perish at the hand of Saul!"

It isn't hard to find yourself in the same sort of situation. If you are a committed Christian (and I underline *committed*) whose life is unreservedly in the hands of God, then you are subject to the constant buffeting of the devil. As the Apostle Paul said, "We wrestle not against flesh and blood, but against principalities, against powers, against the rulers of the darkness of this world, against spiritual wickedness in high places" (Ephesians 6:12).

The committed man of God is against sin, and all the powers of evil are against him. In such a warfare there is no intermission at all. The devil never takes five minutes' vacation! He has an endless variety of methods of attack, and alas, let us acknowledge it, we all know only too well that within our hearts there is many a traitor ready and eager to betray us into his hand. Many times you and I have been saved only by a miracle, but the enemies we thought we had once overcome and slain and left behind years ago have risen up against us with fresh power.

Baffled in one attack against us, Satan may retreat for a moment, but he gathers reinforcements and renews the onslaught. He is bent upon the spiritual destruction of all who name the name of Christ. He is not interested in you as an individual, but he hates that which is within you, the redemptive life of Jesus Christ by the Holy Spirit, and he makes every effort to destroy it.

If that language sounds strange to you, don't congratulate yourself!

It is strange either because you are in the devil's grip and he doesn't have to bother about you; or worse still, as a professing Christian you have given up the fight, and your religious experience is no more than an empty rehearsal of pious evangelical language that is absolutely unrelated to your life and has no spiritual value for your soul at all. These are the alternatives if what I say is strange. But if it is indeed your experience, then no wonder there are times when you are discouraged and at the point of saying, like David, "I shall now perish one day at the hand of Satan."

There is a reason for depression, but see the result of it. Certainly it is never wrong for a man to be depressed. We are only human, and the Lord knows it. We are engaged in a battle which is far too much for us, and constantly there will be reasons for depression. It is not a sin to suffer from depression, but the point is, what do you do about it? What are your reactions to it? Suppose you give in, what then?

Notice a very interesting thing: at first sight it seems that it pays to give in to the devil. "And it was told Saul that David was fled to Gath; and he sought no more again for him" (I Samuel 27:4). The battle is called off; the pressure is released. The enemy withdraws and for the moment what might seem to be peace, but in fact is only stupor, descends upon the soul.

The peace which is the outcome of taking drugs is one thing; the peace which is the outcome of overcoming in the battle is another. Give in to the devil and I promise you without any possible doubt the "enjoyment" of peace immediately. If you want that kind of stupefying drug you can have it: only move, as David moved, into enemy-occupied territory and Satan will get off your neck. There will be three cheers in hell, and you will have a lovely sense of freedom—for a time.

But what is the price of it? At first sight, I say, if you give in to Satan at any point in your life, you will have an immediate release from the pressure, and you will go away saying, "What is the preacher talking about? It's not worth fighting the battle, for I'm having a whale of a time now! It is lovely to be free of conflict." I have heard people talk like that for a short time. But what is the result?

I ask you to notice how dishonoring this was to the Lord. Hadn't God promised David he would be king? Hadn't the Lord said that He would cast out David's enemies like a stone out of a sling? Hadn't every word of God been confirmed to David by Samuel and Jonathan and Abigail, and even by Saul himself? There had been a moment when David had exulted, in the language of Psalm 27, "The Lord is my light and my salvation; whom shall I fear? . . . Though an host should encamp against me, my heart shall not fear . . . in the time of trouble he shall hide me in his pavilion" (27:1, 3, 5).

David, are all God's promises to be discarded? Is all your previous conviction of faith and commitment of trust to be completely denied? Are you going back upon all that?

In this depressed mood David was saying, in effect, "I am afraid the Lord has undertaken something more than He can accomplish. I know that He has kept me so far, but the situation is getting too tough for Him; sooner or later Saul is going to get hold of me. After all, it is stupid to attempt the impossible. I have waited for the Lord long enough, and I'm tired of waiting. It is time I took things into my own hands and used my own wits to get out of this situation."

Oh David! Oh you! Oh me! It is one thing to counsel others, or to condemn them when they give in to the relentless attacks of the devil, but what about our own behavior when the waters threaten to overwhelm us? Are we dishonoring the Lord by refusing to wait and trust Him?

Notice again that this attitude was also harmful to his friends. When David went to Philistine territory, where did he go? Achish gave him Ziklag for a place to live (I Samuel 27:6). Look up Ziklag in the Old Testament: it was a city in the southernmost part that belonged by right to Judah, being allocated to them when Joshua entered the land. Later it was captured by the Philistines, but was never occupied by them. At this period of Saul's reign, though in Philistine territory, it was being occupied by the descendants of Simeon—you find that in I Chronicles 4:30. These people were living in territory that had been given to them by God, but it was controlled by the enemy and they were living in subjection. Evidently "peace at any price" was their motto and they had no stomach for a fight!

The terror of the warning is in my soul as I think about it! God forbid that as I get older in the Christian life I should settle down like that, to live with some area in my life which God has possessed, yet Satan has overcome, and I have no desire to drive him out. God forbid that I should allow him to conquer in one realm after another and say, "Well, I am saved anyway! I am under the blood! If the devil recaptures a bit of the territory, does it really matter?" Oh, perish the thought!

What a disastrous effect this must have had on the fighting qualities of the six hundred men under David! What poison must have been injected into their hearts with tragic results for years to come! I would suggest to you (and you can trace it by studying the Word of God) that out of this episode there came a great deal of idolatry and compromise in marriage. Of course, some of David's six hundred men would no doubt be very thankful for respite from danger and glad to accept the lowered standard of their leader. It would make it easier for them to live to please themselves if he stopped getting under their skin and let them just enjoy living in Ziklag.

Let a Christian leader, a man of God, give in to the enemy in the midst of the pressures and battles, and how widespread are the consequences! How thankful some of the people are when a Christian leader falls! It gives them an excuse for the policy of peace at any price. "We want to live in God's territory," they say, "but let us not trouble the enemy too much." When a man descends to that level, how harmful to his friends and how hurtful to his own life!

In the third verse of I Samuel 27, we see David and his men welcomed with open arms by Achish. When we go along that same road we find it makes the devil happy too. And why? The Philistines now had an excellent opportunity of turning the whole battle against the people of God because they had those whom they thought were traitors in the camp.

If you desert to the devil in one issue of your life, he can turn the whole tide of the spiritual warfare in your community. That is what a deserter does: he gives the advantage to the enemy.

Just look at the deceit and the lies and the suffering which became part of David's life at this point. He had to get provisions somehow, and the only way open to him was plunder, so he attacked the occupants of the south country, the Geshurites, Amalekites, and others (I Samuel 27:8). These people were nomad tribes who were the enemies of Judah. In his heart, David was still with the people of God, even though he was in an embarrassing situation. So when he went out to plunder so that he could keep himself and his company alive, he attacked those who were the enemies of his own people.

In order to make Achish think that in fact he was attacking Israel, David was obliged to slaughter the women and children, everybody, to leave no trace at all of his attack. When he was asked for a report of his activities from his newfound lord, David replied that he had been making a raid "Against the south of Judah, and against the south of the Jerahmeelites, and against the south of the Kenites" (I Samuel 27:10).

David, that is a lie! You haven't been doing anything of the kind! But Achish became thoroughly convinced, he "believed David, saying,

He hath made his people Israel utterly to abhor him; therefore he shall be my servant for ever" (I Samuel 27:12).

No wonder the music of this man's life was in the minor key. It is like listening one moment to the magnificence of the "Messiah," and the next moment going to a joint where they play juke-box jazz. A blight descended on his soul and the song in his heart was silenced when he descended to expediency and gave in to depression.

It is a tragedy in the life of a child of God when he yields to the pressure of Satan, and God leaves him on his own. He is reduced to scheming and planning, and when he is driven into a tight corner he can only escape by deceit. Suddenly the man who has given in to depression realizes that he has purchased his deliverance from the pressure of the devil at too great a price. He has obtained release from tension for a moment, but he has exchanged the smile of God for the grin of the enemy. He has exchanged the protection of Jesus Christ for flimsy walls of defeat, as David exchanged trust in the promises of God for the walls of Ziklag, which soon were going to be burned by fire and over which David would weep scalding, bitter tears of repentance. Oh, the harm that is done by a man who gives in to the enemy!

There is, however, a remedy for this. It need not happen to any of us, by the grace of God, if we just listen and pray. What is the answer for such a situation?

Go back a moment to the Scripture for the discovery of what, I believe, lies at the root of David's failure. "David said in his heart" (I Samuel 27:1). There you have it. As we have seen, in other times of emergency he inquired of the Lord. And we will find that when he learned his bitter lesson in these desperate circumstances, once again David inquired of the Lord and the Lord met him immediately (I Samuel 30:8).

David had failed to seek God in the matter of Nabal, being overcome by passion and temper. At Ziklag he was overcome by panic, and he "said in his heart," with no reference at all to the Lord.

Never act in a panic. Never act when your emotions are aroused and your blood is at the boiling point. Wait until your pulse begins to beat steadily again. If at any moment of tremendous pressure you feel that you *must* do something, that moment is the time when you will be apt to make the most tragic mistake in judgment. At that moment—and may I use the word?—*force* yourself into the presence of God, and I mean "force yourself." When you feel like flying off the handle, when you are a victim of depression, when you are in a mood of despair, when you are on the point of giving in, the last thing you want to do is to seek the Lord. You are too ashamed, and you feel that the only thing you can do is to act.

Whatever you do, stand still! Wait until you have a word from the Lord; cast yourself on your knees and cry out to Jesus for mercy and for help. Wait upon God until He makes His way plain. As long as that way is hidden, if He keeps it closed, quite clearly there is no need to do anything. If only you and I applied that principle always in our walk with God, think what damage might be avoided!

While you wait upon the Lord, I would ask you to remember three simple but basic truths which David remembered at another time in his life.

First, remember that God's promises are sure. "The Lord redeemeth the soul of his servants: and none of them that trust in him shall be desolate" (Psalm 34:22). God has provided that we should be acceptable to Him through the blood of Jesus Christ. He has provided for our renewing into the likeness of our Saviour, and for our perseverance in a life of faith because of the perseverance of Jesus, and no one shall ever pluck us out of His Father's hand.

Secondly, remember that His promises are conditional. "The eyes of the Lord are upon the righteous, and his ears are open unto their cry. The face of the Lord is against them that do evil" (Psalm 34:15-16). Not one promise in the Bible can be yours until you repent and believe the gospel. Therefore examine the cause of your depression and fears.

Are you depressed in case God should forget all about you, denying His word and leaving you to perish notwithstanding the fact that you have trusted Him? Then that is criminal. Or are you doubting that you have ever really come to Jesus at all in His appointed way? Then these circumstances that are flying at you from all sides may not be from the devil, it may be that the Lord is driving you to repent and believe. Have you fled to Jesus for refuge? If not, then to trust God for help is sheer presumption.

Thirdly, remember that His promises are corrective. David said, "There is nothing better for me than that I should speedily escape into the land of the Philistines" (I Samuel 27:1). In other words, he allowed the pressure to drive him away from God. But to wait upon the Lord is to prove that all things work together for good to them that love God and that nothing in the whole universe can separate us from the love of God in Jesus Christ. The promise of the Lord is that He will draw us near: "The Lord is nigh unto them that are of a broken heart" (Psalm 34:18). Never let anything drive you from the wounded side of Jesus Christ.

Now the Philistines gathered together all their armies to Aphek: and the Israelites pitched by a fountain which is in Jezreel. . . . Then said the princes of the Philistines, What do these Hebrews here? . . .

Then Achish called David, and said unto him . . . I have not found evil in thee since the day of thy coming unto me unto this day: nevertheless the lords favour thee not. Wherefore now return, and go in peace, that thou displease not the lords of the Philistines. . . .

And it came to pass, when David and his men were come to Ziklag on the third day, that the Amalekites had invaded the south, and Ziklag, and . . . it was burned with fire; and their wives, and their sons, and their daughters, were taken captives. Then David and the people that were with him lifted up their voice and wept, until they had no more power to weep. . . . And David was greatly distressed; for the people spake of stoning him, because the soul of all the people was grieved, every man for his sons and for his daughters: but David encouraged himself in the Lord his God.

And David said to Abiathar the priest, Ahimelech's son, I pray thee, bring me hither the ephod. And Abiathar brought thither the ephod to David. And David enquired at the Lord, saying, Shall I pursue after this troop? shall I overtake them? And he answered him, Pursue: for thou shalt surely overtake them, and without fail recover all.

So David went, he and the six hundred men that were with him, and came to the brook Besor, where those that were left behind stayed. But David pursued, he and four hundred men: for two hundred abode behind, which were so faint that they could not go over the brook Besor.

I SAMUEL 29:1—30:10

CHAPTER 13

RETURN TO SANITY

(I Samuel 29:1—30:10)

IT IS INDEED true that the darkest hour in a man's experience is always just before the dawning of new light. Well might David say at this point, "The sorrows of death compassed me, and the floods of ungodly men made me afraid. The sorrows of hell compassed me about: the snares of death prevented me" (Psalm 18:4-5).

We find David here in real extremity—but when a man is in such a place, God is there too. The man may not recognize it; he may feel himself helplessly adrift in the storm, but always "the Lord is nigh unto them that are of a broken heart" (Psalm 34:18). So we shall find that David proves the truth of the saying, "Man's extremity is God's opportunity." When we really—I say *really* with threefold emphasis— come to the end of ourselves, we are at the threshold of a new world of discovery and adventure in the will and purpose of God.

There is nobody to whom the Lord is nearer than the one who is so weak that he is saying, "But as for me, my feet were almost gone; my steps had well nigh slipped" (Psalm 73:2). I would that such helplessness might be the attitude of each of us, always, in the presence of our Lord, because conscious weakness is always a prerequisite for heavenly reinforcement. When I am weak, then, and then only, am I strong. The entry of self-confidence into a man's experience means the departure of heavenly strength.

May the Lord speak to our hearts as we consider this tremendous moment in David's life, and as we see, in the first place, the plight to which self-will brought him.

In the context we find that David is in a desperate position: over-come by depression and fear of Saul, he has sought refuge among the Philistines and has been staying in the border city of Ziklag.

In the opening two verses of chapter 28, we are told that King

Achish of Gath considered this an appropriate moment for launching a full-scale invasion of Israel. Did he not see that Saul's kingdom was tottering? More and more people were leaving Israel to live within the Philistine area, and therefore Achish welcomed David warmly because he was quite sure that David and his men would be a wonderful addition to his forces. He offered to David, therefore, the position as captain of his troops when they set out to attack the Israelites.

Oh, what a plight! Here is a man of God in the battle all right, but he is on the wrong side. He is in the position of leading the armies of the enemy, marching with the Philistines to attack his own people. In other words, he found himself involved in a hopeless compromise from which there seemed to be no escape.

But, worse still, no sooner did he set out than he found that even the Philistines did not trust him. "Then said the princes of the Philistines, What do these Hebrews here?" (I Samuel 29:3). That was a good question! And in spite of the protest of Achish, those suspicious Philistines insisted on sending David back, as the following two verses say: "Make this fellow return. . . . Is not this David of whom they sang . . . Saul slew his thousands and David his ten thousands?" (29:4-5). Can you picture anything more humiliating than their rejection of him?

Is this merely an interesting Old Testament story? It certainly is not; this is also a twentieth-century experience. I hope you are not among those people who carve up their Bibles to such a point that you exclude certain portions as having no bearing upon our lives today. Of course, I am perfectly aware that we must rightly divide the Word of truth—but at the same time, I am also commanded to declare the whole counsel of God, and "all scripture . . . is profitable . . . for instruction in righteousness" (II Timothy 3:16). Therefore, I am concerned that we should see in this ancient story a graphic illustration of what is happening today to thousands of Christian people who are pursuing the path of self-will as they refuse complete allegiance to Jesus Christ and deny the authority of His Word when He said, "No man can serve two masters." They have sought to live as near as possible to the world, just as close as they dare. Perhaps they don't smoke or drink, but otherwise the line of demarcation between the child of God and the unbeliever is invisible.

The Christian has his devotions, but he lets down the bars and mingles unconcernedly with worldly people. He shares in their godless conversation and never talks about Jesus—why, that would embarrass everyone! He ignores altogether the counsel of the Word that says, "Be ye not unequally yoked together with unbelievers . . . come out from among them and be ye separate, saith the Lord, and touch not the unclean thing; and I will receive you" (II Corinthians 6:14-17).

I fully recognize the danger of the opposite extreme, when separation equals isolation to a point of having no contact at all with unsaved people. Surely the true position of the Christian is to copy the example of the Lord Jesus. He was the friend of sinners, so near to those in desperate need, and yet holy, harmless, separate, undefiled.

Like David, the Christian often finds himself in the wrong camp, going along with the wrong company. He has lowered the standard, and he excuses himself by saying that you must be as like the world as possible; you must imitate ungodly people and not let them think that you are peculiar or unusual. Then he discovers to his humiliation that there comes a point where the unbeliever, who holds a higher standard for the Christian life than he does, suddenly turns to him and says, "What do these Christians here?"

There was worse to follow for David, but we will leave him there right now, that you may see the plight into which self-will had brought him, and then see the patience with which the Lord his God followed him.

I would ask this question, which you may have framed in your own mind already: Does a man who behaves like that find himself forsaken of God? Indeed he doesn't! When God had spoken to Moses about the Israelites possessing the land, He said, you may recall, that when any of the outcasts—outcasts because of disobedience and apostasy—were even in the "outmost parts of heaven," so far from Him that their recovery seemed beyond any possibility, "from thence will the Lord thy God gather thee, and from thence will he fetch thee: And the Lord thy God will bring thee into the land which thy fathers possessed, and thou shalt possess it; and he will do thee good, and multiply thee above thy fathers" (Deuteronomy 30:4-5).

So spoke the Lord Jehovah in Old Testament days, and in the New Testament we find the Lord Jesus Christ saying: "My Father, which gave them me, is greater than all; and no man is able to pluck them out of my Father's hand" (John 10:29).

Listen again to the confidence of the Apostle Paul: "For I am persuaded, that neither death, nor life, nor angels, nor principalities, nor powers, nor things present, nor things to come, Nor height, nor depth, nor any other creature, shall be able to separate us from the love of God, which is in Christ Jesus our Lord" (Romans 8:38-39).

I believe in the perseverance of the saints because I believe in the perseverance of the Lord Jesus Christ. Here in our story is a man reduced to an appalling plight because he has compromised. But it is thrilling to know that no matter how far that man has gone, the blood of his redemption goes further. No matter how far his wanderings have taken him from God, he is never, never beyond the reach of our wonderful Lord.

How the Lord watched over David as he wandered away! Even in that compromising situation, God made the wrath of men to praise Him. How skillfully he protected David from death!

All the time that David was out of God's will and in the wrong company (living a worldly life, as we would put it), what was God doing? Was He inactive or indifferent? Oh, no! Turn to I Chronicles 12 and you will find the names of all the men who came to David in Ziklag: "at that time day by day there came to David to help him, until it was a great host, like the host of God" (I Chronicles 12:22).

Ultimately over three hundred and forty thousand people actually gathered around this anointed exile and helped him secure the kingdom (I Chronicles 12:24-37). But at this point—although he is out of blessing and out of the will of God—the mind of the Eternal is fixed upon His ultimate purpose for David, for a moment ignoring the fact that he has tripped up and fallen out of His will. One by one they came to David from the other side. Some of them actually swam the Jordan when it was in flood (I Chronicles 12:15)! Others of them, the people of Manasseh, came back from the battle with David (I Chronicles 12:19).

Although this man was out of God's blessing and in the wrong company, the Lord was quietly sending reinforcements that he would need for future battles. The Lord never allowed the lapse of His servant into godlessness to divert Him from His eternal purpose for David.

Do I believe that is true today? I most surely do! "For whom he did foreknow, he also did predestinate to be conformed to the image of his Son . . . whom he did predestinate, them he also called: and whom he called, them he also justified: and whom he justified, them he also glorified" (Romans 8:29-30). It is all in the past tense of accomplishment. Although Satan may trip us up and put us on the sidelines, even though we seem to be marching in the devil's army, God silently works along the lines of His eternal purposes. May that word ring the bells of comfort and encouragement and hope for someone who is weak and helpless!

Furthermore, the Philistines thought they were being prudent in sending David back home. But though they were ignorant of it, they were merely the instruments God was using to extract David from his compromised position. In every situation God is sovereign. David's deliverance was so perfectly timed that it enabled him to get back to Ziklag (though not in time to stop its being burned, because God meant it to be destroyed) to discover the fruits of his own self-will and sin, and to see what damage it had done. He was also in time to go after the enemy and recover all that was lost, as we shall see in the next chapter.

It is true that "all things work together for good to them that love God, to them who are the called according to this purpose" (Romans 8:28). Even when I am out of God's will, when I have refused God's discipline, when I have sought to escape His loving chastening, when I have found myself trapped in compromise, when I feel that the Lord must have justifiably forsaken me forever, there is nobody under heaven to whom He is nearer! "If we believe not, yet he abideth faithful: he cannot deny himself" (II Timothy 2:13).

Could you resist a God like that? Could you ever turn your back and your heart upon the Lord who loved like that? You may be saying that in such a case it doesn't matter very much how you behave, because God has hold of you anyway. Now wait a minute! See the point at which salvation met David. All of God's dealings with him, as also His dealings with you and me, are designed with one supreme objective: to bring us to the end of our own resources.

God succeeded with David, but at what a cost! When David and his men returned to Ziklag they found the place they had chosen as a refuge destroyed by fire. "So David and his men came to the city, and, behold, it was burned with fire; and their wives, and their sons, and their daughters, were taken captives. Then David and the people that were with him lifted up their voice and wept, until they had no more power to weep" (I Samuel 30:3-4).

Can you picture that scene? Let the Holy Spirit lay hold of your imagination to picture David here, a man of God despised by the Philistines—he has got in the wrong company and even his enemies have no use for him. Now his family and possessions have all been destroyed or stolen, and worst of all, his own brave men are threatening mutiny (I Samuel 30:6).

Here is David standing among the ruins of his self-will; the outcome of his compromise is lying in ashes around him. He is despised by his enemies—they have no use for a man who compromises. He is blamed by his own people—they threaten to stone him. Apparently he is feeling absolutely down and out, miles away from God.

Can anybody be lower than that? Nobody except Jesus, who went down deeper still to save us all by being completely cut off from God.

But can any of us be in a worse plight than David? What does one do when he gets to such a place? What *can* he do? "David encouraged himself in the Lord his God" (I Samuel 30:6).

Here we find his return to sanity; he was coming back from the madness and stupidity of compromise. Suddenly he snapped right back into the place of blessing, and for the first time in months "David enquired at the Lord, saying, Shall I pursue after this troop? shall I overtake them?" (I Samuel 30:8).

And the Lord must have answered him, "David, I can't trust you now." No, He didn't!

"David, I'm going to keep you on probation for at least six months." No, not that!

"David, you have to go back in training for a long time before I can trust you in My army." No, not that threat of punishment, either!

"And he answered him, Pursue."

Immediately, when David touched rock bottom, he turned back to God. At the very first uplifting of that tear-stained face, the very first moment the Lord looked down and saw His brokenhearted child weeping until he could weep no more, then heaven answered with an immediate word of power and victory, and sent him out to conquer. That moment became for David the gateway into victory, the stepping-stone into blessing, the beginning of the accomplishment of God's purpose for his life.

This is exactly the place to which God wants to bring you today, for this is simply an Old Testament illustration of New Testament principles.

Do you really desire that God may bring you into victory and blessing today? Then the moment you stand with a broken heart amid the ruins of your self-life, acknowledging the futility of fighting against God; when you turn your eyes upon Jesus and lift your tear-stained face to your wonderful Lord, at that moment He not only lifts you up, but brings you victory and sends you out to pursue your enemies—and His. If you want that in New Testament language, here it is:

"I know that in me (that is, in my flesh,) dwelleth no good thing" (Romans 7:18). Nobody says that with genuineness until it is spoken with a sob to the throne of God.

Then that confession brings heavenly reinforcement. There comes a new step and a new song. "I live; yet not I, but Christ liveth in me: and the life which I now live in the flesh I live by the faith of the Son of God, who loved me and gave himself for me" (Galatians 2:20). "Being fully persuaded that, what he had promised, he was able also to perform" (Romans 4:21).

That is the way into the kingdom. It is the only way, and if you want it confirmed from the very lips of our Master Himself, listen to Him say, "If any man will come after me, let him deny himself, and take up his cross daily, and follow me" (Luke 9:23). You must humble yourself and become as a little child, for "of such is the kingdom of God" (Luke 18:16).

If your self-will, your rejection of God's principles of life, your compromises, have driven you into a desperate plight, remember that God loves you, that He is still planning great things for you, and that He alone can deliver you. The moment you stop fighting against Him and humble yourself before Him, when you encourage yourself in the Lord and inquire of Him, *at that moment* He is there. In fact, He is with you right now to do for you as He did for David, give you victory and blessing.

*And they found an Egyptian in the field, and brought him to David.
. . . And David said unto him, To whom belongest thou? and whence
art thou?*

*And he said, I am a young man of Egypt, servant to an Amalekite;
and my master left me, because three days agone I fell sick. We made
an invasion upon the south of the Cherethites, and upon the coast
which belongeth to Judah, and upon the south of Caleb; and we burned
Ziklag with fire.*

And David said to him, Canst thou bring me down to this company?

*And he said, Swear unto me by God, that thou wilt neither kill me,
nor deliver me into the hands of my master, and I will bring thee down
to this company. And when he had brought him down, behold, they
were spread abroad upon all the earth, eating and drinking, and
dancing. . . .*

*And David smote them from the twilight even unto the evening of
the next day: and there escaped not a man of them, save four hundred
young men, which rode upon camels, and fled.*

*And David recovered all that the Amalekites had carried away: and
David rescued his two wives. And there was nothing lacking to them,
neither small nor great, neither sons nor daughters, neither spoil, nor
any thing that they had taken to them: David recovered all. . . .*

*And when David came to Ziklag, he sent of the spoil unto the elders
of Judah, even to his friends, saying, Behold a present for you of the
spoil of the enemies of the Lord; To them which were in Bethel . . .
and to all the places where David himself and his men were wont to
haunt.*

I SAMUEL 30:11-31

CHAPTER 14

REVIVAL OR FUNERAL?

(I Samuel 30:11-31)

IN THREE WORDS, "David recovered all" (I Samuel 30:19), there is a very lovely Old Testament picture of what the Lord Jesus Christ accomplished for us by His death and resurrection: the recovery of everything that had been lost in the rebellion of the human race against God.

Before that great day of recovery and victory, David was in a sorry plight. He had lost everything: possessions, home, family. Why? His loss was only the outward evidence of his spiritual decline. The Amalekites were but the chastening hand of God to bring him back into His will, back into the purpose of God for his life.

David had lost his vision. Chapter 27 begins with David expressing his discouragement, "I shall now perish one day by the hand of Saul." Because he had lost his vision, he had lost his passion also, for that same verse says, "David said in his heart. . . ." He had forgotten to pray; he had turned aside from the place of inquiry at the throne of God. Because he had lost vision and passion he had also lost the ability for Spirit-governed action. Thus we find David (in chapter 28) on the wrong side, marching with the wrong army, and fighting against his own people, the people of God.

These are three things that any group of believers must have if they are to exist and to survive: vision, passion, action. Many churches today stand at the crossroads, facing either a revival or a funeral. People can get away with a great deal today as Christians: living comfortably, listening to good preaching, enjoying it all with very little personal sacrifice. But that kind of easy Christianity is totally inadequate for the real effectiveness of any church.

What do I mean by revival? Vision, passion, action! Vision is the *upward* look toward heaven. Passion is the *inward* hunger and compassion of soul. Action is the *outward* liberation of both vision and passion in Holy Spirit power. But we have lost all three. We have little vision, scarcely any passion, and hardly any heaven-directed action. We cannot go on as we are.

What is vision? What is this upward look?

David had lost his vision because he had forgotten God's promises and ceased to believe in God's power. He had doubted God's ability to protect him against the enemy. Therefore he had lost everything else, because he had become bankrupt of vision.

What have you and I lost? How have we lost our vision?

We say that we believe God and His Word—but do we live every moment of every day with one eye upon the judgment seat of Christ? We must consider every transaction, every gift, every word that we speak about other people, everything we do or say, in the light of the presence of Christ Himself. Belief has one eye upon the throne of God for His orders, and the other on the judgment seat of Christ in responsibility for our words and actions.

Many seem to think that, first of all, the Bible has to be explained, but that is not true. It has to be believed and obeyed! We fail to see the tremendous difference between knowing the Word of God and knowing the God of the Word. Conferences, rallies, missionary conventions, and church services come and go, and we remain unchanged. We are often just a group of unbelieving believers, perhaps never so well equipped, but never so poorly endued.

Isaiah had a vision of holiness which brought from his lips the confession, "Woe is me! for I am undone; because I am a man of unclean lips, and I dwell in the midst of a people of unclean lips: for mine eyes have seen the King, the Lord of hosts" (Isaiah 6:5). This came from a preacher, if you please! He had a vision of sinfulness because the holiness of God made him conscious of his own depravity. This brought to him the word of cleansing: "Lo, this hath touched thy lips; and thine iniquity is taken away, and thy sin purged" (6:7). He had a vision of the hopelessness of his people who were without God, and that brought from heaven the word of commission: "Go, and tell this people . . ." (6:9).

Isaiah's vision of holiness brought confession; his vision of his own sinfulness brought cleansing from sin; his vision of the hopelessness of his people without God brought the heavenly commission to go and preach the Word of God.

But these things don't seem to move us!

In the world today there are fifteen million Jews, three hundred and fifty million Moslems, one hundred and seventy-one million Buddhists, three hundred and fifty million Confucianists, two hundred and fifty million Hindus, ninety million Shintoists—for whom Christ died. But they have not heard the truth, neither do they know the gospel.

In the United States of America there are twenty-seven million people under twenty-one years of age who receive no Christian training at all. Juvenile crime in the big cities is tremendous—sometimes it seems absolutely out of control. Every week one million people are dying without Jesus. In one minute, eighty-five people pass into eternity. In just the brief span of a church service hundreds are passing out into the presence of God. Does that mean anything to you?

It could be that God is more grieved today with the United States and Britain, for instance, than He is with Russia. There millions of people have never heard the gospel, and perhaps there are many who would believe in the Lord if they had the chance.

William Booth, that great founder of the Salvation Army, once said that if he could, he would finalize the training of every man in his Army by suspending him for twenty-four hours over hell. That is the kind of vision we need!

A renowned criminal in Britain, just before going to the gallows, was having Scripture read to him somewhat piously by the chaplain. He suddenly broke in and said, "Sir, if I believed what you say you believe about what you are reading, even if England were covered with broken glass from shore to shore, I would gladly walk over it—on my hands and knees, if need be, and think it worth living to do that—if only I could rescue one soul from that hell about which you have read!"

We give a few dollars to the foreign missionary program and never cross the street to talk to an unsaved friend. We never make any effort whatever to bring one unsaved person under the preaching of the Word. I ask you lovingly, as these things have searched my own soul in God's presence: Have you any vision of the hopelessness of those who are without God and without salvation?

Do we have a vision of sinfulness? I wonder! We may have plenty of vision of the sinfulness of other people, but not of ourselves. The other fellow, we say, has a terrible temper—but with me it is only righteous indignation. Did you ever see such a covetous man as he is? But I am only expanding my business. Look at him, he is so stubborn —but with me it is only real conviction. From the arrow of God's Word and the conviction of the Spirit we cover up for ourselves and put the blame upon our neighbor. Have we a vision of our own sinfulness?

Have we a vision of holiness? Do we reverence God, or in place of that do we try to syncopate the Holy Spirit? How do we prepare our hearts for the Lord's day? How did we prepare ourselves to meet God in His house last Sunday? Did we prepare ourselves the previous night?

What about our passion for seeking God? David had not inquired of the Lord in a long time; that was why he got so entangled in compromise. He had forgotten to pray; he had been absent from the place of prayer for months.

What about your church prayer meeting? Is it tucked away somewhere because there is a busy program in operation and folks have no time to stop and pray? What would happen if your whole Sunday school gathered together for one hour to wait upon God, to beseech Him to pour out His blessing on your church? Too frequently our programs make no room for God's presence or for His power to work. Churches have plenty of people ready to interfere, but very few willing to intercede.

How long is it since you and I forfeited just one hour of conversation with a friend, or one hour of sleep, in order that we might wait upon God? Remember that the man who sins will stop praying, and conversely, the man who prays will stop sinning. The man who gossips about another will never pray for him, but the man who prays for another will not gossip about him. In our church we have what we call a "mutual encouragement fellowship," but many seem to pay it only lip service, and spend many hours gossiping.

Victory in a morning worship service or in the Sunday evening service is won or lost before the preacher enters the pulpit—it is settled on our knees, by your prayers and mine. Why is the penitent form or altar empty? The space before the pulpit is not a place for people simply to sign a card; it is a place where people should die to self and begin to live for God. Is it empty because we do not pray? And by prayer I do not mean the kind of thing like the mischievous little boy who runs up to a house and rings the doorbell, then runs away before the door can be opened. I mean the agony of a Hannah, whose lips moved but whose voice was not heard—the New Testament intercession of the Spirit through us with "groanings that cannot be uttered."

Is the church program so indispensable, our traditions so unbreakable, the comforts of life so dear, success in business so important, that it must be purchased at the price of prayerlessness and spiritual barrenness? On that judgment day there will be multitudes of people whom I will meet for the first time, and who will say to me, "You faithless preacher, you covered up your indifference to us by many texts and sermons, but you did not really care, because you did not really pray." Oh, how this has kept me awake many nights!

Would you do what I have done recently? Would you shut yourself away for a whole day with your Bible and no other visitor than the Holy Spirit? If you, as a child of God, would do that, soon you would either break up or break out in power and revival blessing. Remember that the price of birth is travail—you cannot escape it.

Where is the travail in our churches? Do you think the Holy Spirit delights in programs and plans, machinery and equipment, if the cribs where new-born babes in Christ should be are always empty?

Amy Carmichael prayed,

> O for a passion for souls, dear Lord!
> O for a pity that yearns!
> O for a love that loves unto death!
> O for a fire that burns!
>
> O for the prayer power that travails,
> That pours itself out for the lost;
> Victorious prayer in the Conqueror's Name:
> O for a Pentecost!

The proverb is still true, that "Where there is no vision, the people perish" (Proverbs 29:18). And it is also true that where there is no passion, the church perishes.

David went over to the enemy's side when he became the victim of depression. His great victory over Goliath became only a faded memory as he lived alongside the people of Goliath. His loss of vision and his loss of passion paralyzed all his heaven-inspired activity.

How then did David recover his spiritual and material losses? He returned to God and was given a new breath of vision and a new flame of passion. The two most effective forces in the world are wind and fire; they are irresistible, uncontrollable, unpredictable. At Pentecost the Holy Spirit lit the flame of missionary zeal and kindled revival fire. The Breath of God upon His people quenched the flame of violence and the fire of the enemy.

> Breathe on me, Breath of God,

—that is the wind;

> Till I am wholly Thine,
> Until this earthly part of me
> Glows with Thy fire divine.

—that is the fire.

O that in me the sacred fire
Might now begin to glow;
Burn up the dross of base desire,
And make the mountains flow!
Charles Wesley

If you are going to be a preacher or a teacher of the Word, the wind and the fire from God are what you must have. You can afford to be ten times less clever if only you are ten times more spiritual. When the Holy Spirit is free to move and has room and opportunity, He will destroy the dross of sin and purify our lives. But we act as if we have lost all.

David recovered all—not only his loved ones and material possessions, but also his spiritual vision, passion, and action. In I Samuel 30, we find David inquiring of the Lord again. We find him so passionately concerned for victory that he sets out after the enemy at such a pace that two hundred of his men have to be left behind because they cannot keep up with him.

David repented, and therefore he recovered all. Repentance is not just a few tears at the end of a touching sermon, not just emotion or reformation. It is a change of mind about God and sin. It is the condition of salvation and it is inseparably linked with saving faith. It is also an inevitable factor for revival in the Christian church.

David recovered in a day what he had lost over a period of months and years. When he turned back to the Lord, immediately heaven answered him. And the Lord will answer us immediately if we meet His conditions.

The question is, then: How are you and I living today?

We must have God-given vision—of His holiness and our sinfulness, and of the fulfillment of His promises.

The terrors of hell are real, and souls are dying all around us, but are we caring? Not unless we have Spirit-fired passion.

Then there must be God-directed action. How are you and I serving? Are we living in His will; are we moving only under His orders?

Which do you want, a revival or a funeral in your church? You want a revival, of course. Like David, you want to recover all. How? Then stop criticizing and begin crying out to God; stop shirking His will and begin working under His direction; stop spending on yourself and begin giving to His cause. Repent, return, and the blessings and guidance of God are yours, right now.

PART II

The Man of God:

Lessons in Leadership

Now there was long war between the house of Saul and the house of David: but David waxed stronger and stronger, and the house of Saul waxed weaker and weaker. . . . And it came to pass, while there was war between the house of Saul and the house of David, that Abner made himself strong for the house of Saul. . . . Then was Abner very wroth for the words of Ish-bosheth. . . . And Abner sent messengers to David on his behalf, saying . . . behold, my hand shall be with thee, to bring about all Israel unto thee. . . .

And Abner had communication with the elders of Israel, saying, Ye sought for David in times past to be king over you: Now then do it: for the Lord hath spoken of David, saying, By the hand of my servant David I will save my people Israel out of the hand of the Philistines, and out of the hand of all their enemies. . . .

And when Abner was returned to Hebron, Joab took him aside in the gate to speak with him quietly, and smote him there under the fifth rib, that he died, for the blood of Asahel his brother. And afterward when David heard it, he said, I and my kingdom are guiltless before the Lord for ever from the blood of Abner the son of Ner. . . . So do God to me, and more also, if I taste bread, or ought else, till the sun be down.

And all the people took notice of it, and it pleased them: as whatsoever the king did pleased all the people. For all the people and all Israel understood that day that it was not of the king to slay Abner the son of Ner.

And the king said unto his servants, Know ye not that there is a prince and a great man fallen this day in Israel? And I am this day weak, though anointed king . . . the Lord shall reward the doer of evil according to his wickedness.

II SAMUEL 3:1-39

CHAPTER 15

CORONATION DAY

(II Samuel 3:1-39)

HAVING CONQUERED THE Amalekites and recovered everything that he had lost at Ziklag, David waited patiently for the next step in God's plan for his life. When the news reached him that Saul and Jonathan had died in battle, he must have realized that the throne of Israel would now be his, that God's promise was about to be fulfilled. Yet he had no thought for himself; the joy of this long-awaited moment was forgotten in the amazing and beautiful lament recorded in II Samuel 1:17-29, as he wept over his loss, the tragic deaths of King Saul and his son, David's beloved friend Jonathan.

Quite clearly we can see that David is back at the place where he is waiting upon God. It was for God to give him the kingdom; he refused to reach out and grasp even that which God had promised him, apart from direction from heaven. Humanly speaking, he had every reason to make a grab for the throne at this point, because the Philistines had invaded Israel. After all, God had anointed him king, and it would seem that taking the initiative would be the right thing to do. But no, David had learned his lesson—a bitter one too—that he must wait upon the Lord.

Thus once again David inquired of the Lord (II Samuel 2:1), and on God's instruction he moved up to Hebron, where he was crowned king over Judah. At last a bridgehead was established, and for seven and a half years David reigned as king over Judah in Hebron.

Meanwhile Abner, the captain of Saul's army, took Saul's son Ish-bosheth and crowned him king in a futile attempt to keep from collapse the tottering house of Saul, which God had rejected. There followed a prolonged period of civil war described in II Samuel 3:1, during which David grew stronger and stronger, and the house of Saul became weaker and weaker.

At last Abner realized that he was on the wrong side, that he was fighting against God. He went through the length and breadth of the land of Israel saying to the people, "Ye sought for David in times past to be king over you: Now then do it." This was the moment for action! They had sought long enough to keep Saul's incompetent descendant. It was time to give in and crown David as king!

Though Abner never lived to see it because he was murdered by Joab, David's captain, yet it was not long until the coronation day dawned and David was anointed king over all Israel (II Samuel 5:3).

That is the narrative, but my heart thrills as the Holy Spirit speaks to me—and I trust He will speak to you too—concerning the implications of this Old Testament story in your life and mine. Many of us have been, or may be even now, like those people in Israel to whom Abner spoke. We have sought in times past for David's greater Son to be King over us. We have thought how wonderful it might be to experience the sovereignty of Jesus Christ, how wonderful to be led of God and live a heaven-directed life. What a difference it would make!

We have thought about the prospect, but somehow we have hesitated. The problems are too great; the consequences might be too serious, the complications would interfere too much with our lives. Like David, the Lord Jesus has never enforced His authority; He has taken, as David did, only what we offer to Him. David stepped to the throne at Hebron when it was offered; he stepped to the throne of all Israel when that was offered to him. He never moved one inch until the invitation came.

Similarly the Lord Jesus has only helped Himself to what we have offered of our lives. Some of us, God forgive us, have offered nothing; though perhaps we wouldn't be ready to admit it, we live in open rebellion against the King. Others have offered Him, so to speak, Hebron. We have given Him a little part that wouldn't interfere too much with our own monopoly. But if we have given Him so much and no more, I tell you, we can have no peace.

In the lives of many Christian people today there is raging, literally, a civil war. The flesh—the kingdom of Saul, struggles with the spirit—the kingdom of David, and the conflict is bitter. We do everything we possibly can to hold up the tottering kingdom of self, so that it might exist just a bit longer. If only we could preserve some rights; if only we could have at least part of our own way; if only we could keep this or that at any cost! We feel we must bolster up this kingdom of self, that we cannot let ourselves be crucified with Christ.

Therefore the battle rages on, although church services are attended, sermons are listened to, the message of the Word of God is heard. Oh, how fondly do we cherish the life that God wants to crucify! Yet as long as such a condition is permitted, the tragic evidences of conflict remain in your soul. There is no authority powerful enough to force your life to yield to God the Holy Spirit who alone can give you victory, blessing, power, and usefulness. The tragedy unfolding year after year in the life of some Christians is that they remain on the shelf as far as availability to God is concerned.

Now is the time for action! It is time to say in your heart, "Down with Satan; up with Jesus as Lord! Down with the usurper, up with my Redeemer! Off the throne with sin and self, on the throne with my wonderful Lord!" Oh, what a difference it makes to belong completely to the One who has never lost a battle! Ye have sought for Jesus in times past to be King over you. Now then do it!

There are strong reasons for taking action now, for making this the coronation day of the King of kings in your heart, a day that will live in your memory as the time when you revolted completely from Satan and joined the army of God's King. Recall some of your former impulses toward the Lord Jesus Christ. With respect and love I want to invade the realm of your memory and unlock some doors that may have been forgotten. I trust that the Holy Spirit may pry them open as you look back.

How many times have you been on the verge of making Jesus King? Some of you can recall the influence of godly parents and a Christian home. You can remember when your young heart was tender toward the Lord, and like Agrippa, you were almost persuaded to be a Christian. Now you can see what has happened in your life because you didn't carry it through! If only you could go back to that day, you wouldn't waste another minute! You would make Him King.

Now you have become entangled in circumstances, friendships, sin, failure, breakdown, cares and worries—a thousand and one things. Oh, occasionally since then a sermon has driven you to your knees. Occasionally the invitation has been so strong that you have wanted to respond publicly—perhaps you have even done so. Occasionally sorrow and heartbreak have left you weeping bitterly until, like David, you could weep no more. God has brought you time and again to a standstill, but you have stifled His promptings and have pushed ahead in self-will.

Others may have had no such background or advantage, but many times you have been made to think of Jesus Christ. You have stood, as I have stood in earlier days, amid the catastrophe of war, the wreckage of homes shattered and cities burned. As you have, you have been forced to ponder, "Where is God? What is this all about?"

There have been times when, after you have had your fling, you have lost the sense of glamor and have asked yourself, "Can I ever live right? Can I turn around and go straight? Is cleansing from sin really possible?"

Let me try to illustrate these former impulses by sticking to the narrative in I and II Samuel. There is a parallel in the case of Israel. Whenever Saul's rule became more than usually oppressive they began to sigh for David.

I can tell you from personal experience, and you can corroborate it from your own life, that whenever sin begins to exercise tyranny, we long for escape. For a while sin's fascination grows—the glamor, the thrill, the pleasure, the wine and the song are fun for a time, but it passes. Somehow you lose your taste for these things, and life becomes stale and empty. I know, because I have been through it myself. Then you begin to say, "Oh, wretched man that I am, who shall deliver me?"

Again, when Israel saw their enemies gradually taking over territory which rightly belonged to the people of God, they longed for their young champion David and his sling. Oh, for a return of the daring shepherd boy who caused the downfall of Goliath and the retreat of the Philistines! "What on earth is the use of a poor puppet like Saul?" they would ask themselves. "We are under the wrong authority, we are following the wrong leadership, and it is getting us only defeat!"

Again from personal experience (with which I guarantee you will say "Amen" in your soul), as the enemy of your life begins to infiltrate upon innocence and purity such as it might have been, upon character, habits, and customs, there comes a moment in your life when you stop, when you become terror stricken as you notice the path down which the devil is leading you. The infiltration of evil makes you desperately afraid. "O God, where is this taking me?" your heart has cried out to Jesus.

But worse still—oh, shame on us, for I don't find it difficult to go back in my memory, and perhaps you find this familiar, also—in the light of that wonderful thing the matchless Son of God did for me at Calvary, how mean and despicable that I should say to Him, "Just come in a little way; don't interfere too much. I want an insurance policy to get me to heaven. I know I'm not right, but don't let me carry this religion thing too far. I want to escape from judgment, but don't let people think I'm fanatical. I just want You to be King over a little territory only!" And from that moment there sets in civil war.

If he had a measure of so-called peace in the days when he knew not the Saviour, the professing Christian who has, as it were, let Jesus into only a corner of his life, loses even the peace he once had. In his soul there is a battle raging. He cannot be at rest, although he wants peace and forgiveness and deliverance. He longs that this inner struggle, in which "two masters" are seeking to run his life, might end!

I sometimes wonder as I ponder this story if, when the Israelites occasionally saw one of David's men—alert, keen, on the job, full of authority, a mighty man of war—when the Israelites saw the genuine power of King David, they must have said to themselves, "I wish I could be like that!"

I feel like hiding myself for shame when I have to say that perhaps you have not often seen genuine believers. You have seen people who know a lot in their heads, but not many of the genuine article, the man filled with the Spirit of God: a man who is real—not a mystic, too heavenly minded to be of any earthly good, but a man with his heart in heaven and his feet on the ground, a man who is all things to all men that he might win some, a man who stands absolutely separate from sin. Would that we were all like that!

Sometimes your impulses toward the Lord have been very strong, haven't they? They may have caused you to pray, or to set up a family altar in your home. You have attended church and mended your ways, but nothing real or lasting has come of it. You know that the Christian way is right; you don't question it. You know that Jesus is worthy of being King of your heart, and you have said, "One day when I have made more money—One day when I have dealt with this social situation—One day when I have got to the top—One day when I have pursued my own path and reached my own goal—One day—"

You have ceased even to argue about the desirability of making Jesus your Lord and King, yet you are not one inch nearer deciding the issue for yourself. Some of you are in grave danger of becoming hard and indifferent; indeed, you wouldn't have believed five years ago that you would be as far down the road as you are today.

In the light of these memories that I have brought before you, I would recommend immediate action: "Now then do it." Hesitate no longer! As of old, when Elijah faced the prophets of Baal, the question was, "How long halt ye between two opinions? if the Lord be God, follow him: but if Baal, then follow him" (I Kings 18:21). Don't remain in the absurd and dangerous position of believing what is right but failing to put your belief into action. You can be right in your knowledge but wrong in your heart and go to hell.

I want to make the issue crystal clear. There can be no possible doubt, according to the Word of God: either Jesus must be King, or He cannot be your Saviour. David had to be king over all Israel, or he never could have delivered them from the Philistines. It was absolutely essential that, if David were to secure his right to the crown and lead them to victory, civil war had to stop.

Many are willing to be saved by Christ. But when they come to see that the initial step into Christian living—not a subsequent step when it suits them, or when their savings account is in good shape, or when their life is all settled—is that He must be their Ruler, their Master, their Lord, it causes them to hesitate or to reject Him. Eternity hinges on that one clear-cut issue.

If Christ is not King, indisputably King, then Satan remains on the throne and you are a lost soul. But if Christ is in supreme authority, then He will drive out every one of your enemies. That simply means that the will of Jesus must be your will, the commands of Jesus must be your law, and the example of Jesus Christ must be your model.

This must take place by your personal action. I cannot do it for you, even though I wish I could. What would I give to be able to re-live some of my life—especially the years from about eighteen to thirty! I can't do it, but because of those wasted years I would give anything in the world if only I might put my arm around you and bring you into the thrilling experience of the sovereignty of Jesus Christ.

God won't do it, either! Jesus Christ, I repeat, has never forced His monarchy upon any individual. The Psalmist said, "Thy people shall be willing in the day of thy power" (Psalm 110:3). How we've prayed, how we've cried to God, how we've pleaded, that this might be the day of His power! When the Holy Spirit speaks with authority, then "Thy people shall be willing." You don't need a high-pressure appeal when the Holy Spirit is working, when He comes in answer to the prayer of believing people.

The kingdom of Christ is not one of force but one of love. He insists on having the absolute consent of your will, and that means that His rival must be put down. Do you imagine that Ish-bosheth and David could have been king at the same time? No, nor can you serve Satan *and* the Lord Jesus. May I say firmly that it is your favorite sins that have to go, the ones you secretly adore have to be abandoned. Most important of all, love of yourself and pride in your reputation must go, for to talk about being saved and yet to love your own way is absolute blasphemy. Let us not imagine that the Lord Jesus is going to pamper us in our unholy ways and habits, that He will give us liberty to go on behaving like that and then take us to heaven. That is absolute heresy! He will never let a man do the work of the devil and then crown him with the reward of the godly.

There has to be a clean sweep of the false to make room for the true. If David is to be king, Ish-bosheth must be beheaded and finished. But you will not be able to master even one sin in your own strength. Of course not; God doesn't expect you to! You cannot chop off the head of this habit and that, because if you do, you only drive it in so that it comes out in worse form.

If you want salvation in reality, you have to turn this day with a perfect heart toward God, a heart which is deliberately turning from every falsehood, every sin, and every failure, and is turning in help-lessness to the Lord Jesus in deep repentance.

You say that is not New Testament teaching? Remember, Jesus said, "If thy right eye offend thee, pluck it out, and cast it from thee. . . . And if thy right hand offend thee, cut it off, and cast it from thee: for it is profitable for thee that one of thy members should perish, and not that thy whole body should be cast into hell" (Matthew 5:29-30).

In the name of heaven I would say to you that such is the imperious demand of God the Holy Spirit for repentance. To make Jesus King is to turn to Him with all your heart and trust Him completely. And to trust Him completely will bring into your heart strength and power by which your repentance is transformed into His deliverance.

"Now then do it!" Don't go on just wishing and resolving—may the Holy Spirit push you into decision. There have been times in my life when quite frankly I have felt the Lord pushing me back to the wall. It is as if He had got me in a corner, and I had to face the issue squarely. I hope that now you are feeling the pressure of God's Spirit pushing you back in your seat so that you must face this issue of the Kingship of Jesus Christ.

"Now then do it," for unless you do (and I don't say this to frighten you), your heart has only to miss about half a dozen beats, and you will be in hell—with all your good intentions, with all your resolves, with all your professions of faith, with all your sound theology. You who sought in times past to make Jesus King, you the child of Christian parents, the frequent attender at the house of God, the listener to the Word of God, the hearer of the gospel—all these privileges and benefits will be merely millstones around your neck in a lost eternity unless you make Him your King.

I would reason with you, and give you three arguments for what I say. First, you need Jesus Christ as your King desperately; sin and self have ruled with cruel tyranny long enough. What delight have you found in them?

Second, God has chosen Jesus to be King in spite of all the machinations of men and the tumult of nations. He declared, "Yet have I set my king upon my holy hill of Zion" (Psalm 2:6). Before that King one day every knee shall bow. Could you have a better king for your life than the one whom God has chosen?

Third, it is only King Jesus who has power to deliver you from the predicaments of your life. "Now then do it: for the Lord hath spoken of David, saying, By the hand of my servant David I will save my people Israel out of the hand of the Philistines, and out of the hand of all their enemies" (II Samuel 3:18).

"O wretched man that I am!" cried the Apostle Paul, "who shall deliver me? . . . I thank God through Jesus Christ our Lord" (Romans 7:24-25).

Read now the first three verses of II Samuel 5, and as the Israelites came to David, make your response to the Lord. The Lord had said of David, "Thou shalt feed my people Israel, and thou shalt be a captain over Israel" (5:2).

Lord Jesus, we gladly crown Thee now! Lead us, O Thou great Shepherd of the sheep! Lead us, Thou great Captain of our salvation! We are Thine and Thine alone, and before the face of God our Father, in the name of the Holy Spirit our counsellor, Lord Jesus Christ we bow to Thee, and we submit body, soul, and spirit. We are Thine forevermore, and we crown Thee King of all!

Now then do it!

Then came all the tribes of Israel to David unto Hebron ... and they anointed David king over Israel. David was thirty years old when he began to reign, and he reigned forty years. ...

And the king and his men went to Jerusalem unto the Jebusites, the inhabitants of the land: which spake unto David, saying ... thou shalt not come in hither. ... Nevertheless David took the strong hold of Zion: the same is the city of David.... And David went on, and grew great. ... And David perceived that the Lord had established him king over Israel, and that he had exalted his kingdom for his people Israel's sake. ...

But when the Philistines heard that they had anointed David king over Israel, all the Philistines came up to seek David; and David heard of it, and went down to the hold. The Philistines also came and spread themselves in the valley of Rephaim.

And David enquired of the Lord, saying, Shall I go up to the Philistines? wilt thou deliver them into mine hand? And the Lord said unto David, Go up: for I will doubtless deliver the Philistines into thine hand.... And David ... smote them there, and said, The Lord hath broken forth upon mine enemies. ... And there they left their images, and David and his men burned them.

And the Philistines came up yet again, and spread themselves in the valley of Rephaim. And when David enquired of the Lord, he said, Thou shalt not go up; but fetch a compass behind them, and come upon them over against the mulberry trees. And let it be, when thou hearest the sound of a going in the tops of the mulberry trees, that then thou shalt bestir thyself: for then shall the Lord go out before thee, to smite the host of the Philistines. And David did so, as the Lord had commanded him; and smote the Philistines. ...

II SAMUEL 5:1-25

CHAPTER 16

SOVEREIGNTY CONTESTED

(II Samuel 5:1–25)

IMMEDIATELY FOLLOWING DAVID's coronation day, some important events took place in his life. These events recorded in II Samuel 5 show in Old Testament picture form the events which take place in the life of a child of God when the Lord Jesus Christ has a coronation day in his heart.

I trust that the Lord has stepped into His rightful place in your life, and that He is undisputed King. If He has entered upon the throne of your heart, you are able to say, "It is no longer I, but Christ." This is just the gateway into abundant life, but it is the *only* gateway into that fullness of blessing which is ours in Jesus Christ.

The little slogan, "Let go, and let God," is not what the New Testament teaches—at least that is only part of the truth, for the act of total submission to the sovereignty of Jesus Christ is but the beginning of a new régime in your heart. No longer is the puppet king Self upon the throne, but the great King of kings and Lord of lords has stepped in to take over the government of your life. When that revolutionary change takes place, surely there ought to be some evidences of it. These evidences I wish to consider with you right now.

What happens when Jesus is King? Look at our text for a moment: what happened when David was king?

In the first place, the sovereignty of David was immediately confirmed, and it was confirmed in two ways. If you look at II Samuel 5:7, you will see the first: David "took the strong hold of Zion."

Probably you know the history of the people of God in the land of Canaan well enough to remember that the city of Jerusalem was always a thorn in their side. In spite of the fact that the whole land had been given to them, they had so far never been able to possess it all. The city from which God's King was destined to reign, the most strategic city in the whole land was, alas, a city in which the enemy was deeply entrenched. The Jebusites were far too strong for the children of Israel; they could not cast them out (Joshua 15:63). Later we discover that the Benjamites settled down in Jerusalem on the basis of a peaceful co-existence with the enemy (Judges 1:8, 21). This could not be allowed to continue; when David became king of all Israel, we are told, he immediately took the stronghold of Zion.

The conquest which had baffled the Israelites through their whole history became amazingly easy when David was king. One of the first evidences of the enthronement of Jesus Christ in our lives will be that deeply entrenched habits of evil will be put under subjection to our risen Lord, who will inhabit that temple of the Holy Spirit, your body and mind. That stronghold of sin which has defied our best efforts, that which has caused us many a heartache and many a tear and many a feeling of remorse and frustration, that which has almost made us give up the fight altogether—how wonderful, when Jesus becomes King it is put under His feet. He comes into our lives to establish His kingdom, and to inaugurate it by giving us the first taste of deliverance and victory over the power of inbred sin.

Have you ever noticed how the Lord Jesus liked to deal with long-standing complaints? How many instances we find in the New Testament of men and women who for years had been bound by infirmity and sin, crippled and helpless and hopeless until the Lord came!

I will remind you of just one New Testament example. When Peter and John went to the temple to worship and found at the gate a man who had been lame from birth, Peter looked at him and said, "Silver and gold have I none"—the church boasted in its bankruptcy in those days—"but such as I have give I thee: In the name of Jesus Christ of Nazareth rise up and walk" (Acts 3:6). Immediately the man leaped to his feet, delivered from his lifelong infirmity by the power of the risen Christ.

I want to say to you in the name of the Lord Jesus that there is no habit that has gone so deep but the power of the blood of Jesus can go deeper, and there is no entrenchment of sin that has gone so far but the power of the risen Lord, by His Holy Spirit, can go further. In our lives, the first mark of the sovereignty of Christ is that the habits of years, which have baffled all our efforts and mocked all our struggles, the things which have brought us in shame and confession of failure time and time again to the Lord in contrition and repentance— their power is broken when He is upon the throne.

Furthermore, the sovereignty of David was not only confirmed by this conquest of the stronghold of Zion, but it was also confirmed in that "David went on, and grew great" (II Samuel 5:10: margin, "went on going and growing"). In other words, the sovereignty of David was expressed in ever-increasing areas of the kingdom.

What was true in David's kingdom is true also in the life of a Christian. Jesus Christ upon the throne is but the initial step of a lifetime in which you will discover that His sovereignty is ever growing and ever extending and becoming an ever more blessed experience. You remember that when the angel announced to Mary the birth of our blessed Lord, he said to her, "The Lord God shall give unto him the throne of his father David: And he shall reign over the house of Jacob for ever: and of his kingdom there shall be no end" (Luke 1:32-33).

What is true prophetically is also true experimentally: of the kingdom of Jesus Christ in your life there is no end. It is impossible to be a Christian unless Jesus Christ is your Lord. "If thou shalt confess with thy mouth Jesus as Lord, and shalt believe in thy heart that God raised him from the dead, thou shalt be saved" (Romans 10:9, ASV). You cannot be a Christian unless He is crowned Lord of your life, but the initial coronation day of the Lord Jesus is immediately followed by a succession of coronations, in which He becomes Lord over an ever-increasing area of your personality.

I would bear humble testimony to the fact that when the Lord Jesus came into my life, at that moment, up to the limit of my understanding, He was Lord of all I had and all I possessed. But I did not know then what would be involved in surrender to His sovereignty. How thankful I am that I didn't!

I admit I do not always like the sovereignty of Jesus Christ. Often, alas, I have disputed it; but every time I have disputed it, that act of resistance has been followed by weeks and months of spiritual stagnation and failure when, although I did not lose my relationship with Him, I lost something almost as wonderful—the sense of His presence and the reality of His fellowship. I lived for weeks and months, alas, even sometimes for over a year in darkness, because I had again raised myself and said "No!" at some point to the sovereignty of my Lord.

At any point in life you can resist His sovereignty, but at that moment God puts you on the shelf: you are useless to Him. Oh, you can carry on preaching sermons, teaching a Sunday school class, using the same pious language and singing the same hymns, but the unction and the uplift have gone. The liberty of the Holy Ghost has gone; the reality has gone. The Lord is in your heart, but you have quenched His Spirit.

But I would also bear testimony to this: every step of faith and obedience has immediately brought a new demand that my Lord's sovereignty be displayed in another area of my life. One mark of the sovereignty of Christ in a man's life is that deeply entrenched habits are overthrown at last, and there is freedom, glorious freedom. Another mark of His sovereignty is that every step of faith and obedience is followed by the increasing demands of our risen Christ that He may occupy a new area of our personality.

Do you find yourself putting the label "sin" somewhere in your life today that you would not admit five years ago? Do you find the Holy Spirit gently and lovingly, but firmly, putting His finger upon something and saying, "You have been a Christian too long for that; it has got to stop"? You may not have thought about it even a year ago, but as you have sought to grow up in Him, the Lord Jesus has led you on to an increasing experience of His sovereignty. Of His kingdom there is no end—His sovereignty is confirmed forever. Is it being confirmed in your heart?

Are you rejoicing in liberty and freedom under the sovereignty of the Saviour? Are you finding your submission to the Lord an increasing, expanding experience? Praise the Lord! You are in the apostolic succession!

In the second place, the sovereignty of David was not only confirmed, but it was immediately challenged.

Notice that the Philistines gathered themselves together and came up to attack him; they spread themselves in the valley of Rephaim (II Samuel 5:17-22). They had not been unduly concerned as long as David was satisfied to be king over Judah; but now that he ruled over the whole kingdom they feared his power and they made an immediate counterattack.

Also immediately, when Jesus Christ becomes your Lord, your act of submission will be followed by a massive counterattack from the powers of evil.

Will you notice how pointed was this attack of the Philistines: "They spread themselves." Isn't that typical of the devil? The Philistines spread themselves in the valley of Rephaim. Where is that? Practically under the walls of Jerusalem!

Christian, mark this very carefully: they spread themselves around a focal point where, for many decades, they had been occupants, although they had no right to claim it. They had defied all the attempts of the people of God to throw them out since Joshua first conquered the land. But once they had been thrown out, they immediately tried to recapture the stronghold.

I want to be careful not to be misunderstood on this point, but I don't think it concerns the enemy unduly when a Christian, in joining a church, signs a doctrinal statement which says, "I no longer smoke, I no longer drink, I no longer play cards, and I no longer gamble."

Oh, do not misunderstand me! I do not advocate any of those things, and I think it would be a great pity if you did them. But the definition of sin and worldliness which enables a man to say, "Because I do not do these things, therefore I am a consecrated Christian," is completely superficial. Such a child of God has not begun to understand the meaning of the Lord Jesus when He said that it is not from without, but "from within, out of the heart of men, proceed evil thoughts, adulteries, fornications, murders, Thefts, covetousness, wickedness, deceit, lasciviousness, an evil eye, blasphemy, pride, foolishness: All these evil things come from within and defile the man" (Mark 7:21-23). When a man really gets concerned about the sinful state of his own heart, he begins to cry in the language of Charles Wesley:

> Thou who at Pentecost did'st fall,
> Do Thou my sins consume:
> Come, Holy Ghost, on Thee I call:
> Spirit of burning, come!

When a man gets that desperate, when he cannot go on as he has been living but cries out to God with all the hunger of his soul, "Lord Jesus, set me free; cleanse my heart from secret sin," at that point the devil launches an all-out attack.

Satan counterattacks pointedly and he counterattacks persistently. He will never admit defeat; if you have crowned Jesus Christ as Lord, you are in for a life of constant warfare. The devil didn't have to bother too much about you before, but if you become determined never to accept a peaceful co-existence with the enemy on any point, if you become concerned that the Lord might create in you a clean heart, that He might give you a blessed experience of deliverance by the power of the indwelling Christ, then I say to you that such holy living is a menace to the powers of darkness.

In this twentieth century the church desperately needs men like that, those who have so submitted to the Lord Jesus that they have a testimony of deliverance from sin.

The sovereignty of Christ in the believer's life is counterattacked at every point, persistently and relentlessly. But the sovereignty of Christ is also communicated to the Christian by the Lord Himself.

What am I to do in the midst of the battle? How am I to face an enemy who is too powerful for me? How am I to deal with all the devil's besetting temptations that spread themselves around my life? Now I hope you understand that temptation is not sin: the Lord Jesus was tempted in every point like as we are, yet without sin. And may I go a step further in that definition, and say that sinful thoughts are not sin, either. Have you ever heard people say, "The other day, this thought passed through my mind . . ."? That's wonderful—just let it pass right through! Satan has no other way of attacking us except by eye-gate and ear-gate and thought-gate. As he flings his poison into our hearts, as he will continuously and persistently, what is a child of God to do about that?

Let me tell you this—and I do it with such a thrill in my soul: the sovereignty of Jesus Christ is communicated! How? Look at the story again. Victory was communicated to David, in the first place, by prayer. "David enquired of the Lord" (II Samuel 5:19, 23). On both occasions here, when the enemy came to attack, we find that David went right to his knees and said, "Now Lord, I look to You."

My friend, it is just as well he did so on both occasions, for do you notice that the divine strategy for victory in the first instance was totally different from the strategy in the next? The first time, he was told to go and attack; but in the second battle he was to sit still and wait. If David had followed the strategy of yesterday in the battle of today, he would have missed His divine resources and would have been humiliated by defeat.

What do I do in the face of the enemy who attacks me when Jesus Christ becomes my Lord? I get on my knees! Or if I'm not in a place where I can do that, I lift up my heart and say, "Now Lord, I have no might or power; I know not what to do, but my eyes are upon Thee."

The victory of yesterday does not put into me strength for today. I discover, as I go on in life, that the flesh is totally corrupt, and is good for nothing. I begin to understand that, in the language of the Apostle Paul, "In me (that is, in my flesh,) dwelleth no good thing" (Romans 7:18). Such is not the language of a backslider; it is the language of a man illuminated by the Holy Spirit who has discovered that God expects nothing from him but total failure and that he can never be any different.

I have been along the road thirty years now as a Christian, and every experience of the grace of God and the cleansing power of the blood of Jesus has only convinced me more deeply than ever of the corruption of my own heart. Basically, Alan Redpath is no different from what he was when he was saved—probably a lot worse by nature, potentially. But I know this: the battle is not mine, but God's; and therefore, during every moment of every testing He communicates to me power as I look to Him.

"Watch ye and pray," said the Lord, "lest ye enter into temptation" (Mark 14:38). We will always be faced with it, but there is no need to run headlong into it. Watch and pray! Seek the Lord, and His sovereignty will be communicated. Always listen to His answer: sometimes it is the word saying, "Go out and attack," but more often it is the word telling us to wait for "the sound of a going in the tops of the mulberry trees" (II Samuel 5:24).

What is that "sound of a going"? Surely it is the same as what happened when 120 disciples had waited and prayed for ten days in an upper room: suddenly there was the sound as of a rushing, mighty wind, and God the Holy Spirit came down upon them and empowered them, sending them out to blaze a trail for Him.

That is how God communicates constantly to my poor and needy heart His sovereignty: in the person of the Holy Spirit. He gives the power of His Spirit in answer to the man who has acknowledged his own bankruptcy and submitted to the Lord's sovereignty, and who waits upon Him for the word from heaven.

But let me say this: we do not move away *from* the Lord Jesus *to* the Holy Spirit. No, He said to His disciples, "When he, the Spirit of truth, is come . . . He shall glorify me: for he shall receive of mine, and shall shew it unto you" (John 16:13-14). And He prayed, "As thou, Father, art in me, and I in thee, that they also may be one in us . . . I in them, and thou in me" (John 17:21, 23). The sovereignty of God is communicated by the Holy Spirit imparting the life of the risen, victorious Christ into my heart and soul. The Holy Spirit points my heart upward to the throne, and from that throne there is communicated to me the victorious resurrection life of our precious Saviour.

Remember that we are no match for the counterattacks of the enemy! I've had enough experience with him to know that the devil is far too clever and far too powerful for me. But he is no match for my Lord, and he is no match for the Holy Spirit. In my heart today, and in your heart, if there is submission to Christ, there is life from the throne of heaven which can enable you to live victoriously. All the strength that you will ever need, in every situation, is in the power of God the Holy Spirit.

Have you begun to see the answer to your need? Is the Holy Spirit moving upon you in conviction? Has this message been something more than theory to you? Has it been life, and has it been victory, and has it been power?

Then listen: what does the Bible say next? Bestir yourself! "And let it be, when thou hearest the sound of a going in the tops of the mulberry trees, that then thou shalt bestir thyself: for then shall the Lord go out before thee" (II Samuel 5:24).

What are you going to do about this tremendous potential of the life of victory? Are you going to discard it because you don't understand it? Or are you going to listen to God as He speaks, and reach out for all that the Lord Jesus has for you of the enabling grace and power of His Holy Spirit? Bestir yourself: act and obey. Oh, that the Lord Jesus may now fill your heart and that through it may flow that life-giving river, the power of a risen Christ, by His Holy Spirit!

Again, David gathered together all the chosen men of Israel, thirty thousand. And David arose, and went with all the people that were with him from Baale of Judah, to bring up from thence the ark of God, whose name is called by the name of the Lord of hosts that dwelleth between the cherubims.

And they set the ark of God upon a new cart, and brought it out of the house of Abinadab that was in Gibeah. . . . And David and all the house of Israel played before the Lord on all manner of instruments . . .

And when they came to Nachon's threshingfloor, Uzzah put forth his hand to the ark of God, and took hold of it; for the oxen shook it. And the anger of the Lord was kindled against Uzzah; and God smote him there for his error; and there he died by the ark of God. . . . And David was afraid of the Lord that day, and said, How shall the ark of the Lord come to me? So David would not remove the ark of the Lord unto him into the city. . . . And the ark of the Lord continued in the house of Obed-edom the Gittite three months: and the Lord blessed Obed-edom, and all his household.

And it was told king David, saying, The Lord hath blessed the house of Obed-edom, and all that pertaineth unto him, because of the ark of God. So David went and brought up the ark of God from the house of Obed-edom into the city of David with gladness. And it was so, that when they that bare the ark of the Lord had gone six paces, he sacrificed oxen and fatlings. And David danced before the Lord with all his might. . . .

And as the ark of the Lord came into the city of David, Michal Saul's daughter looked through a window, and saw king David leaping and dancing before the Lord; and she despised him in her heart. . . . Therefore Michal the daughter of Saul had no child unto the day of her death.

II SAMUEL 6:1-23

CHAPTER 17

PREPARATION FOR SERVICE

(II Samuel 6:1-23)

THERE ARE IN this chapter some very important principles for Christian living which are illustrated in David's life now that he had been crowned king and assumed the place of God's appointment. Ahead of him lay a life of responsibility and leadership.

David faced this moment with a great desire that all he did might be to the glory of God. As so often happens when a man reaches such a place, stepping into the center of God's plan for his life, David encountered some experiences that left their mark upon him for the rest of his days.

Of the things that happened to him at this time, some were good, others unpleasant. I feel, however, that God knows best how to train His own for His service and to prepare them for eternity. Some of the experiences He gives us we would not exchange for anything in the world, and others we have found distasteful; yet in them all, as we have submitted to Him, He has proved again and again that "all things work together for good to them that love God" (Romans 8:28).

We might correctly entitle the first ten verses of this chapter, II Samuel 6, "The sanctity of the presence of God." The one thing above all else which David wanted was that, having assumed the responsibility of this position, he should know constantly the presence of God with him. He could not possibly rule in authority and power and victory without the Lord's guidance. It would be essential for every battle, for every judgment, for every action. That David should receive and enjoy the continuous presence of Jehovah was absolutely vital.

Therefore, he determined immediately to restore the ark to the place where it should be—in the very heart of his kingdom. He had in mind later on, of course, to build the temple. But at this point it was a question of getting the ark back into the center of their national life, because the ark in Old Testament times was the symbol of the presence of the living God. The ark contained the tables of the law, and above it was the mercy seat, overshadowing which were the cherubim.

Most important of all, the Lord had said, "there I will meet with thee, and I will commune with thee" (Exodus 25:22). This is what David desired with all his heart. This is what he knew he needed, an available place of meeting with God, an opportunity for constant communion with Him.

For almost seventy years the ark had been missing from its rightful place. To begin with, it was captured by the Philistines. However, they found it a perpetual embarrassment to them, so they built a nice new cart and sent it back. For decades it had languished at the border of Judah in the household of Abinadab, and from there David determined to rescue it.

There is nothing more important in any life than the constantly enjoyed presence of the Lord. There is nothing more vital, for without it we shall make mistakes, and without it we shall be defeated. Without the sense of His abiding presence and a place of constant communion and fellowship, how far wrong we will go!

I know, of course, that the presence of the Lord is not now localized as it was in David's time. The Lord Jesus said that "where two or three are gathered together in my name, there am I in the midst of them" (Matthew 18:20). Nevertheless, in our personal experience, the presence of the Lord may not be a reality. And anyone who has experienced the joy of fellowship with the Lord Jesus is bereft if that fellowship is taken from him. This is the thing that matters most in the life of a Christian: that the ungrieved Holy Spirit is indwelling his life in power and authority.

I often hear others pray, and I often pray myself, "O Lord, grant me today the sense of Thy presence! Without Thee my purpose faints; without Thee my spirit grows weak; without Thee I shall make so many mistakes and go wrong in so many decisions. Lord, this day I desire above all else the conscious sense of Thy presence in my life."

You see, your desire was David's desire. It is not such an old-fashioned story after all, is it? Except that the greatest things in life are old-fashioned! To desire the presence of the Lord is always a good thing, but I am confident that our desire is not always accompanied by an understanding of the significance of His presence with us.

We find in this story that David set out with thirty thousand men to recover the ark. But the ark itself was placed on a nice new cart, which was exactly what the Philistines did long ago. The people of God evidently thought that the best thing to do was to copy their neighbors, so they made the cart, which was driven along the road by Abinadab's two sons. After all, the ark had stayed around their house for a number of years, and it was only natural that they should be chosen to drive it. In the course of the journey, however, because the road was a bit rough, one of them put out his hand to steady the ark. To the horror of the whole crowd, he fell to the ground and died on the spot.

"David was displeased ... and David was afraid of the Lord that day" (II Samuel 6:8-9). Well, naturally! His first attempt to satisfy his desire for the presence of God had met with disaster. Perhaps he said to himself, "Lord, it isn't fair! You know I wanted Your presence. You know that I need the ark, so why did this have to happen? Why should this man be killed because of it?"

I suggest to you that if David had inquired of the Lord (as had become his usual practice, although apparently he had omitted it in this case) he could have avoided the catastrophe. Why *should* this thing have happened? Surely it seems a bit tough of God to strike a man dead simply because he did the thing that was natural. After all, the ark might have fallen off the cart altogether. Surely it was all right to touch it and keep it steady. But the point is, you see, the ark should never have been on that cart at all!

In the construction of the ark, as commanded by God in Exodus 25:12-15, it was made with rings and staves for carrying it. There was nothing mechanical about the ark of God whatever; it was a divine institution. When it was moved it was to be carried exclusively by the Levites, and even they were not allowed to touch it, as we find in Numbers 4:15. The ark was nothing less than the burden of the Lord, and the burden of the Lord was to be carried on the hearts of the Levites.

We want God's presence very much, don't we? But we like to hitch His presence to some of our new carts. We like to add Him to our list of organizations, to load Him on top of the mechanics of a busy life, and then drive. How much of our service is really in the energy of the flesh, I wonder! So often we put forth our hands, but not our hearts. We put forth our hands to the work of the Lord, but somehow our hearts have never really gotten under the burden of the Lord and begun, like the Levites, to carry it.

Always it is a tragic thing to die under the judgment of God, but I suggest to you that the biggest tragedy of all was to die right alongside the ark of God's mercy. To be slain by the hand of God's judgment within reach of privilege and fellowship is the greatest disaster that could happen to anyone. But that is what happens when we only put forth our hands to work, and we don't put forth our hearts to the Lord. Of course, we long for His presence, but only when the burden of the Lord is upon our hearts can we know the living presence of the Lord Jesus. One thing, therefore, that David learned at that moment—and I'm sure he never forgot—was the sanctity of the presence of God, His untouchable holiness.

You may think that this is only Old Testament law and somewhat harsh. But remember, in the re-establishment of the kingdom under the leadership of David, the essential thing was that all the ceremonial law God had given them should be put in the place where He desired, and that the people should recognize that the Lord they worshiped was absolutely holy. Back of everything that happened on that day was a demonstration that you cannot push or drive God. He is altogether holy and demands not only the putting forth of our hands to work, but also the putting forth of our hearts to worship.

This experience of David's was accompanied by another which I would describe as satisfaction in the service of the Lord. We could write over II Samuel 6:11-19 that title: "The satisfaction of God's service." In verse 11 we find David tired and resigned. He had given up the project, and for three months the ark rested in the house of Obed-edom, who was just one of the porters in God's house. He was the custodian, as it were, a very humble, ordinary individual.

During the three months the ark stayed in this man's house, David seems to have learned at least two things. First, he learned that he had tackled the situation in the wrong way, attempting to get God's presence without recognizing God's holiness. Therefore he, the king, had been dealt with in judgment. But then he heard how apparently this very significant man who had the awesome presence of God in his home was being blessed. In other words, the ark of God was as Paul wrote in II Corinthians 2:16, "To the one . . . the savour of death unto death; and to the other the savour of life unto life."

This is something that God has been showing me to comfort as well as to challenge my own heart, that the presence of the Lord Jesus in His purity and holiness is always one or other of these things—either a savor of death or of life. In the home of an ordinary, humble man like Obed-edom, the presence of the living God blessed his whole household. In the life of David and the rest of the people of Israel at that point, as they tried to get the presence of God in the wrong way, the ark became an instrument of judgment.

Whenever God comes into our lives by the power of His Holy Spirit, He comes either to blast or to bless, either to condemn or to comfort, either to destroy or to deliver, either to judge or to save. Somehow, the presence of the ark which brought blessing in the house of Obed-edom reminds me of the words of the risen Lord: "Behold, I stand at the door, and knock: if any man hear my voice, and open the door, I will come in to him, and will sup with him, and he with me" (Revelation 3:20).

I think David learned something else, too. Those three months gave him time to think and pray: "Then David said, None ought to carry the ark of God but the Levites: for them hath the Lord chosen to carry the ark of God, and to minister unto him for ever" (I Chronicles 15:2).

Just to make it simple I will put it this way: apparently David had been reading his Bible! He had taken these three months to get alone with God and say, "Now, Lord, what has gone wrong? You know that I want Your presence with me; I need Your power for my testimony and service, but look what has happened. What is the matter?" As he thought and prayed about it, the Lord evidently directed his mind to the books of Moses, and he saw where he had made his mistake. Nobody ought to carry the ark but the Levites, he discovered, and consequently he told the people, "because ye did it not at the first, the Lord our God made a breach upon us, for that we sought him not after the due order" (I Chronicles 15:13).

"So the priests and the Levites sanctified themselves to bring up the ark of the Lord God of Israel. And the children of the Levites bare the ark of God upon their shoulders with the staves thereon, as Moses commanded according to the word of the Lord" (I Chronicles 15:14-15).

Now they were doing the right thing in the right way! They were seeking for the living presence of Jehovah, and they were going about it in the divinely appointed manner. King David, back at the task again, was approaching God in the right way: ". . . when they that bare the ark of the Lord had gone six paces, he sacrificed oxen and fatlings. And David danced before the Lord with all his might" (II Samuel 6:13-14).

You want the presence of the Lord, and you need Him desperately for your life. Yet when you seek His presence, I wonder if sometimes He has not dealt with you in a degree of judgment so that you may come to recognize His holiness and His sanctity. If this is true, how bereft and helpless you are!

No man can know the indwelling presence of Christ in his life except first the blood has been applied to his guilty soul. No man can know the joy of the Lord in his soul until first—as he has sought for the redeeming and restoring presence of a holy God—he has met Him at Calvary and has been washed in the blood of the Lamb. The first time David sought the presence of the Lord there was no sacrifice; this time they had scarcely moved the ark before he offered sacrifices before God, and then David started dancing before the Lord with all his might.

Romans 5:11 says, ". . . we also joy in God through our Lord Jesus Christ, by whom we have now received the atonement." That which brings joy to the heart, a shout to the lips, a lilt to the step, and radiance in the countenance of the Christian, is the presence of the living Lord which has been sought in God's appointed way. We must recognize that God is altogether holy and we are completely sinful, therefore we must come by the blood-sprinkled path of Calvary. As the blood is applied, we may walk in the light day by day, having fellowship one with another in the joy of the Lord.

David expressed his joy by dancing before the Lord with all his might. At this time in his life he probably wrote Psalm 132, and this is how he expressed his desire: "Surely I will not come into the tabernacle of my house, nor go up into my bed; I will not give sleep to mine eyes, or slumber to mine eyelids, Until I find out a place for the Lord, an habitation for the mighty God of Jacob" (132:3-5). Then he went on to speak of how he found the ark in the fields of the wood (that is the meaning of Kirjath-jearim) and of how he brought it into God's tabernacle and worshiped at His footstool.

David's desire for the presence of the Lord was of such intensity that he could not rest until he found a place for Him in his life. Have you ever longed for the Lord like that? "Lord Jesus, I just cannot lie down or find any peace until I have made a place for Thee!"

With that desire he faced the question found in Psalm 24:3, which was also written at the same period: "Who shall ascend into the hill of the Lord? or who shall stand in his holy place?" Then David answered himself: "He that hath clean hands, and a pure heart. . . . He shall receive the blessing from the Lord, and righteousness from the God of his salvation" (24:4-5).

What a difference it makes when you do God's work in God's way! What a song comes to the heart when you stop trying to fit God into your schemes and organizations and begin to realize that His life-giving presence is known only by the way of the cross.

There is something else in this chapter: a cloud that came into this happy day in David's life. I believe this experience recorded in II Samuel 6:20-23 left its mark for the rest of his days. I would call it "The sorrow of a lonely heart."

You can imagine the tremendous emotions which had been aroused that day in David—his spiritual hilarity, the sense of joyous liberty now that he had that which he desired so much, the presence of the living God with him. By sacrifice and by worship, God's presence was near and real after all the years of waiting and would be with him for all the years that were ahead. What a wonderful moment it was!

But when the day was over and he went back home, he was met by his wife who chided him bitterly, "How glorious was the king of Israel to day, who uncovered himself to day in the eyes of the handmaids of his servants, as one of the vain fellows shamelessly uncovereth himself!" (II Samuel 6:20).

Later in his life David was cursed by Shimei, but surely nothing hit him to the core like these words from the woman he had first married. Do you remember about Michal? She was Saul's daughter, the king's reward to the young warrior for killing one hundred Philistines. At one time, as I Samuel 18:20 tells us, she loved David, but when he was being persecuted by Saul and hiding in the mountains, she was given to another man, Phalti by name (I Samuel 25:44). As soon as David was approached to be king, he demanded of Abner and Ish-bosheth the return of his wife (II Samuel 3:14-16). David, it would have been better to leave her alone!

Before long we will come to consider the great sin of David's life. Could its root have been right here? Perhaps the thing that started him looking at another man's wife was the bitterness of soul which began when he came back from a day of victory to find the woman of his own heart and house did not enter into the joy of it but despised him for his devotion.

I suggest to you that the trouble with Bathsheba began right there, for the trouble with many a man or woman has begun like that. A person who at one time in his life has given himself over to the will of the Lord may discover as he or she goes on with Him that the life partner has been left behind. Then there has come a day when that partner has despised the other, and that has cut to the quick.

Sometimes I have met men and women, even missionaries, who have fallen into sin as David fell in the matter of Bathsheba. If you had the opportunity lovingly to talk with them as I have and see into the hearts that are broken, you will find that behind most of the trouble there has been a union with someone who has not understood their devotion to Christ and has despised them.

This chapter is like a mirror, and I trust you have been looking into it today. If Jesus comes soon, as we hope and believe, will He find you among these people with new carts, who are putting their hands to the things of God but keeping their hearts back? Or will you be found with your heart under the burden, enjoying His presence?

God grant that you may be found among the faithful, such as David was when he returned again to the task with sacrifice and rejoicing. May you be found among those who know the presence of the living Christ because the blood is constantly being applied to cleanse their sinful lives. This is what brings joy and testimony to the heart!

Now it came to pass, as David sat in his house, that David said to Nathan the prophet, Lo, I dwell in an house of cedars, but the ark of the covenant of the Lord remaineth under curtains. Then Nathan said unto David, Do all that is in thine heart; for God is with thee.

And it came to pass the same night, that the word of God came to Nathan, saying, Go and tell David my servant, Thus saith the Lord, Thou shalt not build me an house to dwell in. . . . I took thee from the sheepcote, even from following the sheep, that thou shouldest be ruler over my people Israel: And I have been with thee whithersoever thou hast walked, and have cut off all thine enemies from before thee, and have made thee a name like the name of the great men that are in the earth. . . .

And it shall come to pass, when thy days be expired that thou must go to be with thy fathers, that I will raise up thy seed after thee, which shall be of thy sons; and I will establish his kingdom. He shall build me an house, and I will stablish his throne for ever. I will be his father, and he shall be my son: and I will not take my mercy away from him, as I took it from him that was before thee. . . .

And David the king came and sat before the Lord, and said, Who am I, O Lord God, and what is mine house, that thou hast brought me hitherto? . . . What can David speak more to thee for the honour of thy servant? for thou knowest thy servant. . . . O Lord, there is none like thee, neither is there any God beside thee. . . . For thou, O my God, hast told thy servant that thou wilt build him an house: therefore thy servant hath found in his heart to pray before thee. . . . Now therefore let it please thee to bless the house of thy servant, that it may be before thee for ever: for thou blessest, O Lord, and it shall be blessed for ever.

I CHRONICLES 17:1-27; II SAMUEL 7:1-29

CHAPTER 18

WHEN GOD SAYS "NO"

(II Samuel 7:1–29; I Chronicles 17:1–27)

I WONDER IF you have had the experience in which you have yielded
your life to the Lord, and then, to quote the language of Scripture, you
have had visions and dreamed dreams, setting your heart upon what
you believed to be God's plan for you. You determined on the very best,
but God said "No!" I think that sometimes He has more to teach us
from His denials than from His permissions. Therefore, I wonder how
you have reacted when He said "No" to you.

In the chapter that we are about to consider together, we find that sort
of situation and its answer. With his kingdom established and all his
enemies subdued, with the ark of the Lord settled in the city of Zion,
David spoke to Nathan the prophet about the dream in his heart. He
revealed to this man of God his desire that he might build a house for
the Lord. David was conscious that he lived in a very lovely home, but
the Lord's house, the shelter of the ark of His presence, was only a tent.

From the context, I have no doubt that David's concern was to some
extent dictated by circumstances, because in I Chronicles 16 we are told
that he appointed certain Levites to minister before the ark of the Lord.
At this time, it would seem, there was set up the plan of temple service
which operated until after the time of Jesus when Herod's temple was
destroyed. There were twenty-four courses of priests, numbering
twenty-four thousand Levites, together with four thousand musicians
and four thousand people on guard over the ark. This was a tremendous number of people who assembled around the ark of God and the
palace of the king, and they all needed housing.

Such a situation might have caused David to make this decision, but
I am confident that he also had a deeper motive. Surely his heart was
full to overflowing with love for the Lord and a deep desire to serve
Him, to show his gratitude for all that God had done for him. So here is

a young man, still under forty years of age, upon whose heart has dawned a great vision and into whose life has come a holy purpose. Somehow this picture opens up a whole area of truth for our lives.

In II Samuel 7 we see, first, heaven's denial of a great resolve. David was evidently inspired by the highest motives, which he expressed in II Samuel 7:2, "See now, I dwell in an house of cedar, but the ark of God dwelleth within curtains."

A similar motive has gripped the hearts of thousands of people since who have dedicated their lives to God for His service, perhaps on the mission field or in the ministry. Indeed, I question whether anyone has had a real encounter with the risen Lord Jesus at Calvary but that into his or her life has come a heavenly vision, a great determination, a holy resolve to be the very best for Him—a glad, happy surrender of everything to the Master.

Some of them, like David, have achieved their "house of cedars" but unlike David they have forgotten those sacred moments of consecration and the secret covenant with the Lord. As the Lord Jesus tells us in the parable of the sower, some seed falls upon ground that is choked with the cares of this world and the deceitfulness of riches, and it becomes unfruitful. Oh, the sadness of a life whose high resolves of dedication and covenant with God have been neglected!

That was not so in David's case, for he was ready to act on his holy resolve, this great determination that he should respond to God's blessings with his uttermost efforts. In the first instance he received a favorable answer from Nathan (II Samuel 7:3). But it very quickly became evident that the answer of God was "No!" The language of this chapter seems a little uncertain, but it is quite clear in the account given in I Chronicles 17:4. When David had made his resolve known to Nathan, that very same night God came to Nathan and said, "Go and tell David my servant, Thus saith the Lord, Thou shalt not build me an house to dwell in."

There you have it—a clear, unequivocal statement from God that His answer to David was "No!" He gave no explanation: it was simply a loving, firm refusal. It was wrapped up in some wonderful promises, but nevertheless, this man who offered his life for a tremendous task was met by the divine "No!"

In later years David understood why, for God told him. He could not have taken it at the time, but the reason finally became clear. David said in I Chronicles 22:8, looking back on this incident as he charged Solomon with the building of the temple, "The word of the Lord came to me, saying, Thou hast shed blood abundantly, and hast made great wars: thou shalt not build an house unto my name, because thou hast shed much blood upon the earth in my sight."

A hand stained with blood, a life which had been responsible for the killing of others, a man who had been deeply involved in the battles and bloodshed of warfare, could never be entrusted with the building of a house for God which was to be the symbol of peace and rest, and therefore God said "No!"

I wonder if something like this has happened in your life? Perhaps you can recall a time when God said "No" to you, and there was no explanation at all. You offered your life for missionary service, or for the ministry, for the Lord's work in some aspect, and it became perfectly clear as the weeks and months passed by that God had said "No." Perhaps you became dogged with illness and were rejected by the mission board because of your health. Perhaps you never even got that far; you had to stay in your home providing for a widowed mother or caring for a lonely father while the vision of your early years became impossible of fulfillment. Today you are still at your office desk; you are still in your home.

Or was it perhaps that in your heart you had a very real dream of a home and children? But the years have slipped by, and God has said "No." Some day you will understand, because God has a reason for every denial. He may give us no explanation at the time. He may simply ask us to trust Him.

It comes as a shattering blow when the missionary recruit is rejected, or when the youthful dream of glorious service becomes impossible because of some home situation. It is a hard thing, as the years go by, to attend the valedictory services and watch others going out while you are left behind. Perhaps even harder to take is the disappointment when the vision of home and family fades and vanishes and God gives you no explanation. One day you will understand, maybe in this life, but certainly in the next; you will see that God's way has been best.

A few years ago it was my privilege to visit in Paris, France, a very famous old building quite near Notre Dame Cathedral called Sainte-Chapelle, the "chapel of the saints." The outside of that building is the drabbest and dirtiest thing imaginable. It is so very old, and the windows are covered with dust. But go inside (and all who visit Paris go inside Sainte-Chapelle), for when you stand looking in a certain direction, you can see the world-famous Rose Window. I doubt if there is any more beautiful stained-glass window in the world than that. You could stand there for hours spellbound by the loveliness of it. Outside you had your back to the light and you saw nothing but blackness. Inside, as you face the light streaming through the glass, you see nothing but beauty. It all depends on your point of view.

If God has said "No!" to you, with your back to the light in your failure to understand, the situation looks so dark. But if He has not already done so, perhaps as you meditate on these things the Lord will take you inside His heart and turn you around so that you may face the light and see the glory of His will.

The most important thing is how you react when God says "No!" Therefore, I want you to look with me here, in the second place, at the heart's response to God's refusal.

When the early dream and vision are unfulfilled, there is nothing more likely than that you want to sit down in despair and let your life go to waste. Not so with David—as a matter of fact, God's refusal became to him the occasion of tremendous blessing.

Not only was it accompanied by mighty promises, but it was supported by a word from the Lord. In II Chronicles 6, when Solomon had completed the temple and was dedicating it, he said, "Now it was in the heart of David my father to build an house for the name of the Lord God of Israel. But the Lord said to David my father, Forasmuch as it was in thine heart to build an house for my name, thou didst well in that it was in thine heart: Notwithstanding thou shalt not build the house; but thy son which shall come forth out of thy loins, he shall build the house for my name" (6:7-9).

Although God refused David's request, He said to him, "It was well that it was in thine heart." Wasn't it good of the Lord to tell him that? Surely it left a permanent glow in David's life.

Do I speak to someone who is going right along with me in your heart because you know that all I am saying is true of your life? God has said "No" to you about something. Remember, the rejected missionary is on a far higher level before the Lord than the person who has never felt the pull to the mission field at all. The soul that is tied to the office or to the home (I was going to use a word that perhaps you would have used in thinking about it in the first place—"doomed"—but that is quite the wrong word), who has to spend day after day in that routine, unnoticed kind of service, yet has a heart aflame toward God and burdened for others who know not the Saviour, I believe will be credited in heaven with a harvest as great as he would have reaped on the mission field.

I am quite sure that in heaven David will have the glory for the building of the temple, not Solomon. If you want authority for that, I would refer you to a passage in the Book of Revelation, where in the very last chapter the risen Lord Jesus speaks of Himself: "I am the root and the offspring of David, and the bright and morning star" (22:16). Solomon is not mentioned there—in fact, the Lord Jesus Christ did not come from Solomon's line at all, according to Luke 3:31. I am sure that on that great day David will have credit for the temple, and I am sure on that day some life who had a dream unfulfilled, to whom God said "No," will be credited with a great harvest.

God never says "No" coldly; He whispers into the heart that is attentive to His word, "It was well that it was in thine heart." Encouraged by this, David gave himself wholeheartedly to the task of gathering the materials. In I Chronicles 29:2-3, where David spoke to his people concerning Solomon and the temple, he said, "Now I have prepared with all my might for the house of my God the gold . . . the silver . . . the brass . . . the iron . . . and wood; onyx stones . . . and all manner of precious stones . . . because I have set my affection to the house of my God, I have of mine own proper good, of gold and silver, which I have given to the house of my God, over and above all that I have prepared for the holy house." This man, who had been denied the fulfillment of his vision, instead of sulking about it, gave himself completely to the task in the best way he knew how, preparing that which he himself would never be able to complete.

If you cannot build, you can gather the materials; if you cannot go, you can send somebody else. If God has said "No" to you, you can make it possible for someone else to fill that place on which you had set your heart. The vision need never have been in vain, even though it remains unfulfilled, for God's refusals in life are loaded with immeasurable possibilities of blessing. It all depends, however, on whether at the moment when God has said "No" you sulk or you seek—if you seek, you will find that God is right there with blessing such as you have never experienced before.

Notice from this chapter that, although there is heaven's denial of his great resolve, there is also heaven's recognition of the desire in David's heart. How wonderfully God made it up to David, and how wonderfully He makes it up to us when He says "No." He stooped over David's life at this time with unlimited blessing; through Nathan, God gave David some tremendous promises and wonderful comfort.

The Lord reminded David that he had been called from a very

humble background: "I took thee from the sheepcote, from following the sheep, to be ruler over my people, over Israel" (II Samuel 7:8). Then He showed David how He had preserved him from innumerable dangers and exalted him to the throne of Israel, giving him rest and victory over all his enemies.

No wonder David was at a loss to express his gratitude. We read in verse 18 that he went in and "sat before the Lord." Isn't that an interesting statement? He didn't fall on his face or stand on his feet, he just sat before the Lord and said, "Is this the manner of man, O Lord God?" Is this the way men deal with each other? Indeed, it is not! It is peculiar to our wonderful God to give even His most unworthy people the greatest of His blessings and the reality of His presence.

Has God said "No" to you? Then before you turn away, before there creeps into your life some resentment, just sit down before the Lord and think about His blessings. He gave us the capacity to know Him, and that puts a touch of dignity upon human life. Though by nature we are sinful and deserve only His judgment, yet God cared enough to give His Son to die for us. Although in ignorance we have trampled underfoot the blood of the everlasting covenant, He sent His Holy Spirit to reveal Jesus Christ to our hearts and to fit us for heaven.

"Is this the manner of man, O Lord God?" Indeed not! A man will bestow honor upon another because he is great and noble, but God goes much farther than that. Do you remember the prayer of Hannah in I Samuel 2:8? This is what she said, "He raiseth up the poor out of the dust, and lifteth up the beggar from the dunghill, to set them among the princes, and to make them inherit the throne of glory."

That is how God deals with His people. David was chosen from following sheep, but look at the place from which God chose you and me: guilty, sinful, incapable of restoring ourselves to God's favor at all, yet He set His love upon us and lifted us up into His kingdom. David was preserved from earthly enemies, but the Lord has preserved us from many spiritual foes, from the powers of evil which we could not possibly contend against except by His grace, by the blood of Jesus, and by power from heaven.

Of course, for David to be an ancestor of Christ was a very great honor, but to be united to the Lord Jesus, to be made with Him an heir of glory forever, is a greater honor still.

Before you turn from God in disappointment after He has said "No" to you about something very fine and desirable, remember that your election was from a far more degraded state than David's, and your elevation will be to a far higher throne than David's. Your preservation is from far greater perils, and your destiny is to far greater honor.

David was absolutely overwhelmed; when God had surrounded His "No" with the reminder of all that He had done for him, David cried out, "Who am I, O Lord God? and what is my house, that thou hast brought me hitherto?" (II Samuel 7:18).

How seldom does God find any of His children sitting before Him like that! How faint and cold is our love! Perhaps some of you have never even spent a single hour sitting before the Lord in reflection upon His goodness, especially at a time when He has said "No." God's refusal to David was accompanied by a reminder of His goodness that made David speechless.

I hope I am not reading too much into this story, but I love verse 20. As David sat in the presence of the Lord, thinking of God's goodness in spite of His negative answer, he said, "And what can David say more unto thee? for thou, Lord God, knowest thy servant."

It was not "What can *I* say more unto thee," but "What can *David* say more unto thee?" When a little child is in real need, she will say, "Mommy, Mary Ann has such a bad pain!" She won't say, "I have a pain," but will use her own name. Have you noticed how children do that? "Daddy, Johnny wants to go for a walk with you." Of course, they grow out of it very quickly, but that is characteristic of a little child.

"What can David say more unto thee?" As this man faced a negative answer, as he sat down before the Lord and worshiped in the recognition of God's goodness until he was speechless, he became as a little child before the presence of the Lord. I am sure that is one reason why God said "No," just to make him like that. Has He done that for you?

Notice one further thing that David learned as he faced God's denial of his great purpose. He was brought to a place where he really began to claim God's promises for himself, personally. David found it in his heart to pray for the blessing of his own house because he came to rest in the promise of the Lord: "The word that thou hast spoken concerning thy servant . . . do as thou hast said. . . . For thou . . . hast revealed to thy servant, saying, I will build thee an house: therefore hath thy servant found in his heart to pray this prayer unto thee" (II Samuel 7:25, 27).

Notice carefully, especially those of you to whom God has said "No," that there is nothing your soul can ever need but is covered by a promise from the Word of God. Did you know that? But you will never have even one of them until you rest in the Lord and claim them.

What is your need today? Is it for pardon? "I have blotted out, as a thick cloud, thy transgressions" (Isaiah 44:22).

Is it for peace? "My peace I give unto you: not as the world giveth. ... Let not your heart be troubled" (John 14:27).

Is it for guidance? "I will instruct thee and teach thee in the way which thou shalt go: I will guide thee with mine eye" (Psalm 32:8).

Is it for holiness? "Be ye therefore perfect, even as your Father which is in heaven is perfect" (Matthew 5:48).

Is it to be with Him in glory one day? "Father, I will that they also, whom thou hast given me, be with me where I am" (John 17:24).

There is not a need of any one of our lives but is covered by a promise from the Word of God. He has put it into our hearts to ask because first of all it was in His heart to give. And when God has said "No" to the ambition of your life, to something that is very precious to you, He brings you close to His heart and shows you that every need of your soul is met by His promises. He wants to teach you, in the face of His negative answer, to learn to make your own every possible promise in the Book.

"Let us therefore come boldly unto the throne of grace, that we may obtain mercy, and find grace to help in time of need" (Hebrews 4:16).

And after this it came to pass, that David smote the Philistines, and subdued them: and David took Metheg-ammah out of the hand of the Philistines.

And he smote Moab, and measured them with a line . . . two lines measured he to put to death, and with one full line to keep alive. And so the Moabites became David's servants, and brought gifts.

David smote also Had-ad-ezer. . . . And David took from him a thousand chariots, and seven hundred horsemen, and twenty thousand footmen: and David houghed all the chariot horses, but reserved of them for an hundred chariots. . . .

David slew of the Syrians two and twenty thousand men. Then David put garrisons in Syria of Damascus: and the Syrians became servants to David, and brought gifts. And the Lord preserved David whithersoever he went.

And David took the shields of gold that were on the servants of Had-ad-ezer, and brought them to Jerusalem . . . king David took exceeding much brass. . . . And Joram brought with him vessels of silver, and vessels of gold, and vessels of brass: Which also king David did dedicate unto the Lord, with the silver and gold that he had dedicated of all nations which he subdued. . . .

And David gat him a name when he returned from smiting of the Syrians in the valley of salt, being eighteen thousand men . . . and all they of Edom became David's servants. And the Lord preserved David whithersoever he went.

And David reigned over all Israel; and David executed judgment and justice unto all his people . . . and David's sons were chief rulers.

II SAMUEL 8:1-18

CHAPTER 19

MORE THAN CONQUERORS

(II Samuel 8:1-18)

IN THE LANGUAGE of Psalm 2:8, God said, "Ask of me, and I shall give thee the heathen for thine inheritance, and the uttermost parts of the earth for thy possession." That great promise is to His Son, but it was partially fulfilled in the man who wrote that Psalm, King David.

The crowning of David as king over all Israel, together with the establishment of his kingdom, was followed by his all-out attack on the enemies of God's people. David could not be content with anything less than the fulfillment of God's purpose for himself and for the people he ruled.

The narrative is in II Samuel 8; and about this time David wrote the 2nd and 60th Psalms. Their historic background is the experience of David which we find in this chapter. Their prophetic significance is given in Revelation 11 where we are told that "The kingdoms of this world are become the kingdoms of our Lord, and of his Christ; and he shall reign for ever and ever" (11:15). The personal application is found in Romans 6 and 8 and, of course, this is of immense importance to us today.

We are not primarily concerned here with the historical aspect or the prophetic interpretation of Scripture, but with the personal application of David's experience in our own lives. We are studying the making of a man of God, and nothing must be allowed to sidetrack us from this particular goal. Paul said in II Timothy 3:16-17 that "All scripture is given by inspiration of God, and is profitable for doctrine, for reproof, for correction, for instruction in righteousness: that the man of God may be perfect, throughly furnished unto all good works."

"The man of God"—that is our subject. As we consider the battles, the blessings, and the victories of David in II Samuel 8 we shall, I trust, have some instruction in righteousness.

Notice, in the first place, the scope of David's victory. If you could take time to look up all these names on a map, you would see some very significant things, the first being the fact that the victory of David was absolutely complete. First, II Samuel 8:1 speaks of the Philistines who lived in the western area, along the Mediterranean Sea. Verse 2 tells of the Moabites who inhabited the area on the eastern side of the Dead Sea, and verse 6 refers to the Syrians, two companies of them, who came from the north and northeast. Then verse 14 speaks of the people of Edom who inhabited the territory south and east of the Dead Sea. Therefore over this chapter we may write east, west, north, south— total victory in all areas. The Philistines were conquered and the Moabites became David's servants, as did the Syrians and the people of Edom.

All these powerful enemies surrounding Israel were completely sub-dued. Significantly, it was for the first and almost the last time in his-tory up to now that the people of God possessed the whole territory which God's covenant with Abraham said that they should have. Back when Abraham did not possess an inch of the land, God said, "Unto thy seed have I given this land, from the river of Egypt unto the great river, the river Euphrates" (Genesis 15:18).

Here David possessed, for the first time in history, the whole territory. Not content with the bit that he held, David went out and methodically took possession of all that God had promised to His people Israel.

The thing that fascinates me about this complete victory is the utter contempt with which David treated the great power of his adversaries. The Philistines, for instance, who had occupied part of the land and harassed the Israelites for so long, had their chief city taken away from them. In II Samuel 7:1 it is called Metheg-ammah, but that is another name for Gath, "the bridle of Ammah." This implies that the city was a curb or a bridle, and it had been that very thing to the people of Israel. David simply took it out of the hands of the Philistines and then used it against them.

The Moabites, who lived east of the Dead Sea, were the descendants of Lot. Their origin (related in Genesis 19:37) doesn't bear thinking about. They began and continued to be a people who were utterly cor-rupt, and they were responsible many times for the corruption of Israel. When the devil couldn't capture the people of God any other way, he turned them from God by corrupting their moral lives.

David was particularly severe with the Moabites. As a matter of fact, they had killed his parents when he was in exile and had left them under their charge for a time (I Samuel 22:3-4). I don't know if David was taking revenge, but he certainly dealt very firmly with a situation which otherwise would have corrupted God's people again. He laid the Moabites down on the ground, measured them up, and decided to kill two thirds of them, sparing one third alive.

Then there was Syria, the great heathen nation to the north, divided into two groups with capitals at Zobah and Damascus. They united together for protection but found themselves helpless against the might of David.

In a wonderful bit of irony in Psalm 60:8, David mentions those who had thought themselves so powerful: "Moab is my washpot." Of this people, who had defiled and corrupted Israel, David was saying, "I will wash my feet in them! I will take these people who have defiled us and make them a cleansing agent! I will take this land and use it for the glory of God!"

Then, in the same breath, he says, "Over Edom will I cast out my shoe." Edom was the descendants of Esau, a people ready to sacrifice any spiritual birthright if only they could gratify the flesh. To empty out the dust in one's sandal over the head of another was an eastern symbol of claiming a slave. "I will put them under my control. That is what I will do with this powerful adversary!" said David.

"Philistia, triumph thou because of me" is thought to be either satire or sarcasm, or perhaps it should more correctly be rendered, "Philistia, I will triumph over you." In any event, the important thing to notice is that David, God's anointed king, occupied the whole territory which God promised and treated his once-powerful enemies with derision. He took all the power out of their hands to use it in the service of the Lord. He made his enemies to become his servants, bringing them all into complete subjection.

I find this so thrilling to my soul because the language of Psalm 2, where the "heathen rage, and the people imagine a vain thing," and "He that sitteth in the heavens shall laugh" at His enemies, "the Lord shall have them in derision," is also prophetic. It is the language of the Father speaking to the Son in glory: "Sit thou at my right hand, until I make thine enemies thy footstool" (Psalm 110:1). It is the solemn, awesome laughter of God. I am sure that most Bible students know that there is no reference at all to God's laughing except in scorn and derision at the powerlessness of His adversaries.

Here is a sure prophecy of the triumph of the Lord Jesus in that great day when every knee shall bow and every tongue shall confess that He is Lord. But in the language of the Holy Spirit to our hearts, it is also the tremendous declaration that where we have been corrupted and made unclean, where we have fallen into idolatry and materialism, in the realm of the flesh to which we have often yielded as it has cried out for gratification and for which we have sold spiritual birthrights cheaply to gratify the self-life—over every area of our lives can be written, "In all these things we are more than conquerors through him that loved us" (Romans 8:37).

Have you discovered the joy of handing over your battle to the Lord and allowing Him to take command on your behalf? Are you launching into the attack, as it were, with your Lord and Saviour, and letting Him deal with the enemy? To do that is to discover there is nothing that God will not do for the obedient heart. I tell you, the cause of the devil is absolutely hopeless when the Lord takes up the fight. I believe that even the weakest of us can laugh our enemy to scorn, taking the bridle out of his hand and using it for the glory of God.

Do you know this glorious truth of the gospel as applied to your Christian life? Your weaknesses, deficiencies, failures and sins, when handed over to the Lord, can be a source of blessing and power. The Lord does not crush any of us, but He takes hold of all the weaknesses of our lives, snatching them out of the hand of the enemy and making them serve His own ends.

Remember the Apostle Paul, who went to Damascus eaten up with jealousy and determined to slay every Christian he could get his hands on. God met him in Jesus Christ on the road, and years afterward he wrote to the church at Corinth, "For I am jealous over you with godly jealousy" (II Corinthians 11:2). God had taken hold of the thing which was his weakness—his jealousy and bitterness—but He did not do away with it; He transformed and used it. In its place, Paul became filled with a jealous compassion for others on the behalf of Christ. That is how God takes hold of our weaknesses and transforms them by the power of His Spirit, making them serve His own purposes to the discomfiture of hell!

As you think of the scope of David's victory, ask yourself how complete is victory in your own life. A Christian does not have to struggle for it, but simply rest in the Lord who won it for us by His blood and submit to His Spirit who will make it real in our lives.

Have you ever connected Psalm 2:8 with Acts 1:8? The commission is, "Ye shall be witnesses unto me . . . unto the uttermost part of the earth," and the promise is "Ask of me, and I shall give thee . . . the uttermost parts of the earth for thy possession." That is God's plan of deliverance, and we, like David, are called upon never to settle for anything less than possessing all that God gives us in Jesus Christ. There is no victory without a fight; take the initiative and trust the Lord for power. The moment that God sees you doing that, He will work with you, in you, and through you, so that you begin to have complete victory as He has promised.

Notice here also what I would call the strategy of David's victory. His discernment was so significant. First of all, he hamstrung the chariot horses (II Samuel 8:4). Does this sound like savage slaughter? No, David was doing this in obedience to God's command in Deuteronomy 17:15-16, the "king over thee, whom the Lord thy God shall choose . . . he shall not multiply horses to himself."

The purpose of this command was to keep the people of God from putting confidence in anything except in the Lord. Any misplaced confidence in their own weapons of warfare had to be completely destroyed. So David wrote, for instance, "Some trust in chariots and some in horses: but we will remember the name of the Lord our God" (Psalm 20:7). Again the Psalmist wrote, "There is no king saved by the multitude of an host: a mighty man is not delivered by much strength. An horse is a vain thing for safety: neither shall he deliver any by his great strength" (Psalm 33:16-17).

Here was the first strategy for victory—death to everything that could lead David to a misplaced confidence. Secondly, there was surrender.

From the Syrians—and indeed, from all the other enemies whom he had overcome—he captured many valuables: gold, brass, and other articles of great worth. Why? Even though God had said "No" to him about the temple, David still had the temple in his mind, and he was not going to let that vision go. He did not get resentful with the Lord, but brought back the spoils of victory to dedicate them for the Lord's glory. His first action was to burn the enemies' gods; then he dedicated the enemies' gold. Therefore much of Solomon's magnificent temple was built with materials which had been captured from the enemies of God's people.

The third point of strategy for victory we find mentioned in II Samuel 8:13. Because of his victory over the powerful opposition of Syria, "David gat him a name." Watch out when a man of God becomes famous! That is always a dangerous moment, but David refused to touch the glory. In Psalm 60:12 he says, "Through God we shall do valiantly: for he it is that shall tread down our enemies." David knew what to do with fame. When the people applauded him and gave him a name and a reputation, he brought the glory right back to the throne of God and said, "Lord, You have done it all!"

That is the strategy of heaven: the destruction of every false strength, the dedication of the fruits of victory, and the declining of applause. The Book of Revelation says quite a great deal concerning that holy temple unto the Lord, the New Jerusalem. Every living stone built into that temple of God is a soul which has been captured from the grip of the devil. That is how heaven is built; that is how it is occupied; that is how it is populated. It is composed of people in whose earthly lives there has been resident the Person of the Holy Spirit, who have glorified their Saviour, and therefore who, through all eternity, are the temple of the Lord. Every one of them has been seized from the grip of Satan and put into the service of the Lord. That is heaven's strategy. How it must annoy the devil to see God doing it!

That is also the strategy of the Holy Spirit in the conquest of a soul saved by grace. Everything in a life that stands in opposition to God has to be condemned and put to death. Everything in a man's life which can be used to glorify God has to be dedicated and come under new ownership. Before God can ever use our lives they have to be brought to Calvary, and there He picks them up and uses them for His glory, because everything in the temple must proclaim "Glory to God!"

You see, David's strategy is but a picture of heaven's strategy in eternity and the Holy Spirit's strategy in time. Have you accepted this for your life—the crucifixion of the self-life, the condemnation of that which is contrary to God? Then come to Jesus and bring to Him all that is you, that there may be a change of ownership, and that you may know the joy of a life which, because it has followed heavenly strategy, is experiencing Holy Spirit victory.

Then what is the sequel to victory? We have already seen something of the scope of it and of the strategy of it. Now we see the sequel to it: twice in II Samuel 8, in verses 6 and 14, is the lovely statement that "the Lord preserved David whithersoever he went."

It seems to open up a principle: because David obeyed the Lord and followed heaven's strategy, the Lord preserved him. It is an inescapable fact that God will protect and bless the obedient. He will punish and chastise the disobedient, and there is no exception to that rule.

"David reigned over all Israel; and David executed judgment and justice unto all his people" (II Samuel 8:15). As the Lord saved him from his enemies, David exercised his authority and rule. Not only did he have a right to rule; he *did* rule because God delivered him. He possessed all that God had promised him.

David's rule was marked at first by godliness, integrity, and justice. However, it was not long before he forsook those heavenly principles and brought disaster on himself, his family, and his nation. But as long as he maintained God's principles, the Lord was with him in power.

I would remind you of some words in Revelation 19:11-16, "In righteousness he doth judge and make war." History is rapidly converging to that point where Jesus Christ shall come to reign as King of kings and Lord of lords! He comes with a vesture dipped in blood upon which is written that Name. He rules! He reigns! Why? Because He was obedient unto death.

If that be true in eternity, then the New Testament truth concerning your life and mine today is the same, as we are exhorted by the Apostle Paul: "Know ye not, that to whom ye yield yourself servants to obey, his servants ye are to whom ye obey; whether of sin unto death, or of obedience unto righteousness? But God be thanked, that ye were the servants of sin, but ye have obeyed from the heart that form of doctrine which was delivered you. Being then made free from sin, ye became the servants of righteousness" (Romans 6:16-18).

Here is the same principle: the sequel of victory is a righteous and godly life. The strategy of victory is obedience from the heart to the Word of God; therefore, because Jesus is in authority over the enemy, He is able to save you to the uttermost. The scope of victory is through Jesus Christ Himself, for all things are of Him, and He is ours.

God calls us to claim all that Jesus has for us. Are you victorious in the fight today? You can be! By the grace of the Lord you can press home the battle in the name of the Lord. As you do so in obedience to His strategy, there will be slaughter of that which grieves the Saviour—the reckoning of being dead with Christ—surrender of everything that is His, and a sanctification that refuses to touch the glory but gives it all to Him. The sequel to this is that the Lord will preserve you wherever you go, and you will reign where once you were in bondage.

And David said, Is there yet any that is left of the house of Saul, that I may shew him kindness for Jonathan's sake?

And there was of the house of Saul a servant whose name was Ziba. And when they had called him unto David, the king said . . . Is there not yet any of the house of Saul, that I may shew the kindness of God unto him? And Ziba said unto the king, Jonathan hath yet a son, which is lame on his feet. . . . . . .

And the king said unto him, Where is he? . . . Then King David sent, and fetched him out of the house of Machir, the son of Ammi-el, from Lo-debar.

Now when Mephibosheth, the son of Jonathan, the son of Saul, was come unto David, he fell on his face, and did reverence. And David said, Mephibosheth. And he answered, Behold thy servant!

And David said unto him, Fear not: for I will surely shew thee kindness for Jonathan thy father's sake, and will restore thee all the land of Saul thy father; and thou shalt eat bread at my table continually.

And he bowed himself, and said, What is thy servant, that thou shouldest look upon such a dead dog as I am?

Then the king called to Ziba, Saul's servant, and said unto him, I have given unto thy master's son all that pertained to Saul and to all his house. Thou therefore, and thy sons, and thy servants, shall till the land for him. . . . Now Ziba had fifteen sons and twenty servants. . . . As for Mephibosheth, said the king, he shall eat at my table, as one of the king's sons.

And Mephibosheth had a young son, whose name was Micha. And all that dwelt in the house of Ziba were servants unto Mephibosheth. So Mephibosheth dwelt in Jerusalem: for he did eat continually at the king's table; and was lame on both his feet.

II SAMUEL 9:1-13

CHAPTER 20

THE EXHIBITION OF GRACE

(II Samuel 9:1-13)

In this story we reach the high point of David's life. Here was his greatest hour. Tragedy and decline came soon, but at this point David had captured the whole land which God purposed that His people should inhabit and possess; he had driven out all his enemies and was undisputed king over the whole nation.

He took this particular moment to reflect upon his early life, the days of testing, days of suffering, days of rejection. And as he mused over the past and recalled Saul's animosity to him, there came the thought: "I wonder is there any left alive of the house of Saul, that I might show kindness to him?"

Thus we are introduced to one of the most touching chapters in the Old Testament, a vivid illustration of New Testament truth. David's treatment of Mephibosheth is just one of the many pictures in the Bible of God's grace toward His people. Isn't the Lord good to give us so many examples of His love? As we meditate upon David's kindness to Mephibosheth, we shall come to understand and appreciate more than ever God's gracious treatment of us.

To begin with, notice the condition which grace meets. This is not the first mention of Mephibosheth, for in II Samuel 4:4 he is introduced as a child five years old. At that time an accident happened to him. When the news of Jonathan's death in battle, along with his father King Saul, reached the royal households, immediately the child's nurse, filled with panic, picked him up in her arms to run for their lives. So great was her haste that she dropped the child, and he became lame on both his feet for the rest of his life.

We might ask ourselves why all the hurry and panic, but if we think a moment the answer is perfectly clear. Mephibosheth, being Jonathan's son, was heir to the throne after the death of his grandfather and father.

Everyone knew that God had chosen David to be king, however, and therefore Mephibosheth would be in danger. Surely the first thing for David to do when he took the throne would be to eliminate any possible rivals.

Furthermore, the nurse must have reflected on how Saul had treated David, how despicably and jealously he had behaved, until she had become quite convinced that the moment David had opportunity he would take vengeance on any of Saul's family he could find. With this fear in her mind, she picked up the child and ran for safety.

In the ninth chapter we find that Mephibosheth is no longer a child, but a grown man. The significant thing is that he had been careful to keep clear of David. No doubt he had been indoctrinated since childhood to fear the king, for coming to the attention of David might be fatal for him. No doubt the arguments that had led the nurse to run away with him as a little child had been repeated to him many times until Jonathan's son, although a grown man, had a deeply rooted fear of King David. Perhaps he also had a sense of resentment against the man who stood in the way of his own claim to the throne.

Therefore, we find Mephibosheth in this attitude that I am calling "the condition which grace meets." I could describe it in three simple words, the first being *away*—away from God, which is always the condition of the heart apart from His grace. Away, afar off, estranged from God, perhaps indoctrinated by others, we feel that the safest thing is to steer clear of God, not to get on close terms with Him. As the years go by, many of us maintain our distance, away and astray from God.

The Bible says that "by one man's disobedience many were made sinners" (Romans 5:19). From our very earliest days we have known a sense of estrangement from eternity, a feeling of distance from God, which before long develops into my second word: *afraid*. We are not simply afar off, but we are afraid of God. After all, we may argue, we know that our lives are not what they should be, and God, if there be a God, is absolutely perfect and righteous, therefore we cannot face Him. "I am quite sure that He is against me, and the safe thing for me is to keep away!"

Through the years fear accumulates and develops into my third word: *antagonism*. There is even a sense of resentment against God in the natural heart. "Why should God permit the world to be in such a mess? Why should God allow this to happen to me? If He is God, why doesn't He do something?"

These and a thousand other things invade the consciousness of the natural man, and over the years—from childhood through youth, sometimes in manhood and even to old age—he is characterized by these three words in his relationship to God: away, afraid, and antagonistic.

Nothing but grace could meet a condition like that, for the fact of the matter is that our assumptions concerning God, which have kept us away from Him, are simply the lie of the devil. God is not against us. He has shown His love toward us beyond all doubt "in that, while we were yet sinners, Christ died for us" (Romans 5:8). "If God be for us, who can be against us? He that spared not his own Son, but delivered him up for us all, how shall he not with him also freely give us all things?" (Romans 8:31-32).

If you have developed an attitude of antagonism toward God, your fears are built upon the deception of Satan. It is not God who needs to be reconciled to you; it is you who need to be reconciled to God. Atonement has been made for your sin, and the distance between you and God was obliterated at the cross. It is true that when you come into this world you are away from God, that you are out of touch with Him. But the gap has been bridged at Calvary, for "God was in Christ, reconciling the world unto himself, not imputing their trespasses unto them" (II Corinthians 5:19).

It is the lie of the devil which persuades people today to keep their distance from God, while all the time God Himself is pleading that He "so loved the world, that he gave his only begotten Son" (John 3:16). He is not against us, He is for us!

Our separation from God is the condition which is met by the grace of God in Jesus Christ. Therefore, let me say again, that if you are in that condition you are right where His grace can meet your need.

There is also the salvation which grace ministers. Notice how the chapter begins. At the moment of David's triumph, what did he do? He said, "Is there yet any that is left of the house of Saul?" Why? "That I might take vengeance upon him"? No! "That I might retaliate for Saul's persecution of me and eliminate any possible rival"? No! But "That I may show him kindness for Jonathan's sake!"

"Is there any left of the family or household of the man who tried to kill me with a javelin, who pursued me from mountain to mountain, from stronghold to stronghold? Is there anyone related to this man who made my life so unbearable? Not that I might take vengeance, but for Jonathan's sake—my beloved friend Jonathan, with whom I entered into a covenant which covers all his children—that I might show them kindness."

David found a servant of Saul's named Ziba, who told him about Mephibosheth. At once David sent for him where he was living in the land of Lo-debar. That word means "the barren land," a place of emptiness and dissatisfaction. That was where Mephibosheth lived. I can imagine that he was filled with fear when he heard that King David wanted an interview with him! He came, however, and immediately fell on his face before David, calling him master and lord. When David spoke to Mephibosheth there was no chiding or anger: "Fear not: for I will surely shew thee kindness for Jonathan thy father's sake, and will restore thee all the land of Saul thy father; and thou shalt eat bread at my table continually" (II Samuel 9:7).

Observe that last little phrase, which finds its way no less than four times into II Samuel 9, in verses 7, 10, 11, and 13. When the Holy Spirit says something four times, it is obvious that He intends to grip our hearts with an important truth.

Here is the salvation which grace ministers, and again I want to give it in three simple words. The condition which grace meets is that of being away, afraid, and antagonistic. God always takes the initiative in bringing His blessing to a life. It is not you who take the first step; you are incapable of doing a thing. It is God who makes overtures to you; it is God who by grace steps down to you where you are, who comes to meet you in your need.

The first word is *acceptance*. "Is there any of a lost race of people," asks God, "who have kept Me out of their lives, who have ignored or defied Me? Are there any such people that I may show them kindness for Jesus' sake? I have made a covenant with My Son that shall cover all His family, down to the end of time, a covenant sealed with His blood that can reach out to the person who is farthest away, to the one who is the most afraid of all, even to the most antagonistic. Is there anyone like that to whom I may show kindness for Jesus' sake?"

Yes, "when we were enemies, we were reconciled to God by the death of his Son, much more, being reconciled, we shall be saved by his life" (Romans 5:10). It is a tremendous thing that God, infinitely righteous and absolutely holy, is able, while upholding the justice of all His created universe, to reach down to the depths of human need and say, "Are there any here to whom I may show kindness, in spite of their treatment of Me?"

How is He able to do it? He is able to do it for Jesus' sake, because Jesus at Calvary has borne the responsibility of our antagonism and rebellion. He paid the price for it by His own absolute submission to the will of the Father and His absolute obedience to the justice of God. Therefore, because of His blood that was shed, God is able to seek a people who are far away from Him, who are afraid of Him, who are antagonistic toward Him, and to such He is able to say, "Are there any of you to whom I may show kindness for Jesus' sake?"

My second word is *abasement,* for David who sent for Mephibosheth is but a picture of God who calls by His Holy Spirit the man who is afar off. If I know anything of what it is to live in antagonism and at a distance from God (and alas, indeed I do!), I can understand something of the meaning of this word "Lo-debar"—the place of barrenness, dissatisfaction, and frustration.

That is the inevitable condition of a man whose life is in maladjustment to God, who has never been born of the Spirit of God. That describes where he is living, and it is the reason for his misery, unhappiness, and defeat, because he is far away from God. It is to him there, right there, that the Holy Spirit comes to bring him into the very presence of the King. The moment he gets face to face with the Lord, in recognition of the grace of God and the marvel of His love, like Mephibosheth he falls at the feet of the Master and looking up into His face says to Him, "My Lord and my God!"

A few verses later, we find that Mephibosheth called himself a dead dog (II Samuel 9:8). The grace of David poured out upon this man brought him to a recognition of his baseness and lifelessness. Grace always does that. Grace never leaves a man with his self-righteousness and pride. The cross brings us down to the very feet of our Lord in recognition that we are impotent, lost, and barren.

We look up into His face, as did the Apostle Paul on the road to Damascus, and say to Him, "Lord, who art Thou?" And when we have discovered who He is, we say, "Lord, what wilt Thou have me to do?" There is no revelation of grace to the heart that does not produce this effect of self-abasement.

> When I survey the wondrous cross,
>   On which the Prince of glory died,
> My richest gain I count but loss,
>   And pour contempt on all my pride.
> *Isaac Watts*

I wonder if God's grace has produced that abasement in you. Has it brought you down there? If not, you have room to question whether you have really met Him and received His grace.

The first word in connection with the salvation which grace ministers is acceptance by virtue of the merit of another. The second word is abasement by the revelation of that grace bestowed upon us in Christ. My third word is *abundance.* "I . . . will restore thee all the land of Saul thy father," said David to Mephibosheth, "and thou shalt eat bread at my table continually" (II Samuel 9:7).

Abundance! "Blessed be the God and Father of our Lord Jesus Christ, who hath blessed us with all spiritual blessings in heavenly places in Christ. . . . But God, who is rich in mercy . . . hath quickened us together with Christ . . . and made us sit together in heavenly places in Christ Jesus: That in the ages to come he might shew the exceeding riches of his grace in his kindness toward us through Christ Jesus" (Ephesians 1:3; 2:4-7).

"Thou shalt eat bread at my table continually," said David.

I tell you, there is no poverty in God's salvation! There is no stinting, no just scraping through by the skin of our teeth! Ours is a super-abundant salvation; in Christ we are more than conquerors! In Him there is a constant supply of life to the helpless and penitent sinner who has come to the foot of the cross. At Calvary he discovers real satisfaction. Instead of barrenness in his life, there is fruitfulness; instead of being afar off, he is made near to God by the blood of Jesus.

From that moment on, he is the object of God's outpouring of blessing. All the resources of heaven are made available to meet his need and to take him safely through the journey of life until one day he will be presented faultless at the throne of God.

Meditate on this thought, that Mephibosheth was to eat bread at the king's table continually. He went through his life lame, but at the king's table his deformed feet would be safely hidden. God didn't choose to heal him physically, so he remained a cripple. Those were the marks of his running away from God, of his fear, and they were with him forever.

It is a strange thing how often in the Bible you find that, far from healing people, God crippled them. He crippled Jacob, so that even though he was renamed Israel, "a prince with God," he "halted upon his thigh" from the day he met and wrestled with God (Genesis 32:31).

I am sure that very often as Mephibosheth sat down to eat at the king's table he said to himself, "I am not worthy of being so close to the king. When I think of how far away and resentful I have been, why should I be treated like this?" Then the thought would come to him,

"But I am not here for my own sake. I am here for my father Jonathan's sake!"

The man who has been brought back from waywardness and antagonism, who has been accepted by God on the merit of Jesus Christ, and who has become aware of the abundance of his salvation and the glorious supply of God's grace toward him, is often brought to say, "But Lord, I am not worthy of this. If I got my just recompense I would be in hell, judged by God and sent to a lost eternity. I don't deserve these privileges, the joys of an open Bible and of an indwelling Christ!"

But as we sense our unworthiness almost to the point of despair, we are reminded that we are not receiving any of these blessings on our merit, but for Jesus' sake. We enjoy the abundance of our salvation and continued fellowship at the table of the King of kings because God has sealed by the precious blood of His Son a covenant that has taken you within its scope to protect and keep you throughout life and for all eternity.

Also, we are told in II Samuel 9:10 that Ziba had fifteen sons and twenty servants. Why did the Holy Spirit put in a detail like that? I'll tell you what they were for: to look after Mephibosheth! They were part of God's superabundance, an Old Testament picture of the New Testament truth that if I seek first the kingdom of God and His righteousness, all manner of things within the will of God shall be added unto me (Matthew 6:33). What an abundant supply God provides to enable His children to triumph day by day through grace!

There is a postscript to this story which is very precious, and without which it would be incomplete. It is not found in II Samuel 9, but in chapter 19, and it shows a response which grace merits.

Many years had gone by, and there had been a breakdown in David's life. Even though he confessed and was cleansed and forgiven, he bore the consequences of his sins—note that. David's disgraceful behavior left its mark upon his family and home life, and for a time he was even rejected from being king; his son Absalom revolted against him and he was forced into exile. The rebellion ended after Absalom was killed, and when David returned to Jerusalem he met Mephibosheth face to face. What had he been doing all this time of David's exile? We are told in II Samuel 19:24, "And Mephibosheth the son of Saul came down to meet the king, and had neither dressed his feet, nor trimmed his beard, nor washed his clothes, from the day the king departed until the day he came again in peace."

Our first word concerning the response which grace merits is *absti-*

nence. This man who had been the recipient of David's grace, through all the time of his rejection and exile had maintained a life of absolute loyalty to him. The very way he dressed and the way he lived signified that he was sharing the sorrow and hardship and suffering of his rejected king.

It was all the harder for him to do that because his servant Ziba had slandered him. When David asked Ziba what Mephibosheth was doing, he answered, "Behold, he abideth at Jerusalem: for he said, To day shall the house of Israel restore me the kingdom of my father" (II Samuel 16:3). That was a lie, but it convinced David that Mephibosheth was betraying him. The king said to Ziba, "All right, everything that I have given to Mephibosheth shall be yours."

But when David came back and saw Mephibosheth bearing all the marks of suffering and sorrow which he had shared with him, David said, "Mephibosheth, why didn't you go with me?" And he told the king the truth, that Ziba had slandered him. As he spoke, David saw the mistake he had made and said, "I suggest that you and Ziba divide the land." "And Mephibosheth said unto the king, Yea, let him take all, forasmuch as my lord the king is come again in peace unto his own house" (II Samuel 19:30).

Here, then, is abstinence: separation and identification are the marks that we are Christ's and that He is our Lord and Master.

The second word is *abandonment*: "Let him take all, David, I am not interested in the land. What matters to me more than anything is that you have come again in peace to your own house. All I want is *you*—not your blessings, or wealth, or possessions, but yourself!"

This is the response which grace merits. One of the evidences that grace has been genuine in a man's life is that there is something about him of abstinence: something about his character, his speech, his behavior, his dress, that indicates he shares in the suffering and rejection of Christ until He comes again.

Deeper even than the outward signs, however, is the transaction about which the world knows nothing (although it will see evidence of its reality in his life) that comes when he lifts up his face to the Lord Jesus and says, "Lord, I am not interested in Your blessings; all I want is that You should reign in peace in Your own house. Let them take all the material things, Lord. But I am Your property; my body is the temple of the Holy Spirit. I am Your blood-bought child, Lord Jesus, and therefore I belong to You completely."

Do you see it, friend? Oh, how poverty-stricken are words to speak on such a subject! Are you in the condition which grace meets? Then think about the salvation which grace ministers to you: you are accepted by virtue of the blood of the cross, because of what He has done for you. That truth brings you in abasement to the foot of the cross, and because you come like that, there is ministered to you the abundance of God's salvation.

Then there comes the response which grace merits from your life—an abstinence from the world, an abandonment to God in Jesus Christ which enables you to say with the Apostle Paul, "But God forbid that I should glory, save in the cross of our Lord Jesus Christ, by whom the world is crucified unto me, and I unto the world" (Galatians 6:14).

David sent Joab, and his servants with him, and all Israel; and they destroyed the children of Ammon, and besieged Rabbah. But David tarried still at Jerusalem. And it came to pass in an eveningtide, that . . . from the roof he saw a woman washing herself; and the woman was very beautiful to look upon.

And David sent and enquired after the woman. And one said, Is not this Bath-sheba, the daughter of Eliam, the wife of Uriah the Hittite? And David sent messengers, and took her; and she came in unto him, and he lay with her; for she was purified from her uncleanness: and she returned unto her house. And the woman conceived, and sent and told David, and said, I am with child.

And David sent to Joab, saying, Send me Uriah the Hittite. And Joab sent Uriah to David. . . . And David said to Uriah, Go down to thy house, and wash thy feet. . . . But Uriah slept at the door of the king's house with all the servants of his lord, and went not down to his house.

And when they had told David saying, Uriah went not down unto his house. . . . David wrote a letter to Joab . . . Set ye Uriah in the forefront of the hottest battle, and retire ye from him, that he may be smitten, and die. . . . Then Joab sent and told David . . . Thy servant Uriah the Hittite is dead. . . .

But the thing that David had done displeased the Lord. And the Lord sent Nathan unto David. . . . And Nathan said to David, Thou art the man. Thus saith the Lord God of Israel. . . . Wherefore hast thou despised the commandment of the Lord, to do evil in his sight? . . . Now therefore the sword shall never depart from thine house. . . . The Lord also hath put away thy sin; thou shalt not die. Howbeit, because by this deed thou hast given great occasion to the enemies of the Lord to blaspheme, the child also that is born unto thee shall surely die.

II SAMUEL 11:1—12:14

CHAPTER 21

HOW ARE THE MIGHTY FALLEN!

(II Samuel 11:1—12:14)

IT IS QUITE remarkable how easily many of us can cast aside impressions made as the Word of God has been preached, and how quickly we can revert both in manner and in conversation to purely social and secular things. We may often have a service of which we say, "Well, we had a good time and a helpful message," but somehow there has been no real word from the Lord to our hearts, no vital impact from the Holy Spirit, and therefore no lasting response. May this study be a stab from the Spirit of God to grip our hearts and consciences with conviction.

The real question for us all is: Are we prepared to face sin? Not to discuss someone else's sin, but to face our own; not to be appalled at the domination of communism, but to be appalled at the domination of the devil; not so much to be alarmed at juvenile delinquency, but to be concerned about our own delinquency. We need to hear the Spirit of God speak to us with such authority and in such a personal way as to drive us into a corner from which we must cry out for mercy, as He says, "Thou art the man."

We have been studying the life of David by exposition from the Word of God. We have risen with him to the pinnacle of the great days in his life, great days of victory, but suddenly we are hurled down to an abyss.

Let us consider for a moment the relationship of this part of David's life to our own times. What saps the vitality of this country today? What undermines our national strength of character? What is the real menace to the power of the United States? What brings shame upon the Christian church? What causes more heartbreak and sorrow than anything else in the world? It is the same sin of which David was guilty.

The casualties from accidents in the air and on the road are insignificant compared with the casualties of broken homes and ruined lives, and this is not confined to ungodly circles. Of course, I recognize that Satan is very clever and powerful, and one of the cleverest things he does is to glamorize sin. One of the features of recent movie advertising has been the glamorizing of sins of people in the Bible. When that industry attracts its patrons by announcing a film on the subject of David and Bathsheba, everyone knows what they are going to show.

Satan specializes in making sin popular; he implies, "Well, it doesn't really matter. That is what everyone does." The success of his strategy may be partly due to the fact that we have ceased to think about the horror of sin. A student somewhere is preparing for the ministry, and suddenly he drops out of school—soon you hear that he has been hastily married. Or a member of the faculty isn't in class one morning, and he is not seen again. Or there is the pastor of a church who cannot be found, a deacon who doesn't appear for the services, a church member who cannot be traced any more.

It is the sin of David that has come to light, and as Nathan said to him, "By this deed thou hast given great occasion to the enemies of the Lord to blaspheme" (II Samuel 12:14). May the Lord have mercy upon us, and lay bare our hearts before Him!

I am quite certain that until we are prepared to put the label "Sin" where God puts it—taking not our own estimate of it, but God's—and until our hearts are broken and we are brought to acknowledge before Him that we have failed, there will be no breaking through of the power of God in victory and blessing.

I want to remind you, as we come to this solemn subject, that "where sin abounded, grace did much more abound" (Romans 5:20). If we learn about the heinousness of David's sin—and we leave it at that— we have learned little, because we know it; but if we learn about the mercy of God, then we surely have learned something tremendous.

Remember the background of this story from the study of David's life; remember the great heights he reached before he crashed. He was a shepherd boy, the one who kept the sheep, and who was despised by his family. You remember how strong and athletic he was: he leaped over a wall, outran a troop, killed a lion and a bear. He was a master in the use of a sling; with unerring aim his first stone landed right in the forehead of Goliath, and down went the giant! David had a handsome face that glowed with health and a warm heart that was tender toward God. He was also a poet, with all the characteristics and temperament of a poetic soul.

The Lord was his Shepherd, David declared, and he was completely dedicated to his duty in the Lord's will. One day, you will recall, Samuel came and anointed him as the king chosen of God. In his childhood he had known the quickening of the Spirit, but now he knew the anointing of the Spirit—and there is a difference. There are many people who unquestionably are Christians, who know God's regenerating power, but something is tragically and obviously lacking in their lives. They have not that ability given by the Spirit of God to live above circumstances. They need what electricity is to the wire: spark, power, authority. The Holy Spirit is in them, but He has not come upon them.

The flame of God's Holy Spirit had descended upon the burnt offering of David's life; the Lord had met him in his sacrifice and surrender. He knew the reality and the power and the heavenly authority of God's anointing. The Lord was his Rock, his Redeemer, his Great Shepherd. In weariness David knew where to go for green pastures; when he was thirsty he knew about the still waters; when he was perplexed he knew the sustenance of God's presence. How easily he conquered the giant! How gracious he was in his treatment of Saul, how lacking in spite and animosity! All this was possible only because the Holy Spirit was upon him.

David was called "a man after God's own heart." That was the caliber of the man, the height to which he had risen. He had become king of all Israel, and he had defeated all his enemies. He had risen now to the peak of his life and career—when suddenly the devil tripped him up.

Oh, from what heights of blessing it is possible for a man to fall! To what depths of sin a man can descend, even with all that spiritual background! The higher the pinnacle of blessing, authority, and publicity he has attained by grace, the deeper and more staggering can be his collapse. There is never a day in any man's life but that he is dependent upon the grace of God for power and the blood of Jesus for cleansing. If ever you pray for men in positions of Christian leadership, you are praying for those who are the special targets of the attack of the devil.

This was David's background. Here was the sort of man who slipped, whom Satan defeated and humiliated, the man who crashed so low. "Wherefore let him that thinketh he standeth take heed lest he fall" (I Corinthians 10:12). As I think of what happened (the events are recorded in II Samuel 11), of this I am sure, it did not happen all at once. This matter of Bathsheba was simply the climax of something that had been going on in his life for twenty years. Indeed, those of us who have been studying his life perhaps will have seen certain symptoms indicating that there was this kind of trouble ahead. I purposely have not gone into any detail about it, knowing that I would come to this particular point in due course.

For instance, we read: "David took him more concubines and wives [plural, many of them] out of Jerusalem, after he was come from Hebron" (II Samuel 5:13). This was a direct violation of God's command. In Deuteronomy 17, God laid down specific laws for the one who would be king over His people. There were three things from which he had to abstain: "he shall not multiply horses to himself" (17:16); "neither shall he greatly multiply to himself silver and gold" (17:17); and the third was "neither shall he multiply wives to himself, that his heart turn not away" (17:17).

From previous studies you will recall that David, when he was victorious in battle, slew the horses in obedience to God's command. He dedicated the silver and gold, bringing them to the temple in obedience to God's command. But on the deeper issue, the thing that was not outside himself but in him—when it came to the matter of the opposite sex, he broke God's law.

Why did God make those three rules for a king? Because there is a price to pay for leadership; such a man cannot afford to live as near as he dare to that which is wrong. If you would attain to any position of Christian leadership, you must recognize that there is a price to pay. Sometimes it is the price of loneliness; sometimes it is being misunderstood or having but few friends. It may be something else, but one thing is certain: there is the price to pay of keeping your life transparently right with God. On that issue David failed.

Twenty years before David saw Bathsheba, he had sown the seeds of fleshly indulgence, but we see here in II Samuel 11 how this particular incident began. It was the time when kings went forth to battle and Joab, David's faithful commander-in-chief who stood by him through thick and thin, was at the battle front, while "David tarried still at Jerusalem" (II Samuel 11:1).

In an indolent, lazy mood, in a moment when he was off-duty and alone, there came, to quote the words of Nathan, "a traveller," a thought, which led to a look, which developed into a desire, which formed itself into action. To satisfy that thought he went, in effect, to the house of a poor man who had but one ewe lamb, in spite of the fact that he had so much himself: "his own flock" (II Samuel 12:3-4).

I notice that Scripture puts the entire blame for the situation upon

David; it doesn't implicate Bathsheba. Before the king she was obliged to yield, and in a few moments this great man had blackened his character, imperiled his kingdom, dishonored the name of His God, and caused the enemies of the Lord to blaspheme. It was all because there came "a traveller" and he yielded. Later came that awful moment when the truth dawned on David that his sin could not be hidden, and his blood ran hot and cold. Bathsheba sent him the news that he was going to be found out; a child would be born.

Somehow this thing must be covered up, so he sent a messenger to Joab at the battlefront demanding that Uriah be sent back home. Bathsheba's husband came back at David's command, but he was a brave soldier who would not indulge himself as David had done. He refused to go to his own house, even when David made him drunk. Therefore the king sent him back to the battle with orders to Joab, "See to it that Uriah is put right in the front line of the battle and leave him there to die." When Uriah was dead, he could not disown the child that would be born.

I wonder what Joab thought when he received his king's command that amounted to murder. "It is a strange thing how my master can write wonderful psalms and can worship God so beautifully, yet behave like this!" But Joab saw to it that Uriah died. In fact, he conducted the battle in a ridiculous fashion, going right up to the very walls of the city and asking for trouble! When he sent back news of the battle, and the death not only of Uriah but of many brave soldiers who also fell, he said to the messenger, "If David is angry because we have lost the battle, tell him that Uriah is dead. That will satisfy him!"

David's reply was to say, in effect, "I don't mind about losing the battle—that can happen in war. Uriah is dead: that is what matters to me!" Now that Uriah was dead, he had covered up; the story would never be revealed.

Ah, David, you have reckoned without one vital factor: "The thing that David had done displeased the Lord" (II Samuel 11:27). David thought that killing the man would settle the issue, but he forgot that everything was done in the sight of God. It was all known to Him, and soon David and the world would hear more about it, too!

What a tragedy it was—that a man who had walked with God, a psalmist, a warrior, a king, a great spiritual leader, had trampled all that in the dust in a few moments because of "a traveller"!

You know the perils of an indulgent life, of unguarded moments, of leisure hours, of slackness and lack of discipline with the flesh. I want you to notice that middle life for David (for he was over fifty at this time) did not mean that there was immunity from the attacks of the enemy; there was no lessening of the need for buffeting the body and keeping it in subjection.

Oh, that you and I might finish our course without a blemish like that! You may say, "But David's sin hasn't been my sin." Are you sure about that? Before you clear yourself completely, read Matthew 5:28; the Lord said that "whosoever looketh" is guilty.

Perhaps you are just beginning an association with someone which is out of God's will—or at least, if the association is in God's will, the way you are behaving is not, and you are sowing the seeds of trouble. Who knows but that the climax of disaster is just around the corner!

Young man, listen to me. God will save you from any temptation if you lean upon the Lord Jesus; but if you deliberately seek companionship where you are going to be tempted, you will have to take the consequences. If you deliberately walk into a situation where the devil can trip you up, heaven will not help you until you have learned your lesson, that the only way of escape is to steer clear of trouble.

Have you attained a place of authority in Christian circles? Have you become a missionary, a teacher of the Word, a preacher, an evangelist? If you have slackened in the discipline of your own personal life, you may get dragged down by this kind of net. May the Lord deliver you from it!

Notice David's penitence here! The implication is obvious—I need not go into detail, but for at least twelve months David hardened his heart and refused to acknowledge his fault. It was only after the child was born that he eventually came to his senses. Do you wonder what that year was like? David tells us in Psalm 32:3-4: "When I kept silence, my bones waxed old through my roaring all the day long. For day and night thy hand was heavy upon me: my moisture is turned into the drought of summer. Selah."

"Selah"—think of that! David, David, what a price to pay!

This was a man who had walked and talked with God and had known the power and authority of the Holy Spirit. But as he resisted the pressure of the Spirit and fought against confession of sin, his "bones waxed old." All the moisture of heaven lapsed into drought; everything was dry and barren in his soul.

But one day Nathan came and told him a parable about a rich man and a poor man who lived in the same city. The rich man had much and the poor man had only one precious little ewe lamb. There came a hungry traveler to the rich man's house, and instead of taking from his own flock, which was large, he stole all that the poor man had, the one little lamb. Almost before Nathan was through with his story David burst out, "Why, that man should be killed, and restore fourfold that which he had taken!"

I must pause to ask that you notice how David had become very harsh toward other people. The law did not say anything about the robber of a lamb being killed, although it certainly said he had to restore fourfold. But David said that a man who behaved like that should be killed also.

Have you observed that when you excuse sin in your own life you become very critical of it in other people? The person who hides an uneasy conscience and a sense of guilt may flash out in anger against the sin of another. Is that why some of us are so merciless with the Christian who is tripped up? Is that why we have no gospel for the believer who falls? It may be not because we are very holy, but because we are so unholy, that we condemn the thing in another as we refuse to judge it in our own lives. Let us not forget the words of our Master, "He that is without sin among you, let him first cast a stone" (John 8:7).

At David's outburst the prophet turned to him with the arrow of God that drove right home: "Thou art the man!" Notice how firmly God, through Nathan, reminded David of His goodness over the past years in II Samuel 12:7-9. Those words hit David right down at the roots of his soul and all he could say was, "I have sinned against the Lord." David's only answer to God was Psalm 51; its language reveals the sob of a man whose heart has been broken.

The first impulse, when conviction hits a man, is to run from God, as David did for a year. But the second thought of a man of God is to rush to the wounded side of the Lord Jesus for safety—like Peter who said, "Depart from me, for I am a sinful man, O Lord"; yet later, on that post-resurrection morning by the seashore when John said, "It is the Lord," Peter jumped out of the boat and ran to His side. That may be where you need to go today.

What about God's forgiveness when a man's heart is really broken with conviction, when he puts the label "sin" where God points it out and acknowledges to the Lord, "Against thee, thee only, have I sinned"? David's sin was not against Bathsheba only, it was not against Uriah, but supremely his sin was against God.

Nathan told David, "The Lord also hath put away thy sin; thou shalt not die" (II Samuel 12:13). That was like music to his soul! Sin is desperate and dangerous, and it always brings judgment, yet it cannot quench the love of God. If we confess our sin specifically as David did, then He will forgive us our sin and cleanse us from all unrighteousness.

But there is a word following that bit of comfort which sends a shiver down my spine: "Howbeit. . . ." Yes, there is immediate forgiveness, immediate cleansing, immediate restoration to fellowship with God, but what about the consequences? "Howbeit, because by this deed thou hast given great occasion to the enemies of the Lord to blaspheme, the child also that is born unto thee shall surely die" (II Samuel 11:14).

His sin was forgiven, but the consequences he had to take! When God forgives us and restores us to favor, He uses the rod, too, and life is never quite the same again. Oh yes, He restores His repentant child to fellowship, but sometimes a man has to drink the bitter cup; a forgiven man may still have to reap what he has sown. We will come to this harvest later in our studies on David's life, but remember that this child died. Then one of David's sons treated his sister as David had treated Bathsheba, and his son Absalom became a murderer and a usurper of his father's throne. David went through stormy days, but he knew it was not the judgment of God; it was the chastisement of a loving heavenly Father, "For whom the Lord loveth he chasteneth" (Hebrews 12:6).

As that chastisement cut David's heart to the very depths, then, praise God, the Lord healed the wound. The pendulum began to swing back again the other way, voices began to speak kindly to him again, and love came to his path again at the end of his journey. The people's loyalty returned to him, and before he went to be with the Lord he could still say, "Many are the afflictions of the righteous: but the Lord delivereth him out of them all" (Psalm 34:19).

The Lord sets all our sins in array before His face; even our secret sins are revealed in the light of His countenance. He breaks our hearts and humbles us and brings us to confession and repentance in order to make us holy, to restore to us the years that the locust has eaten, and to present us even yet "faultless before the throne."

Now therefore the sword shall never depart from thine house; because thou hast despised me, and hast taken the wife of Uriah the Hittite to be thy wife.

II SAMUEL 12:10

And it came to pass after two full years, that Absalom . . . commanded his servants, saying . . . Smite Amnon; then kill him, fear not: have not I commanded you? . . . And the servants of Absalom did unto Amnon as Absalom had commanded. . . .

II SAMUEL 13:23-29

And Joab sent to Tekoah, and fetched thence a wise woman, and said unto her, I pray thee, feign thyself to be a mourner. . . .
And the king said unto her, what aileth thee? And she answered . . . thy handmaid had two sons, and they two strove together in the field, and there was none to part them, but the one smote the other and slew him. And, behold, the whole family is risen against thine handmaid, and they said, Deliver him that smote his brother, that we may kill him. . . .
And the king said unto the woman, Go to thine house, and I will give charge concerning thee. . . .
And the woman said . . . the king doth speak this thing as one which is faulty, in that the king doth not fetch home again his banished. For we must needs die, and are as water spilt on the ground, which cannot be gathered up again; neither doth God respect any person: yet doth he devise means, that his banished be not expelled from him. . . .
And the king said, Is not the hand of Joab with thee in all this? . . . And the king said unto Joab . . . bring the young man Absalom again. . . . Let him turn to his own house, and let him not see my face. . . .

II SAMUEL 14:2-24

CHAPTER 22

THE PERIL OF A DIVIDED HOUSE

(II Samuel 12:10—14:33)

THE TITLE OF this message gives but a symptom of something that took place at this period in David's life. I think you will see the connection as we pursue this meditation. I would speak about the safeguards which God places upon the forgiven sinner.

"Now therefore the sword shall never depart from thine house," was the message of God that Nathan delivered to David (II Samuel 12:10). But the prophet also declared, in answer to David's confession, "The Lord also hath put away thy sin" (II Samuel 12:13). This man experienced forgiveness, but God's sentence remained: "The sword shall never depart from thine house."

You will discover in these chapters that David not only received divine pardon for his transgression, but he also began to reap that which he had sown. Something seems to have snapped somewhere: the bonds of integrity in his home life collapsed, and David seemed utterly unable to cope with it. Amnon, his eldest son, treated his half-sister Tamar in the same way David had treated Bathsheba. Absalom, David's spoiled child, treated his brother Amnon as David did Uriah. Meanwhile David, with the awful sense of guilt in his own soul, watched his home and family going to pieces and seemed powerless to do anything about it. Of course he was!

"But when king David heard of all these things, he was very wroth" (II Samuel 13:21). Yes, but as far as discipline was concerned, he was incapable of exercising any. How could he rebuke his son for the crime against a sister when the memory of Bathsheba was in his own heart? How could he possibly discipline Absalom for murder when the death of Uriah was on his own conscience?

Therefore David faced the humiliation of seeing his house divided and his kingdom in danger of collapse because of his personal break-

down. There were very few happy days in his life after this; the storm
set in. David's halfhearted forgiveness of Absalom and his inability to
cope with the whole situation led to rebellion, and before long David
found himself an exile. "For whatsoever a man soweth, that shall he
also reap" (Galatians 6:7).

Is this how God forgives? When God forgives, doesn't He forget?
When a man is cleansed by the blood of Jesus Christ, surely his sin is
wiped out and the consequences of it vanish! Wait a moment! I want
to make a statement and then justify it from this portion of Scripture.
Each of us is either under the judgment of sin which God has never
forgiven, or we are suffering from the chastisement of our heavenly
Father because of sin which He has forgiven.

That which happened in David's home during these years was not in
spite of the fact that God had forgiven him, but because God had forgiven him. The man whom God forgives sometimes has to drink very
deeply of the well which his sin has tapped. In this easy day when we
want cheap forgiveness this may shock you, but I have a responsibility
in the name of the Lord to substantiate these things from Scripture, and
to show you how the chastening hand of a loving heavenly Father is a
very different thing from the judging hand of a holy God.

In order that we may get the picture clearly, let me show you David's
forgiveness of Absalom. The story is in II Samuel 14. Absalom had
become infuriated because of his half-brother's crime against his sister,
so he waited for an opportunity to murder him, and then he ran for
his life from the judgment of his father. What a poor sort Absalom
was! He was a spoiled child with a child's petulance and an old man's
passion. He was extremely proud of his long hair, and he lost his life
because of it. Poor, weak Absalom!

You don't need to be clever to start a lot of trouble. Absalom certainly started plenty, and therefore he had to run for his life. I am
interested to note that David became rather sentimental. A man who
had been tripped up like that often gets sentimental about people, and
in II Samuel 14:1 you see that his soul is longing after Absalom. Of
course, as king he knew that he must punish the evildoer, but as a
father he wanted his son near him.

Captain Joab, faithful but ruthless, came to the rescue. He called for
a wise woman of Tekoah, asking her to put on an act for David's benefit. She sought an audience with the king and told him a story: "I am
a widow with two sons. One of them has killed the other, and now all
my relatives are coming around saying, 'Hand over the murderer to

justice. Let him be killed!' But," she said, using her quaint terminology, "if I do this my coal will be quenched," meaning that she would have no children left (II Samuel 14:2-7).

David by this time was so eaten up with emotion that he promised, "Just leave it to me," and with an oath in the name of the Lord he said, "As the Lord liveth, there shall not one hair of thy son fall to the earth" (II Samuel 14:11).

He guaranteed safety at the expense of justice, and immediately the farsighted woman captured him in her trap. Turning to him she said, in effect, "All right, why don't you practice what you preach? You should welcome Absalom back home instead of banishing him. David, I want you to be like God: He doth devise means that his banished be not expelled from him" (II Samuel 14:12-17).

David, duly impressed with the story, agreed to restore Absalom, but notice how he did it. Joab brought Absalom back, but when that young man returned to the city the king refused to see him (II Samuel 14:21-24). David attempted to keep up some kind of punishment, and Absalom dwelt in Jerusalem for two years without seeing his father's face. The king finally had to give in to pressure because his son had become very difficult to handle, as Joab found. Therefore, the king welcomed his delinquent son back into his presence without any evidence at all on the young man's part of penitence or sorrow. What was the result?

Before David recognized what was happening (at this point he evidently spent a great deal of his time shut away by himself), Absalom was winning the hearts of the people. He sowed seeds of distrust against the king and made himself popular by his attractiveness. He put on a show of luxury as he went around in a chariot with some fifty attendants and, just as surely then as now, luxury will always slacken devotion to God's king. Presently Absalom secured a sudden revolt, and David found himself running for his life.

Perhaps one of the hardest things of all was that Absalom drew away Ahithophel, David's favorite counsellor. "Yea, mine own familiar friend, in whom I trusted, which did eat of my bread, hath lifted up his heel against me" (Psalm 41:9). He was the one the king thought he could trust. But after what David had done, why should he have trusted the man who was Bathsheba's grandfather (cf. Eliam in II Samuel 11:3 and 23:34)? Ahithophel had promptly joined Absalom in the conspiracy against the king.

The sort of forgiveness that David gave to his son Absalom only sowed the seed of a worse rebellion. The king welcomed him back into his presence, but the next thing David knew, he found himself betrayed by the very son whom he had forgiven. From Absalom there was not any show of sorrow, any evidence of repentance or sign of a broken heart.

What kind of forgiveness is that? I will tell you: it is the kind we want from God, but we never get. "O God, forgive us, but please let us go on doing what we are doing! Don't demand of us repentance! Don't demand a broken heart! Don't demand from us a turning away from sin! Lord, please forgive us, for we need to be forgiven; but don't, please don't expect any change!" God refuses those terms altogether; He will never forgive at the expense of justice. In this instance David proved the utter futility of any attempt to do so.

Such was the total inadequacy of David's forgiveness of Absalom, against which I would in contrast point you to the way that God forgives a soul. I must draw upon the woman of Tekoah for this, because she has given me one of the best gospel texts in the Old Testament. As this wise woman said to David: "Neither doth God respect any person: yet doth he devise means, that his banished be not expelled from him" (II Samuel 14:14).

His banished! I wonder how much of the reality of this truth she understood, but I would say that she certainly described you and me: "His banished." We are banished because of sin, and not merely banished, but in flight from God as Absalom was in flight from David, condemned and guilty before Him who is absolutely holy and just. In so many instances, therefore, we drift into a life of practical atheism, even in church circles. God is not in all our thoughts, nor is He really relevant in our daily lives. Even in our religious experience we seek things that stir our emotions rather than the reality of His presence.

Banished and in flight—the degradation of our soul is surely revealed in imagining that we are free and happy as long as we live like that. Don't let us get too near God! Let us keep ourselves free, or the situation might become difficult and awkward!

Banished and in flight, but God loves us. He loves His banished. We are still His, no matter how much we may run away from God. Even if we turn away from the King of kings saying, "Lord, I don't want you too near," we are still His. We belong to the Lord by purchase and creation, and this is a relationship that none can deny. We are still His banished, His property, and He wants us back at His side. As David longed for Absalom, so the Lord longs far more for the banished soul; but because He is a holy and righteous God, there are obstacles in the way.

Let me remind you of them. Forgiveness, that is, the removal of the consequences of sin and restoration to the favor of God, is not so easy as we may imagine. The popular idea is, of course, that God is love, therefore He must forgive. But if forgiveness is to be adequate, it must accomplish two things. In the first place, the gulf between sin and righteousness must be maintained. There must be absolutely no compromise, no attempt to reduce the absolute purity and holiness of God, and no attempt to minimize the depths of degradation of the human soul. Sin is sin; righteousness is righteousness. Of course, that kind of theology is very unpopular today, when so many people just lower the standard of righteousness and laugh at sin and put the two together. But it is not so with God!

To say that God will forgive us, that He must forgive us anyhow because He is love, may be charitable, but it is cruel. If God forgives on the basis of lowering His standard of righteousness and winking at sin, then the whole foundation of His sovereignty melts away, and His absolute authority and holiness crash to the ground. Of course He must pardon, but only on the condition that there is no tampering with justice. He will pardon only if there is no tendency to say, "It didn't matter very much anyway that I did that."

May God write it on your soul: if the pardon you want is that God should wink at your sin, He will not do it. If all you lean upon is that God has ignored your transgressions, that what you have done doesn't really matter to Him, then you are banking your eternity on a broken reed. The first thing that God must do in offering forgiveness is to maintain that righteousness is still righteousness, and sin is called sin, and those two will never be brought together.

The second thing that God must do if He would pardon is to turn that man who is forgiven from the secret lust of the old nature to a heart-cry for purity of life. Otherwise, forgiveness will only foster the sin that it has pardoned.

Unless you learn somehow to hate sin, then you will have to be crawling to God every five minutes for more pardon, because you will simply go on sinning. A superficial sense of sin is satisfied with a superficial forgiveness. But let a man once see himself, his real self, then I tell you he wants more than a little twig on the river bank to clutch as he flounders in the foul and muddy water. He wants something firm to which he can hold, something that will never let him down. He begins to say, "Oh, to be saved from myself, dear Lord!"

Does this world look like a place to which we should offer easy forgiveness? With its filth and its vice, its immorality and awful breakdown, is it a place to come with a sunny and syncopated gospel that says, "Come on, get your sins forgiven and go to heaven"? Can I go into the grimness, the sordidness of any great city today with a kind of gospel that says, in other words, "Travel now, pay later"—a kind of easy, jazzy forgiveness? Can I offer pardon without any demand for repentance? I cannot because God does not. He "devises means," and that word is "He plans plannings, He thinks thoughts." God cannot arbitrarily forgive the man who has collapsed: His nature forbids it, His law forbids it, and our good forbids it. Therefore He plans means.

If God's Holy Spirit has brought to you some measure of conviction, I would point you to

> . . . a green hill far away,
> Outside a city wall,
> Where the dear Lord was crucified
> Who died to save us all.
> *Mrs. C. F. Alexander*

It is the cross, and only the cross, which meets God's requirements. At Calvary the gulf between a holy God and sinful man was bridged. That is the miracle of grace!

Think of that great gulf between sin and goodness. Where is there such proof that the wages of sin is death as at the cross? Where is such a demonstration of the holiness and purity of God's law as when my Saviour submitted to it utterly? Where can we learn the hideousness of sin and the hatred of God for it better than in seeing His beloved Son rejected and taunted and crucified? Where do we realize the misery of being banished from the presence of God more than when we hear Jesus cry out, "My God, my God, why hast thou forsaken me?" (Matthew 27:46).

It is only at the foot of the cross that the man who is forgiven learns to hate the sin that separated him from God. God's forgiveness of the human soul can only take place when a guilty soul and a holy God are brought together by faith which claims the price Jesus paid.

David's forgiveness of Absalom was completely inadequate, leading to a further outbreak of sin. God's forgiveness of a man's soul is completely adequate, and a great deterrent to continued sin.

Notice David's reaction to God's forgiveness (II Samuel 15:30). He left the city under the pressure of Absalom's rebellion, going up by the ascent of Mount Olivet, weeping as he went, with his head covered but his feet bare. He was not suffering the sentence of a judge, but the discipline of his heavenly Father.

If David could speak to us today we might ask him, "Why the tears? Because you have been turned out of your kingdom? Because you have lost your throne?" Surely he would answer, "No indeed!" When he went out from Jerusalem what broke his heart was the evidence of his sin in his children and in his kingdom. He had seen everything go to pieces, and the sense of guilt and shame just broke him down.

In II Samuel 16:5-8 is recorded one of the worst things, perhaps, that David had to face. That wretched man Shimei watched him from the other side of the river and cursed him, hitting him when he was down in the dust. Yet David was able to say to Abishai and to all his servants, "Behold, my son, which came forth of my bowels, seeketh my life: how much more now may this Benjamite do it? let him alone, and let him curse; for the Lord hath bidden him" (II Samuel 16:11). David even received the cursing of his enemies as part of the discipline of God: "It may be that the Lord will look on mine affliction, and that the Lord will requite me good for his cursing this day" (16:12). David had no desire to avenge himself. All the curses and abuse that could ever come to him were simply the ministry of God to help him toward perfection and restoration.

That is the kind of forgiveness that God offers at the cost of Jesus' blood. That is what I mean when I say that every man and woman is either under the judgment of God's holiness for sin that has never been taken to the cross, or he is experiencing the chastening hand of a loving heavenly Father. "Whom the Lord loveth, he chasteneth" (Hebrews 12:6).

In spite of all David's failures, as he reacted to the chastening of God he was still the man after God's own heart. You can kick against His chastening and harden your proud heart against it; you can resist and refuse to accept it; you can deny it and become hard and callous, though still fundamental in doctrine.

David's acceptance reminds me of the words of Frederick W. H. Myers as he wrote of St. Paul:

> Yea, Thou forgivest, but with all forgiving,
> Canst not renew mine inner sense again.
> Make Thou, O Christ, a dying of my living!
> Purge from the sin, but never from the pain.

Can you say that to the Lord today? "Lord, don't take off Your chastening hand! May I never go through life feeling anything but pain for the sin of which I have been guilty. Make my living to be a dying in the will of God. May I accept all that comes to me as part of His plan to take the clay that has been spoiled in the hand of the potter and make it again another vessel."

If you want to know what David was saying in his soul, turn to Psalm 3. There we see him accepting his chastening from God and coming to rest in the Lord. He went to sleep quite happily, awakened in the morning quite brightly, for the Lord was his helper. "I laid me down and slept; I awaked, for the Lord sustained me" (Psalm 3:5).

Such is God's forgiveness that I have tried to portray to you. It is not an easy or a cheap thing, but very costly. As you submit to it in your soul and receive the chastening of your heavenly Father, what a precious thing it becomes as it conforms you to the image of His dear Son!

And it came to pass after this, that . . . Absalom said moreover, Oh that I were made judge in the land, that every man which hath any suit or cause might come unto me, and I would do him justice! And it was so, that when any man came nigh to do him obeisance, he put forth his hand, and took him, and kissed him . . . so Absalom stole the hearts of the men of Israel. . . .

And Absalom sent for Ahithophel the Gilonite, David's counsellor . . . the conspiracy was strong; for the people increased continually with Absalom.

And there came a messenger to David, saying, The hearts of the men of Israel are after Absalom. And David said unto all his servants that were with him at Jerusalem, Arise, and let us flee. . . . And the king went forth, and all the people after him . . . and all the Gittites, six hundred men which came after him from Gath, passed on before the king.

Then said the king to Ittai the Gittite, Wherefore goest thou also with us? . . . And Ittai answered the king, and said, As the Lord liveth, and as my lord the king liveth, surely in what place my lord the king shall be, whether in death or life, even there also will thy servant be. . . .

And David went up by the ascent of mount Olivet, and wept as he went up, and had his head covered, and he went barefoot: and all the people that was with him covered every man his head, and they went up, weeping as they went up.

And one told David, saying, Ahithophel is among the conspirators with Absalom. And David said, O Lord, I pray thee, turn the counsel of Ahithophel into foolishness. And it came to pass . . . behold, Hushai the Archite came to meet him with his coat rent, and earth upon his head: Unto whom David said . . . return to the city, and say unto Absalom, I will be thy servant, O king . . . then mayest thou for me defeat the counsel of Ahithophel. . . . So Hushai David's friend came into the city, and Absalom came into Jerusalem.

II SAMUEL 15:1-37

CHAPTER 23

THE FELLOWSHIP OF HIS
SUFFERINGS

(II Samuel 15:1-37)

As WE HAVE studied the life of David as the making of a man of God, we now come to the subject of identification with a rejected king as one of the great principles that is necessary in the life of a child of God today. When this principle is lacking, the life is only a heap of ashes on the grate—no fire but all smoke. This principle of identification with a rejected king is something strange and unusual, but so vital that when it grips the heart it sets it on fire. It causes us to speak to the Lord Jesus as Ittai spoke to David in the hour of his rejection.

One of the saddest episodes of the whole Bible is the story of David's flight from Absalom; it was one of the most tragic moments in his life. Perhaps the most pathetic thing of all was that deep down in his heart he was conscious that he deserved what he got. As we have seen in a previous study, this was the chastisement of a heavenly Father because of the sin of his life. He was now being put through the fire, through the testing, by the hand of a loving God.

His attitude at this moment was surely one which honored the Lord. His heart-cry is found in the language of Psalm 62. They are familiar words, but have you ever recognized them in their true context? King David, rejected by his people, was going out into the loneliness and desolation of exile. His son and most of his relatives and friends, who had hailed him "Hosanna, welcome to the king!" were now in revolt against him. Then listen to him say, "My soul, wait thou only upon God; for my expectation is from him. He only is my rock and my salvation: he is my defence; I shall not be moved. In God is my salvation and my glory: the rock of my strength, and my refuge, is in God" (Psalm 62:5-7).

As David left Jerusalem, he paused at the city limits and looked

215

around at the company of people who followed him in this moment of rejection. And whom did he see? A great company from the people of Israel? No, they were all against him. His family? No. He saw a group of rough, rugged Philistines—all of them foreigners—six hundred of them headed up by Ittai of Gath. How have such people come to be identified with David? Why are they true to the king when others, those who had been so excited and devoted at the moment of his coronation, have now turned their backs upon him? Why has this rough troop of hard men decided to follow the king even into exile?

I'll tell you why. These men had watched him in the difficult days before his coronation. They had been with him in Gath when, though anointed, he had fled from Saul, and they had watched his reactions. Something in him had brought from them great admiration and love. The ruggedness of their hearts had been melted as they walked and talked with David, and now gushing rivers of living water flowed from them in dedication to his cause. In the moment of his rejection, that is what made them say, "In what place my lord the king shall be . . . there also will thy servant be" (II Samuel 15:21).

Whatever David's fate, they were going to share it. Although his back was to the wall and his own people were rebelling against him, they refused to desert him. Following him meant danger or even death, but their declaration was "whether in death or life, even there also will thy servant be."

These rugged Philistines have preached a sermon to my heart. Are these the only people, this rough heathen-born crowd, who will remain true to him now that his subjects have turned away in revolt? The vow of loyalty in which this group of men pledged themselves to David gives us words in which you and I may express with our lips and hearts our dedication to our rejected King Jesus: "As the Lord liveth, and as my lord the king liveth, surely in what place my lord the king shall be, whether in death or life, even there also will thy servant be."

In the lives of this group of men there is unquestionably a surrender to the will of the king, a yielding that is not slavery, but a happy and blessed liberty. It is not enforced by compulsion; it arises freely from hearts that are tender, hearts from which the hardness has been dispersed. Therefore, as David went out of the city, this group of men— all tough warriors—were the ones who committed themselves to the king's cause and to his will, while David's lukewarm supporters chose the winning popular side.

Let me say to you very lovingly that Jesus is only King when your will and His will agree together. Where His will and yours coincide there is strength and a quality of divinely imparted life. Where they differ, there is weakness. Vital Christian experience is so simple: Christ's will is your will. You are only Christian to the extent that this is true; you are not one inch further than that in spite of all your professions. The word "Christian" means "Christ's man," and whenever your will diverges from His will, then at that point you are not His man. You belong to Him only when you think as He thinks and love as He loves and will as He wills. When you accept His commandments as the principle of your life, His example as the pattern to follow, and His providence, whether it seems to be for good or ill—when you accept thankfully all that is sufficient for your need, then you are His man.

If you think that this is slavery, I would remind you that it is the kind of sacrifice you give to someone you love. You give it to husband or wife; you give it to mother or child. You see it in friend for friend; you see it in all sorts of intimate relationships. But what a tragic thing it is to contrast that devotion on the human level with our lack of devotion in relationship to the God who loved us and gave Himself for us.

Jesus once said, with a coin in His hand, "Whose is this image and superscription?" To whom did it belong? He answered His critics, "Render therefore unto Caesar the things which are Caesar's; and unto God the things that are God's" (Matthew 22:21).

To whom do you belong? As plainly as the emperor's head was on that coin, so the image of Christ is stamped upon your life and therefore you belong to Him. Your heart can only rest in a love that is perfect, a will that is absolute, a holiness that is complete. Frustration is the inevitable result if you surrender your will to other people, and fail to do it in your relationship with the Lord.

"In God is my salvation and my glory: the rock of my strength, and my refuge, is in God," David said (Psalm 62:7). God comes to your life in the person of Jesus Christ, who gave Himself utterly for you on Calvary, and He asks you to yield yourself wholly to Him saying, "He that loseth his life for my sake shall find it" (Matthew 10:39).

Have you ever paused to contrast the affection that flows from your heart to husband, wife, parent, child, lover, or friend with the coolness of your heart toward the Lord? Did you ever stop to contrast the willingness with which you sacrifice for other people and the grudging way in which you sacrifice anything for the sake of Jesus? Have you ever paused to contrast the sense of desolation when some loved one is taken from you with your comparative indifference to the presence and reality of the Lord Jesus?

Yet, if you are truly His, the measure of your power to love somebody is the measure of your obligation to love your Lord. Your capacity to love, to sacrifice, to surrender, which so often is given to others but withheld from God, is the measure of your responsibility to love Him with all your heart. Surrender to the King is real only when it comes from personal devotion and love for Him.

This little band of foreign men, whose hearts had felt the warmth of David's presence, who had seen his patience in the time of suffering, who had walked with him in the days of his rejection, these men who were close to David loved him. Living so close to him made them conscious of his greatness, and his love broke up the hardness of their hearts. So in the day of crisis, while other people, who were what you might call fair-weather followers, were deserting him, this group of men followed him and shared the fellowship of his sufferings.

Are you a fair-weather follower of Christ? There never was a time in all history when a clear identity with Jesus Christ in the day of His rejection is more needed than in this world that cares nothing for the things of God. But His service would be slavery and pure legalism unless it springs from a life that walks and talks with Him, and a heart that loves Him. Therefore, surrender to the will of the King is not a forced obligation; it must be a glad devotion of the heart.

There is another part to the sermon that this rugged crowd preaches to us: self-sacrifice to the purpose of the king. Their declaration of loyalty was no lighthearted promise given when David was a popular hero. Far from it! Their pledge wasn't given in a moment of enthusiasm, when everything was going right. It was given when everything was going wrong! It was commitment in the time of rebellion, when David's kingship amounted to nothing and his authority was unrecognized. At that time they offered the sacrifice of their lives for his sake. They just believed that it was right to be with David instead of with Absalom, that it was better to be with the few who followed the king than with the crowd who rejected him.

That is the kind of obedience Christ wants today. Whose side are you really on? Are you ready to surrender much that other people enjoy, much that the self-life would be only too thankful to have? Then your self-sacrifice for Christ will cause you to say, as Nehemiah used to say, "So did not I, because of the fear of God" (Nehemiah 5:15).

Self-sacrifice for the purpose of the King involves identity with His will and His way at the cost of refusing to listen to other claims that might be legitimate or delightful, but which are not His will for you. To take orders from the King of kings and to say as David said, "My soul, wait thou only upon God; for my expectation is from him," is to discover that something happens in your life, exactly what happened to this rugged crowd—their hardness of heart was melted.

I understand that an expert astronomer could point out to us a star in space which had been quite insignificant, almost invisible, until suddenly it seemed to have caught fire and now it stands out in shining brilliancy, flaming with light. When the thing that we are talking about happens in the life of a fellow or girl, a man or woman, when they see that the only thing in life that matters is to be on God's side completely, when they recognize this principle of self-sacrifice for His purpose, when their surrender is inspired by love for the Lord, I tell you, that Christian begins to take fire. I have seen it so often.

A fellow has come up and said, "Why, I have been saved for years, but it didn't make much difference in my life. I was forgiven; I knew I was a child of the King, but it was more theory to me than reality. Suddenly I saw the simplicity of the victorious life: it is just submission to the totality of the will of God, a surrender of my all to the purposes of the King." That is when the fire begins to burn.

But my heart is heavy for many who profess so much, yet go through their whole Christian life and never seem to know that truth at all. Surrender may have been theory, but it has not been reality for them. What a reckoning it will be for them on that great judgment day! The fire has never burned, the heart has never been softened, the temper has never been controlled. They say they are "Christ's men," but I wonder!

Yet the answer is so basic and simple. The need is not more theological learning, nor more intelligent appreciation of the Bible, nor a greater understanding of truth. It is that measure of spiritual crisis which brings a man—body, soul, and spirit—unreservedly to the feet of the King of kings in total commitment to Him. I wonder how many of us have really arrived at that place. But when the fire begins to burn and we know that our vow unto the Lord has been accepted, we would never go back.

Self-sacrifice for the purpose of the King is something that this group of Philistines teaches us from this Old Testament story. But there is another part still, and I would call it absolute satisfaction with the presence of the king.

I think there is nothing so sad in a man's life as when his heart's surrender is misdirected, when other people claim what Jesus Christ deserves, when the Lord is given only the little bits left over, the things that don't count and don't cost, when home and material things, or even human affections, crowd out the one relationship for which we were made.

In a dramatic story from the Book of Daniel, when the heathen king Belshazzar had his drunken feast, the writer tells us that they used the golden vessels that were taken from the house of God at Jerusalem. The Babylonian king and his princes, his wives, and his concubines drank toasts to their gods from these vessels.

But how often our hearts, with the mark of Christ's ownership upon them (for whether we recognize the ownership or not doesn't make any difference in the fact), have been filled with the poison of other affections as we have served other gods. We have devoted our surrender and sacrifice to things that are utterly unworthy of those who claim to be children of the King.

David himself said in Psalm 119:165, "Great peace have they which love thy law": the peace of conscience, the peace of self-surrender, the peace of casting the whole burden upon His shoulders—the limit of our responsibility is to walk the road of His choosing. That is the tranquil life, the resting life, the life that has found peace.

To lay down your will before God is to find the place of rest and of satisfaction with the presence of Jesus Christ. To yield to Him and to obey His will makes your life quiet and strong and confident. That is the secret of removing tension. That kind of person has found his rest because he has faced the simplicity of total surrender to all the good and perfect and acceptable will of God. Oh, the satisfaction that comes to a heart that is yielded like that! The only true peace and satisfaction that a man can ever get in this life comes from the presence, the power, and the reality of Jesus Christ in the life.

When our rejected King returns one day, those who shared in His sufferings, those who have been identified with Him in His rejection, those who have followed Him right through whatever the path may have been, they are the ones who will reign with Him forever. "As the Lord liveth, and as my lord the king liveth, surely in what place my lord the king shall be . . . even there also will thy servant be" (II Samuel 15:21).

What does this sermon say to your heart? From the example of this group of men who in the day of David's rejection walked loyally with him into a future that was unknown, whose hearts had been softened, and out of whose lives there flowed the rivers of devotion, I am suggesting to you these simple, basic things that lie at the heart of Christian experience: total surrender to the will of God, sacrifice for the purpose of God in the life, and satisfaction in the presence of Christ day by day.

Those of you who profess to have known the Lord Jesus for many years and to be His followers, is this something you have failed to face? Is that why our cities do not feel the impact of Christianity? Is that why multitudes go on their way casually rejecting the Lord? Is it because they never meet people who are identified with Christ in His rejection, who really have put Him first in their hearts, to whom His will matters more than anything?

When you come to Him in surrender, the fire will begin to glow in your heart, and the reality of His indwelling power and authority will bring heaven very near and make Christ precious and real to your soul. But how dull and how dangerous it is to go through life like a machine, grinding out the work, going through the feverish routine, the irritations and the frustrations, with lack of rest and lack of reality!

If from your heart you can say to the Lord Jesus who loved you and gave Himself for you, "Lord, as Thou dost live, in whatever place my King shall be, even there will Thy servant be also," out from your being will shine the glowing flame of the Spirit of God, the reality of the presence of Christ, and your life will be different forevermore!

And it was told Joab, Behold, the king weepeth and mourneth for Absalom. And the victory that day was turned into mourning unto all the people . . . the king cried with a loud voice, O my son Absalom, O Absalom, my son, my son!

And Joab came into the house to the king, and said, Thou hast shamed this day the faces of all thy servants, which this day have saved thy life. . . . In that thou lovest thine enemies, and hatest thy friends. . . . Now therefore arise, go forth, and speak comfortably unto thy servants. . . . Then the king arose, and sat in the gate. . . .

And all the people were at strife throughout all the tribes of Israel, saying, The king saved us out of the hand of our enemies. . . . And Absalom, whom we anointed over us, is dead in battle. Now therefore why speak ye not a word of bringing the king back?

And king David sent to Zadok and to Abiathar the priests, saying, Speak unto the elders of Judah, saying . . . Ye are my brethren, ye are my bones and my flesh: wherefore then are ye the last to bring back the king? . . . And he bowed the heart of all the men of Judah, even as the heart of one man; so that they sent this word unto the king, Return thou, and all thy servants.

So the king returned, and came to Jordan. And Judah came to Gilgal, to go to meet the king, to conduct the king over Jordan. . . . And all the people went over Jordan. . . .

Then the king went on to Gilgal . . . and all the people of Judah conducted the king, and also half the people of Israel. . . . And the words of the men of Judah were fiercer than the words of the men of Israel.

II SAMUEL 19:1-43

CHAPTER 24

BRING BACK THE KING!

(II Samuel 19:1–43)

WHEN DAVID WENT into exile he left a friend of his in the court of Absalom, Hushai the Archite, in order that he might defeat the counsel of Ahithophel, David's one-time friend who had deserted him. When Absalom decided on his strategy for attacking David, the counsel of Hushai prevailed against the counsel of Ahithophel. David was warned; his army was prepared, and he turned the scale of battle against Absalom.

Ahithophel committed suicide when his advice was rejected, a man embittered and frustrated in his attempt to get revenge for David's treatment of his granddaughter Bathsheba. The rebellion was completely broken when Absalom was killed by the ruthless Joab, in spite of David's plea that whoever found him should deal kindly with him.

Now the way was wide open for David to return to Jerusalem and claim his kingdom. However, we find in II Samuel 19 that David didn't lift a finger to re-establish his authority. It would seem a golden opportunity, while the rebel forces were in confusion, for David to come straight back to Jerusalem and enter the city in great triumph. But the moment of David's return was not a dramatic entry into the affairs of Jerusalem, or by his intervention to crush the opposition. His return to sovereignty was decided by the voluntary submission of his kinsmen and by their loving obedience to his will.

That is clearly brought out in the language of II Samuel 19:12. It is the voice of David speaking, the voice of the exiled king, waiting to come back and assume authority over his people, but refusing to do so without a unanimous vote in favor of his return from those who were his own brethren, his own tribe. David refused to move in and establish his authority until he was asked, until he had the submission and obedience of his people. Why should that be? Why shouldn't David have

gone back to Jerusalem immediately and assumed his authority, putting
an end to the confusion?

I'll tell you why. You remember that Judah was to be David's law-
giver; he said so himself in Psalm 60:7. The ancient promise given by
Jacob in the blessing of his children was that "The sceptre shall not
depart from Judah, . . . until Shiloh come" (Genesis 49:10). It was
through Judah that David's authority was going to be made effective.
The position of Judah was one of privilege and responsibility. They
were his own people, and until they submitted and gladly obeyed him,
his reign would not be established.

Therefore, David waited while Israel debated and discussed the subject, until there came a momentous crisis described in II Samuel 19:14-
15: "He bowed the heart of all the men of Judah, even as the heart of
one man; so that they sent this word unto the king, Return thou, and
all thy servants. So the king returned, and came to Jordan."

I want to flash New Testament truth upon this Old Testament story,
a truth that somehow challenges my heart. How often we say, as Christian people, that we are living on the verge of our Lord's return. We
believe in the personal and imminent return of the Lord Jesus Christ
to reign in authority and power. We do not believe that this world
will ever be Christianized; we do believe that it must be evangelized,
but there is a big difference. This world will not become Christian by
the preaching of the gospel, but it will know peace and happiness only
under the personal reign of our Lord Jesus Christ.

How often I hear people say, "Things can't go on much longer as
they are. Surely Christ must be coming soon!"

Has it ever occurred to us that we have a personal responsibility to
fulfill before our Lord can come again? Will it shock you when I say
that I do not believe that it is possible for Him to come today? I want
to substantiate that statement from the Word of God, and to give you
three basic propositions from this Old Testament story to bring out
New Testament truth. I pray that these things may burn into your
heart and soul.

My first proposition is that the return of the King is demanded by
the suffering of the world. You get a glimpse of that in II Samuel 19:1-
10, the kind of thing that happens when the king is rejected: "And all
the people were at strife throughout all the tribes of Israel, saying, The
king saved us out of the hand of our enemies, and he delivered us out
of the hand of the Philistines; and now he is fled out of the land for
Absalom. And Absalom, whom we anointed over us, is dead in battle.

Now therefore why speak ye not a word of bringing the king back?"
The absence of David meant the presence of strife and frustration.
The folly of their allegiance to Absalom was clear—it had brought only
misery and confusion. They were on the wrong side; they had rejected
their true king, and therefore the situation was full of unrest.

In the absence of the Lord Jesus Christ (for remember He is absent
in His person, although He is present within His body the Church by
the Holy Spirit), the only true Prince of peace, what is the condition of
the world today? Is it not intensified suffering and unrest? The longer
He is absent, the greater the suffering, until the pressure of the cloud of
fear is almost at the bursting point.

This statement is supported not only by evidence in the world around
us, but by the words of the Lord Jesus Himself, "Ye shall hear of wars
and rumours of wars: see that ye be not troubled: for all these things
must come to pass, but the end is not yet. For nation shall rise against
nation, and kingdom against kingdom: and there shall be famines, and
pestilences, and earthquakes, in divers places. All these are the beginning of sorrows. Then shall they deliver you up to be afflicted, and shall
kill you: and ye shall be hated of all nations for my name's sake"
(Matthew 24:6-9).

Again, in Paul's second letter to Timothy we read this: "This know
also, that in the last days perilous times shall come. For men shall be
lovers of their own selves, covetous, boasters, proud, blasphemers, disobedient to parents, unthankful, unholy, Without natural affection,
truce-breakers, false accusers, incontinent, fierce, despisers of those that
are good, Traitors, heady, highminded, lovers of pleasures more than
lovers of God; Having a form of godliness, but denying the power
thereof: from such turn away" (II Timothy 3:1-5).

Exploding world populations, the cry from underprivileged nations
for freedom at any cost, the staggering increase in crime—these and
many other symptoms with which we are only too familiar give ample
support to the descriptions of the time just before His coming which I
have read to you from the Word of God. The desperate need of this
poor world is for peace and rest, for liberty and freedom, for justice and
deliverance. None of these things are possible except under the rule of
the King of righteousness. The return of the King is demanded by the
suffering of the world. The anguished cry of humanity is begging for
the return of the only One by whose reign and power the suffering
can be ended.

Then why doesn't He come?

My second proposition is this, that the return of the King is delayed by the sinfulness of His people. David said, "Ye are my bones and my flesh: wherefore then are ye the last to bring back the king?" (II Samuel 19:12).

Our Lord said, "And this gospel of the kingdom shall be preached in all the world for a witness unto all nations: and then shall the end come" (Matthew 24:14). "And the gospel must first be published among all nations" (Mark 13:10). These are the Master's own words. Of course He must return to reign in power and glory. There must be a millennium in which Jesus Christ personally rules out of Zion for a thousand years. God's Word says so! Then why—with the cry of suffering humanity to which there is no answer except the coming of Jesus Christ—why doesn't He come?

It is because we haven't obeyed His command. Peter writes something that stirs my heart. "Seeing then that all these things shall be dissolved, what manner of persons ought ye to be in all holy conversation and godliness, Looking for [listen to this!] and hasting unto the coming of the day of God" (II Peter 3:11-12). The English Revised Version has it, "Looking for and hastening the coming of the king."

Is it possible for us to hasten the day when Jesus comes? Yes, it is. Is it possible for us to delay it? It certainly is!

For a thousand years His authority is going to be demonstrated through people who have submitted to Him and obeyed Him, and who will live and reign with Him on earth. Through the church will be made known "unto the principalities and powers in heavenly places . . . the manifold wisdom of God" (Ephesians 3:10). Through a body of believers obedient to all His commands, Jesus Christ is going to establish His rule throughout the earth. But the disobedience of His church delays the fulfillment.

Only 9 per cent of the world's population speaks the English language, and ninety per cent of Christian work is being done among that 9 per cent. In other words, only 10 per cent of Christian people are among the 91 per cent who speak other languages. I believe that the population of the world is somewhere around two billion eight hundred million people. Of those, only eight hundred million call themselves Christian. That means that two billion are still pagan. Of the three thousand different languages of the world, the Bible—or at least part of it—is translated into only one thousand languages as yet. Actually, I believe the figures are that the complete Bible is in just over two hundred languages, and the New Testament in some two hundred fifty more, and at least one Gospel in over six hundred languages.

Two thousand tongues are without the Book, without any portion of the Word of God, and yet we read, "Thou art worthy . . . for thou wast slain, and hast redeemed us to God by thy blood out of every kindred, and tongue, and people, and nation" (Revelation 5:9). That means that when we get to heaven there will be people there not from some tongues, not from some tribes, not from some nations, but from every tribe and every tongue and every nation. There will be no exception; out of every one of them will come those who have been redeemed by blood.

Yet today as we sit in our churches, there are multitudes—tribe after tribe, nation after nation—who have never yet heard the gospel of Jesus Christ. As the suffering of this world intensifies, as the cry of humanity arises for peace, liberty, and justice, we know that there is only one answer: the coming of the King. What then is our alibi before God for failing to take the message to the uttermost parts of the earth? That is why I believe that Jesus Christ cannot come today: because His people have failed to obey His command to preach the gospel to every creature.

As I was reading recently in the Book of Ezekiel, I came across these words which, although their primary application is to Israel, certainly have an application to us today: "So thou, O son of man, I have set thee a watchman unto the house of Israel; therefore thou shalt hear the word at my mouth, and warn them from me. When I say unto the wicked, O wicked man, thou shalt surely die; if thou dost not speak to warn the wicked from his way, that wicked man shall die in his iniquity; but his blood will I require at thine hand. Nevertheless, if thou warn the wicked of his way to turn from it; if he do not turn from his way, he shall die in his iniquity; but thou hast delivered thy soul. Therefore, O thou son of man . . . speak, saying . . . As I live, saith the Lord God, I have no pleasure in the death of the wicked; but that the wicked turn from his way and live: turn ye, turn ye from your evil ways; for why will ye die, O house of Israel?" (Ezekiel 33:7-11).

Do you get the significance of that portion? We may long for the return of the Lord Jesus, and believe that the only hope for our suffering world is that He should come back, but our disobedience to His command to preach the gospel to every creature delays His coming and prolongs and intensifies the suffering. What is it going to be like one day to face the judgment seat of Christ in the light of these facts?

My third proposition is that the return of the King is dependent upon our submission to the vision.

See what had taken place to make it possible for David to come back: "He bowed the heart of all the men of Judah, even as the heart of one man; so that they sent this word unto the king, Return thou, and all thy servants. So the king returned" (II Samuel 19:14-15).

David had made his appeal to Judah, "You are my people, you are bone of my bone, flesh of my flesh. Why are you the last to bring back the king?" And that appeal had reached their hearts—not simply their minds, but their hearts. He had bowed the heart of his people, and made them willing, and therefore he would come back to rule. Through his people who were obedient he was enabled to return and demonstrate the power and blessedness of his authority.

What did it take to bring David back? The unanimous surrender of the people of God to the purpose of David—that was what opened up the way for his return.

What is it going to take to bring Jesus back? Exactly the same, and nothing less than that. The longer we fail in surrender and obedience, the greater is our judgment. The Lord looks down upon us, His people, and He says, "Ye are My brethren, ye are My bones and My flesh [ye are My body—that is what the church is]: wherefore then are ye the last to bring back the King?"

The return of the King is dependent upon our submission, our obedience to the vision, and may I say that obedience begins right here at home. What about the ignorance of the people in our cities concerning the gospel? I am reminded of the words of the Apostle Paul, which sometimes we relegate to a foreign missionary context, "For whosoever shall call upon the name of the Lord shall be saved. How then shall they call on him in whom they have not believed? and how shall they believe in him of whom they have not heard? and how shall they hear without a preacher? And how shall they preach, except they be sent?" (Romans 10:13-15).

Let me ask you one or two personal questions in the name of the Lord Jesus. Is your life related to God's purpose? As He looks down today, does He say to you, "Why are you the last to bring back the King?" Is your life hastening the return of Christ, or is it delaying it? Have you spoken a word of bringing back the King into some life this week?

Would you make this slogan the resolve of your heart: "In obedience to the vision"? Only when we are surrendered and obedient can Jesus Christ come to rule. In that great millennial kingdom He is going to rule through an obedient people who have obeyed Him now. He will exert His authority here on earth to end all the suffering, unhappiness, and misery in the world. But that great day is held back because the church hasn't completed His commission.

You say to me, "What can I do about that?"

You can first, right now in your own heart, speak a word to bring back the King. Call upon Him: speak from the depths of your soul to the heart of God that you desire the King to take His place of authority in your life. Then you can speak a word to your neighbor, or friend, or family, of bringing back the King, to bring Him into His rightful place in their lives. You can begin right there at home.

You can begin to give sacrificially to the Lord's work, to see that nothing takes precedence over getting the gospel to the last tribe and nation of the world. Everything else is secondary to that purpose; no matter how great our programs and how much we may give to our home-base work, nothing is so important as getting the gospel out to the uttermost parts of the earth.

I think one of the greatest sins of the church today, if I may dare to say so, is the millions of dollars spent on up-to-date buildings and the latest equipment and enormous church plants—when all the time there are multitudes who have never heard, and missionaries ready to go, but without support. This thing is wrong, and I believe that God is judging His people for it.

Nothing matters so much as sending out people supported by the church to spread the news of the Saviour's love. Before God I say that this must have priority in our work and testimony, that in this generation the gospel shall be preached to the uttermost limits of the world until the King comes back.

David the son of Jesse . . . the sweet psalmist of Israel, said . . . He that ruleth over men must be just, ruling in the fear of God. . . . Although my house be not so with God; yet he hath made with me an everlasting covenant, ordered in all things, and sure: for this is all my salvation and all my desire. . . .

These be the names of the mighty men whom David had . . . Adino the Eznite: he lift up his spear against eight hundred, whom he slew at one time. And after him was Eleazar the son of Dodo the Ahohite, one of the three mighty men with David. . . . He arose, and smote the Philistines until his hand was weary, and his hand clave unto the sword: and the Lord wrought a great victory that day; and the people returned after him only to spoil. And after him was Shammah the son of Agee the Hararite . . . he stood in the midst of the ground, and defended it, and slew the Philistines: and the Lord wrought a great victory. . . .

And David longed, and said, Oh that one would give me drink of the water of the well of Bethlehem, which is by the gate! And the three mighty men brake through the host of the Philistines, and drew water out of the well of Bethlehem, that was by the gate, and took it, and brought it to David: nevertheless he would not drink thereof, but poured it out unto the Lord. And he said, Be it far from me, O Lord, that I should do this: is not this the blood of the men that went in jeopardy of their lives? therefore he would not drink it. . . .

And Abishai, the brother of Joab, the son of Zeruiah, was chief among three. And he lifted up his spear against three hundred, and slew them. . . . And Benaiah the son of Jehoiada . . . had the name among three mighty men. . . . And David set him over his guard. Asahel the brother of Joab was one of the thirty . . . Uriah the Hittite: thirty and seven in all.

II SAMUEL 23:1-39

CHAPTER 25

VALIANT IN THE FIGHT

(II Samuel 23:1–39)

EPHESIANS 6:13 IN THE Weymouth translation reads: "Therefore, put on the complete armour of God, so that you may be able to stand your ground in the evil day, and having fought to the end, to remain victor in the field."

We hear from all over the world something of the pressures and problems of missionary service today. Everywhere on the mission fields tensions are increasing. Some have their source in the demand of nations for independence and freedom. In most places missionary personnel is barely adequate to maintain present positions, quite unable to extend the message to the uttermost parts of the earth to hasten the coming of the King. Missionaries also have their own individual burdens: problems of ill health, incompatibility on the field, lack of supplies, and personal spiritual battles.

It is impossible, therefore, for us to regard the mission fields of the world as far-off places which are detached from our own personal life and Christian ministry at home. Missionary service is not one thing over there, and the place of service that we occupy here something quite different. The field is the world, and it is more than ever "one world." As we think of the tremendous responsibility that confronts the church in this missionary task, what is the answer to all the problems and difficulties? I am perfectly sure that the basic need is not just more money, or more equipment, or even more missionary recruits—the answer is on a deeper level than that altogether.

Wherever we may be placed in the will of God, in whatever circumstances we find ourselves, each Christian is a fort of resistance in the name of heaven against all the forces of evil in the world today. When the church is complete and Jesus comes to take to Himself His body, the church, then the world will know the agony of evil which is unresisted by the presence of the people of God. But today the Christian stands in the name of the Lord wherever he is, as a point of resistance to the enemy of righteousness. He doesn't stand alone; he is one of a great army, that company of people who have been redeemed by the precious blood and who share together the life of their Lord, although scattered in different parts of the world.

The triumph of the church as a whole depends upon the personal victory of every Christian. In other words, your victory, your life, your personal testimony, are important to the cause of God today. What happens out in New Guinea, down in the Amazon jungle, over in disturbed Congo, is not unrelated to what happens in your own personal relationship with God and your personal battle against the forces of darkness. Victory for the church on the whole world-front depends upon victory in your life and in mine; "home" and "foreign" situations cannot be detached.

Therefore the answer is not, I repeat, in more money, more equipment, more people; but it is in dedication, commitment, abandonment to God. This we find illustrated by three outstanding men among David's army.

At this point in the story we are looking back from a high peak. David the King, although for a time rejected, had returned and was administering his kingdom. In II Samuel 23 are listed the names of the men who stood with him through thick and thin, men who were identified with him at any cost.

We will mention just three of them. The first was Adino, who slew eight hundred of the enemy on his own (II Samuel 23:8). Another was Eleazar who, when the people of God were in rout and confusion, defied the Philistines to the point of complete weariness until, when the battle was over, he could not unclasp his fingers from his sword (II Samuel 23:9-10). The third, Shammah, stood his ground against an attack of the enemy, defended it, and slew the Philistines (II Samuel 23:11).

These men won victories which had some common factors. In each case it was victory against overwhelming odds. It was victory in the face of utter exhaustion. It was victory when the people of God were in confusion and retreat. It was victory that was won only in the power of the Lord, for we read in two places, "The Lord wrought a great victory that day" (II Samuel 23:10, 12).

Jeremiah said, "I cannot hold my peace [can find no peace], because thou hast heard, O my soul, the sound of the trumpet, the alarm of war"

(Jeremiah 4:19). I believe that the whole missionary enterprise in this century is at stake until we have this Old Testament illustration (which is amplified in New Testament truth in Ephesians 6:13) translated into twentieth-century experience, not only in the lives of a few missionaries in Borneo or South America or Africa, but in the lives of every ransomed soul. There must be the same spirit of dedication in the face of overwhelming odds, in the face of confusion in the ranks of the people of God who are so often in retreat, in the face of absolute physical and mental and often spiritual exhaustion. In the face of all these things we must be able to stand our ground and to remain victor in the field, to be able to say, "The Lord hath wrought a great victory this day!"

But this, I repeat, should be not simply Old Testament history, but your experience and mine in the personal spiritual battles of our lives.

I think of one of our missionary families in New Guinea battle line with the problems of Bible translation into the language of the tribespeople. Another couple, in Southeast Asia, after repeated physical setbacks are again working at the task of getting the Word of God into the language of their people. I think of an elderly missionary, deprived of his loved ones and refusing to retire, spending his last years on the field, and of another couple who have spent their lives in Africa—if you ask them when they will retire, they retort, "Only when we get to heaven!" Another couple, who have served in South America for nearly forty years, first in evangelism, then teaching, followed by a Bible Institute ministry, are now confirming the local churches, traveling ceaselessly to strengthen believers in the Lord.

We receive letters that tell of overwhelming odds, of absolute exhaustion, of weariness of mind, weariness of soul, weariness of body. I begin to ask myself, "What do we know of a life on that level of sacrifice?" Victory in those key battle fronts depends upon victory in your life and mine right now where we are today.

In order to reinforce this truth, let me draw from Ephesians 6. Here Paul writes to the Christians of his day to tell them of a position that must be maintained: "that ye may be able to stand." In other words, where I am in the will of God, in my circumstances, I am to stand my ground.

It was for this purpose that the Lord Jesus Christ threw Himself into the battle on our behalf. Without Him we were not only down, we were conquered and helpless. But now, "being justified by faith, we have peace with God through our Lord Jesus Christ: By whom also we have access by faith into this grace wherein we stand" (Romans 5:1-2).

The power of the cross in a man's life puts him on his feet and enables him to stand in this evil day. Without God and without salvation he was down and helpless, but the Lord has come and lifted him up and set his feet on the Rock. In the spiritual battles that come upon a man of God who is dedicated to the will of God, he is called upon never to flinch, but to stand firm against the adversary in the power of Jesus Christ our Lord.

Is that position being maintained? Are we standing our ground against the enemy of our souls? This is illustrated in the life of Shammah who, in the midst of a Philistine raid, when the people of God were running helter-skelter from the enemy, stood his ground and defied them until he had slain so many that they had to retreat.

Ephesians 6 says not only that we must stand our ground, but that we must wrestle. Our enemy is not flesh and blood, but "the world rulers of this darkness" and "the spiritual hosts of wickedness in the heavenly places" (6:12, ASV). Every man of God is engaged somewhere in the depths of his soul in a spiritual battle. There he has to fight with everything he possesses, not only to maintain his stand (in the passive sense) but, as Paul emphasizes, to wrestle. This is the language of personal conflict, toe to toe with the enemy of our souls to resist evil in the name of the Lord.

It is quite easy for Christian people somehow to avoid the sense of battle and conflict and to take their ease. "Woe to them that are at ease in Zion," says Amos 6:1. Many of us quite readily become so occupied with material things and with our work that it is a long time since we really fought a battle against sin alone on our knees. How much do I really know, and how much do you know, about prayer that resists the powers of darkness and refuses to give in? Have I spent half an hour alone each day this week on my knees in prayer like this? Have you?

Our prayer life, our whole spiritual witness, can lose its priority and become mechanical so that it has no flavor of life or conflict in it at all. Yet victory on the whole battle front depends upon maintaining our position in the name of the Lord Jesus, so that when the enemy flings his fiery darts, we wrestle and stand our ground by God's grace, we fight and refuse to give in.

Are you engaged in this spiritual warfare? Are you standing your ground? In your home life, in your personal walk with God, in your prayer life, in your testimony and witness among your colleagues at the office and your family at home, are you standing your ground today? In the position where God has put you, are you resisting the enemy or are

you in retreat? Have you said, concerning missionary service, "If I pay
my pledge, that is all that is required of me. If I write a letter occasionally, that is all I am expected to do. But as for the impact of spiritual
warfare upon my soul, I know nothing of that—in fact, I have kept
clear of it! It is surely only for the few"? No, no, this is a position to be
maintained by us all.

Paul speaks further of a provision that has been made in order that
we may stand our ground. "Wherefore take unto you the whole armour
of God, that ye may be able to withstand" (Ephesians 6:13). Let us look
briefly at this armor which God has provided in Jesus Christ to enable
the child of God to stand. Here are the details of the power by which we
may resist the devil.

Paul mentions first the girdle of truth about our loins: in other words,
a man's strength derives from his character of godliness and truthful-
ness. He speaks of the breastplate of righteousness, which indicates a
conscience void of offence before God and man, a rightness of life and
conduct that relates a man's belief to his behavior. The shoes of pre-
paredness make feet ready to run errands for the King of kings, ready
to follow the Master wherever He may lead, ready to obey His commands and spread the message of the gospel—next door or anywhere
for Jesus.

Speaking of the shield of faith, Paul says it is "above all." I have no
doubt but that as he was describing this armor he had his eye upon the
Roman soldier who guarded him in the prison from which this letter
was written. He saw the great shield that reached from the man's neck
almost to his feet, covering his body entirely. This part of the Christian's
armor is his complete confidence in the ability of the Lord Jesus to defeat the enemy. Then there was vital protection in the helmet of salvation, and divine power in the sword of the Spirit.

I observe, as I am sure you have, that there is no armor for the back of
the Christian, no provision for running away from the enemy. It is all
for the front and the head: retreat is not considered a possibility for the
child of God. He is to stand his ground.

There is only one offensive weapon, the sword of the Spirit. All else is
for defense, for security against the attacks of the enemy; the Christian
is given only the sword of the Spirit, the Word of God, for subduing the
enemy.

I would remind you that this armor was forged by the Lord Jesus
Christ. That is why He came, that is why He lives to make intercession
for us today. When He entered into Jerusalem the word was, "Behold,

thy King cometh!" At Bethlehem, at Nazareth, in Judea, in Galilee, at Calvary, from the door of the open tomb, He forged this armor for His people. The Bible tells us that "the weapons of our warfare are not carnal, but mighty through God to the pulling down of strong holds" (II Corinthians 10:4).

May I say that one of the greatest perils for us as individual Christians in this day is not simply that we neglect the armor and try to escape the spiritual battle, looking upon the missionary as a unique specimen who faces it in distant lands; one of the greatest perils of our time is that we substitute for heaven's armor something of our own imagination. I could sum up all the pieces of this armor that we have been talking about in one word: character. The very character of the Lamb of God, His integrity and righteousness, purity and holiness, faith and salvation, is the sum of it. Character is the armor that God supplies, and in place of it the church tends to substitute equipment, gimmicks, money, and all kinds of other things in order that somehow it might make an impact upon our day and generation. We have forgotten that our weapons are *not* carnal, but spiritual. However, if we claim and use them, they *are* mighty through God to the pulling down of the strongholds of Satan.

God has made provision in Jesus Christ to enable you to stand your ground right where you are, in your immediate circumstances. Our armor is not outward things, not material equipment or money or anything like that. It is character, the godliness and righteousness and loveliness and sweetness and grace—the very life of Jesus Christ imparted to you and me so that we may be equipped to wield the sword of the Spirit for Him.

No man can use his Bible with power unless he has the character of Jesus in his heart. No man can have impact for God through the use of Scripture in preaching, teaching, or witnessing, if to him it is merely a textbook. His life must be filled with the very life of Jesus Christ. Our offensive weapon depends upon our wearing all the defensive armor; the power to attack depends upon being completely equipped for defense against Satan with every bit of the character of our Lord Jesus. If we are to maintain our position in this evil day, if we are to fight through to the end and remain victor on the field, then we must put on the whole armor of God. If we wear it, then we are able to wield the sword of the Spirit in the power of God.

This is the provision that heaven has made, for it is "not by might, nor by power, but by my spirit, saith the Lord of hosts" (Zechariah 4:6).

Jesus stooped from the throne to the cross in order that He might forge for us a complete armor of His holy character.

There is one other supremely important thing that I must say here, for if you would understand the secret of victory in your own life, there is a Person whom you must meet.

When the Lord Jesus gives us this armor, He is not giving us something apart from Himself. The armor is Christ—not simply His blessings, not just righteousness or truth or faith or salvation or the sword of the Spirit. It is not these apart from Him, but Christ Himself. Paul said also, "Put ye on the Lord Jesus Christ, and make not provision for the flesh, to fulfil the lusts thereof" (Romans 13:14).

All the wealth that is in our wonderful Saviour, of which Satan tries to rob us, all our personal walk with God from which Satan tries to drag us away, and all the victory we need in the warfare, is in the Person of our living Lord from whom Satan tries to keep us separated so that he can defeat us.

I have a serious question to ask you: Have you really met God in Jesus Christ at this level? Do not let that question slip by, because I am persuaded that one reason for our lack of dedication and devotion to the missionary call, and often our lack of ability to stand and win through where we are in the name of the Lord, is because we have not really met God in Jesus Christ like this.

When Joshua had crossed the River Jordan with the people of God, he went out for a walk to survey the first great city that stood in his way, Jericho. As he looked at its battlements, no doubt calculating his resources and how he could use them in order to overcome this mighty obstacle which he dared not leave in the rear, which had to be attacked and possessed—suddenly he encountered a man with a drawn sword in his hand. Joshua challenged him, "Art thou for us, or for our adversaries?" (Joshua 5:13).

The answer came from this One who was none other than the Lord Jesus Christ Himself, who often appeared in this way in the Old Testament: "Nay; but as captain of the host of the Lord am I now come." Immediately Joshua fell on his face before Him asking, "What saith my lord unto his servant?" This mysterious Commander, the living God, answered him, "Loose thy shoe from off thy foot; for the place whereon thou standest is holy" (Joshua 5:15).

On that day the leader of God's people in his day met God in Jesus Christ at a new level. He saw Him as one whose sword was drawn in His hand, whose very presence was holy ground.

What a poor illustration is the story of Eleazar, who fought through one day against the Philistines to the point of absolute exhaustion, so that he could not unclasp his fingers from his sword! What a pale reflection he is of the One who stood by Jericho with a sword in His hand, and who has never, never withdrawn His hand from the battle since He won it for us at Calvary! He imparts His authority to men like Joshua, who meet Him at a new level and recognize that the responsibility of the battle is not their own but God's.

It was not a question of what resources or equipment Joshua had, or the numerical strength of his people. The situation was under the control of the Captain of an invisible host, who could defeat any strategy of the enemy. Joshua gladly handed over the battle entirely to Him.

The word came to Joshua, as it had to Moses, that the ground whereon he stood was holy. As a matter of fact, Joshua was on his face in worship and surrender. But the man who is on his face before God is always standing against the enemy. It is only the man who has met God in Christ, whose heart has been broken at the cross, who has been brought on his face before the Lord, who can stand before the enemy.

If I try to stand before God in my own puny self-righteousness, in self-confidence and arrogance, thinking that I have equipment that can see me through to a life of victory, then I shall fall before the devil. But if I fall before the Lord, I find that I am enabled to stand before the enemy.

I trust that you have come to see that the whole missionary enterprise scattered throughout the world today, with its problems, testings, suffering, shortage of manpower and material and finance, is that way because Christian people in the homelands have not met God in Jesus Christ like that. God is calling, not simply for more money, greater response, more recruits—He is calling for men and women who will fall before Him in surrender that they might stand before the enemy. What is your position today?

And Satan stood up against Israel, and provoked David to number Israel. And David said to Joab and to the rulers of the people . . . bring the number of them to me, that I may know it. And Joab answered . . . are they not all my lord's servants? why then doth my lord require this thing? why will he be a cause of trespass to Israel? Nevertheless the king's word prevailed against Joab. . . .

And God was displeased with this thing. . . . Go and tell David, saying, Thus saith the Lord, I offer thee three things: choose thee . . . Either three years' famine; or three months to be destroyed before thy foes . . . or else three days the sword of the Lord, even the pestilence. . .

And David said . . . let me fall now into the hand of the Lord; for very great are his mercies: but let me not fall into the hand of man. So the Lord sent pestilence upon Israel: and there fell of Israel seventy thousand men. And God . . . said to the angel that destroyed, It is enough, stay now thine hand.

And the angel of the Lord stood by the threshingfloor of Ornan the Jebusite. And David lifted up his eyes, and . . . said unto God, Is it not I that commanded the people to be numbered? . . . let thine hand, I pray thee, O Lord my God, be on me . . . but not on thy people, that they should be plagued. . . .

Then David said to Ornan, Grant me the place of this threshingfloor, that I may build an altar therein unto the Lord. . . . I will verily buy it for the full price: for I will not take that which is thine for the Lord, nor offer burnt offerings without cost. So David gave to Ornan for the place six hundred shekels of gold by weight. And David built there an altar unto the Lord . . . and he answered him from heaven by fire upon the altar of burnt offering. . . .

I CHRONICLES 21:1-30

CHAPTER 26

FIRE FROM HEAVEN

(I Chronicles 21:1-30)

THE ANSWER OF God to the cry of every heart today is fire from heaven. That is the dynamic response of God to the uttermost yielding of ourselves to Him, and I would take this Old Testament story in I Chronicles 21 to show you how this may happen in your life.

By way of introduction, glance with me at the context. The first verse of this chapter has an ominous note about it: "And Satan stood up against Israel, and provoked David to number Israel" (21:1). Here was a direct frontal attack from the adversary focused upon the entire assembly of God's people, but David was the one who bore the brunt of it.

Now this is surely significant. The one whom Satan hates is the Holy Spirit, and therefore his attack is directed against Him as He indwells all of God's redeemed people. But those who bear the brunt of it are, more often than not, those who bear the responsibility of leadership. Satan does not waste time upon the circumference of church life, he goes right to the heart of it. The missionary, the Christian leader, the minister, the ones chosen of God to be undershepherds and to stand in the front line of the battle for Him, are subject to the most dangerous and subtle blows of the enemy of souls.

The particular issue in this case may seem trifling until we consider it through Spirit-anointed eyes. David was determined to number the people, which was actually an evidence of the basic sin of all: pride. It was an indication of his departure from trusting the Lord in every situation to depending upon the flesh. This sin of which David was guilty is the one of which you and I have been guilty over and over again. God will not give His glory to another; he that glorieth must glory in the Lord. In tempting David to pride in his own resources, Satan successfully tripped up the leader of the flock.

Now follow with me as we watch what happens. David learned two things about sin at this time. First of all, he learned that sin inevitably carries with it punishment. Read the solemn words of I Chronicles 21:9-12. David is given the choice of three years' famine, three months to be destroyed before the enemy, or three days in the hand of the Lord. The eternal consequences of sin are forever forgiven in response to confession and repentance, but the temporary consequences of sin, more often than not, have to be faced.

David made a wise choice in verse 13: "Let me now fall into the hand of the Lord; for very great are his mercies: but let me not fall into the hand of man." From the depths of our hearts we would say "Amen" to that. When a Christian leader is defeated by the enemy and his sin exposed, there is little mercy to be found anywhere except in the hand of the Lord; it is the only safe place to be.

Then again, David found that nobody can sin alone. As he saw the angel of the Lord bringing judgment upon the people, seventy thousand men of Israel killed, imagine the agony in his heart as he cried: "Is it not I that commanded the people to be numbered? even I it is that have sinned and done evil indeed; but as for these sheep, what have they done? Let thine hand, I pray thee, O Lord my God, be on me, and on my father's house; but not on thy people, that they should be plagued" (I Chronicles 21:17).

How true this is in our experience! Nobody sins to himself, and so often those who are most affected are those whom the sinner would desire at all cost to escape the consequences. Are you a missionary or a pastor? Have you ever watched the work around you fall apart? Have you ever seen the prayer meetings go to pieces? Have you watched the people to whom you minister face chastisement and times of barrenness? Then, my friend, you know something of the experience of David, as you see the humiliation of your own sin being wrought out in judgment upon others.

Long before, when the people of God entered into the land and were defeated at Ai, the judgment of heaven was, "Israel hath sinned," although it was Achan who was responsible (Joshua 7:11, 20). I wonder how much blessing the church has missed because of the sin of its leaders? God have mercy upon us!

Let us consider in the first place the pressure to which David yielded. David saw, by the threshingfloor of Ornan the Jebusite, the sword of the Lord drawn against him in judgment, "And David lifted up his eyes, and saw the angel of the Lord stand between the earth and the heaven, having a drawn sword in his hand stretched out over Jerusalem" (I Chronicles 21:16). In the city of Jerusalem, where God had planned a Bethlehem, a Calvary, a Pentecost, David had sinned, and his controversy with heaven continued until David could no longer resist the pressure brought to bear upon him. He recognized his guilt and the consequences of it in the lives of others; therefore we read: "Then David and the elders of Israel, who were clothed in sackcloth, fell upon their faces" (21:16).

I wonder if this has been your experience. Perhaps even now God has been speaking to your heart, and you have come to see as never before the sinfulness of sin. But you have seen it outmatched by the everlasting mercy of our God. He has brought all kinds of pressure to bear upon you in the area of your heart where He has planned for you a personal Calvary, a personal Pentecost, and where His blessings must be withheld until, like David, you prostrate yourself in sackcloth on your face before Him.

The pressure of the devil in a Christian's life is one thing, but the pressure of heaven is another. By the grace of God we can withstand any pressures that are brought upon us by the forces of darkness. But when we have grieved the Spirit of God, and the hand of God is upon us with pressure until we repent, that is an experience those who have passed through it will never forget. I do trust that the Lord has brought you to yield as David did.

Observe, then, the price which David paid. The experience of humiliation was to be followed by one of worship. "Then the angel of the Lord commanded Gad to say to David, that David should go up, and set up an altar unto the Lord in the threshingfloor of Ornan the Jebusite" (I Chronicles 21:18).

The place was offered by Ornan to David free, together with the oxen for sacrifice. This man must have been somewhat afraid of the display of heavenly power that was taking place. But David's answer was a firm "No." "I will verily buy it for the full price: for I will not take that which is thine for the Lord, nor offer burnt offerings without cost" (I Chronicles 21:24).

Where did all this take place? We are told in II Chronicles 3:1 that it was on Mount Moriah. Have you ever considered the significance of that mountain in the Old Testament? It was always associated with sacrifice; it was always a place where the price was paid. Up Mount Moriah Abraham took Isaac to offer him. Now we find David offering his burnt offerings there, and on that spot Solomon built the temple at such infinite cost. Hundreds of years afterwards, Satan took our blessed Lord to the pinnacle of the temple there and tried to persuade Him to make public show of His power. Always in Scripture Mount Moriah is a place where the price was paid to the uttermost.

Tell me, have you been up Mount Moriah? I trust you have been up Mount Calvary and there have received forgiveness and cleansing by the blood that was shed for you. You may have been up Mount Hermon and seen a transfigured Lord as you experience the glory of His risen life. But have you ever walked alone up Mount Moriah and there allowed the Lord Jesus to deal with that which is basic in your Christian life? There is always somebody around tempting you to take the easy way out. Satan always tries to persuade you to evade the real and deep issues in your heart. He is quite content for you to deal with the simple things, the secondary things, the trivialities. But when you get down to the basic sacrifice, he will do anything to keep you from facing that, because he knows that when you do, you will receive the inevitable outpouring of Holy Spirit power upon your crucified life.

Jesus only met King Herod once, a few hours before His crucifixion, but He had nothing to say to him. Just one word from our Lord then, and what a difference might have taken place in that man's life, but our Lord would say nothing. Herod asked Jesus many questions, but He gave that man no reply.

Only three years previously, Herod had been faced with one whom our Lord described as the greatest preacher born of women, John the Baptist. That bold servant of God had dared to intrude into Herod's personal life and tell him that he had no business to be living with Herodias, his brother's wife. We are told that when he heard John the Baptist, Herod "did many things" (Mark 6:20). I suppose he smoked a bit less, drank a bit less, and perhaps swore a bit less, but there was one thing he refused to do—give up the woman who ruined his life. That was the basic issue, and therefore Jesus had no word for him.

My friend, that may not be the issue—indeed, I trust it is not in your life—but there is always one point in each life where the spiritual battle is crucial. Have you faced it? Have you gone up Mount Moriah? Have you paid the price? Or has Satan made you feel content that you have dealt with other things, that you have given up much in your life, although you still hold tenaciously to that which you know mars your testimony and makes it impossible for the Lord to work through you in Holy Spirit authority?

You will recall that in Old Testament time the priest used a fleshhook to bring the sacrifice back under the flame so that it would keep constantly burning. That is exactly what God wants to do with us, and sometimes He has to take the fleshhook to pull us back under the flame until our lives are mere dust and ashes. That is all He wants of us, because from that platform where the self-life has truly been crushed and reduced to ashes, the Lord can then display His glory.

There is one other thing here at which we must look, the power which David received. "And David built there an altar unto the Lord, and offered burnt offerings and peace offerings, and called upon the Lord; and he answered him from heaven by fire upon the altar of burnt offering" (I Chronicles 21:26).

The Lord answered him from heaven by fire upon the altar of burnt offering—of course He did! That was heaven's immediate response to this man's utmost surrender. It still is! God always gives His Holy Spirit in fullness to them that obey Him.

"One mightier than I cometh," said John the Baptist; "he shall baptize you with the Holy Ghost and with fire" (Luke 3:16).

> O Thou who camest from above,
> The pure celestial fire impart,
> Kindle a flame of sacred love
> On the mean altar of my heart.
> *Charles Wesley*

That is the language of a man who meant business with God. That is the cry for the precious flame of God's holiness that burns out sin in the soul and burns in His life and power. May the flame of the love of God and a passion for souls constantly burn on the altar of our lives. This is something which not simply *may* happen, but *must* happen; not something which God *may* do but which He *must* do. The answer of heaven to Calvary is always Pentecost, the seal upon the transaction of an everlasting covenant in the precious blood of the Lord Jesus Christ.

Believer, this is your portion and privilege. Have you been up Mount Moriah? Have you paid the price? Then I say to you, step boldly to the throne of God in the merit of the blood of Jesus Christ your Lord, and claim your share in the inheritance of His Holy Spirit. Nothing less than that is full salvation. Nothing less than that will meet the need of the church today so that it may be able to stand against all the powers of darkness.

Perhaps I ought to add a postscript, because it seems to me that I Chronicles 21:27 is one of the most wonderful verses we could ever read.

Here is the peace which David enjoyed: "And the Lord commanded the angel; and he put up his sword again into the sheath thereof."

The sword of God's judgment is back in its sheath, hallelujah! Judgment is over; peace is now deep down in David's heart. Oh, that it might happen to you right now, that your controversy with heaven might end, that the sword of God's judgment which has been against you be put back into its sheath, and you might know His peace! Other battles to come you will have to wage in His name, but if the sword of judgment is in its sheath, you will win them. Until now, perhaps you have been losing many battles with the enemy because God's sword has been against you. What greater thing could happen than that your controversy with God should end and that you should experience the peace of God that passeth all understanding garrisoning your heart and mind through Christ Jesus.

> Peace, perfect peace, in this dark world of sin?
> The blood of Jesus whispers peace within.
> Peace, perfect peace, our future all unknown?
> Jesus we know, and He is on the throne.
> *Edward H. Bickersteth*

And David assembled all . . . unto Jerusalem. Then David the king stood up upon his feet, and said, Hear me, my brethren, and my people: As for me, I had in mine heart to build an house of rest for the ark of the covenant of the Lord. . . . But God said unto me, Thou shalt not build an house for my name, because thou hast been a man of war, and hast shed blood.

Howbeit the Lord God of Israel chose me . . . to be king over Israel. . . . And of all my sons . . . he hath chosen Solomon my son to sit upon the throne of the kingdom of the Lord over Israel. And he said unto me, Solomon thy son, he shall build my house and my courts. . . . Moreover I will establish his kingdom for ever, if he be constant to do my commandments and my judgments, as at this day.

Now therefore . . . keep and seek for all the commandments of the Lord your God: that ye may possess this good land, and leave it for an inheritance for your children after you for ever. And thou, Solomon my son, know thou the God of thy father, and serve him with a perfect heart and with a willing mind . . . but if thou forsake him, he will cast thee off for ever.

Take heed now; for the Lord hath chosen thee to build an house for the sanctuary. . . . Then David gave to Solomon his son . . . the pattern of all that he had by the spirit, of the courts of the house of the Lord. . . . All this, said David, the Lord made me understand in writing by his hand upon me, even all the works of this pattern.

And David said to Solomon his son, Be strong and of good courage, and do it: fear not, nor be dismayed: for the Lord God, even my God, will be with thee; he will not fail thee, nor forsake thee, until thou hast finished all the work for the service of the house of the Lord . . . also the princes and all the people will be wholly at thy commandment.

I CHRONICLES 28:1-21

CHAPTER 27

HANDING ON THE TORCH

(*I Chronicles 28:1-21*)

DAVID'S LIFEWORK WAS over, his years of leadership and service at an end. At the conclusion of the journey he had the opportunity of surveying his progress and asking himself how much of it had been permanent, vital, and effective. As he looked back he recognized that he had only one thing to face, his accountability before God.

That was a tremendous moment in David's life, and it will be an equally great moment in your life when it comes, as it surely will for us all, sooner or later. Only God knows just when, because our times are in His hands. One day our last sermon will have been preached, our last testimony will have been given, our last piece of service will have been rendered. But there is even now the opportunity to ask ourselves, "Has my life been worth while? Has it brought heaven any nearer? Has it made the Lord Jesus more real and more precious to others? How much of my work can stand the test of judgment before a holy God? Has any of it been gold, silver, precious stones? Or has it been only wood, hay, and stubble?"

These are solemn questions, and I think it is good to reflect upon them while there is yet time to make an adjustment in our lives and ministry, if need be, before we face the Lord. We have the advantage of being able to stand with David, as it were, upon the mountain top and look back to survey those things that made him, in spite of all his failures, a man after God's own heart.

In the charge that David gave to Solomon, I think we can see some of the deciding factors which made him what he was and which can make you and me what God wants us to be. I see in this portion of the Word, first, what I would call the blessing of a frustrated desire.

In the second part of I Chronicles 28:2 are these words: "As for me," said David, "I had in mine heart to build an house of rest for the ark of the covenant of the Lord, and for the footstool of our God, and had made ready for the building: But God said unto me, Thou shalt not build an house for my name, because thou hast been a man of war, and hast shed blood." You will recall that David's great ambition was to build the temple, but God had said "No." David's desire was frustrated; God answered his prayer in the negative and told him why: David had been a man of war and had shed blood.

What did David do in the face of a life ambition that was shattered because it was not God's will? Did he become sour? Did he resign and give up? Did he allow his frustration to turn him away from God's work? No; as a matter of fact, he gave himself the more completely to serving the Lord in His will.

In I Chronicles 22:1 David declared, "This is the house of the Lord God, and this is the altar of the burnt-offering for Israel." In other words, he found the site for the temple and purchased it at the full price (I Chronicles 21:24). The temple was to be built on the place where God had commanded him to sacrifice, where God had met him with fire from heaven that came down and consumed his offering. In that place of cleansing, forgiveness, deliverance, and power, David established the site and purchased it. He also gathered and fashioned much of the material for the temple. "In my trouble I have prepared for the house of the Lord," he said, and listed all the metals and woods that he had collected for it (I Chronicles 22:14).

At the last, he gave Solomon this charge, "Be strong and of good courage, and do it: fear not, nor be dismayed: for the Lord God, even my God, will be with thee; he will not fail thee, nor forsake thee, until thou hast finished all the work for the service of the house of the Lord" (I Chronicles 28:20).

David's ambition to build the temple is similar to the ambition that has come into the life of every genuine believer, that he might do great things for the Lord. "Expect great things from God; attempt great things for God" was William Carey's motto, and this has been the desire of everyone who has come to know Jesus Christ as his Saviour and Lord: to do something for Him to extend His kingdom.

The building of the temple in the Old Testament is but a picture of the building of the church in the New Testament. As Peter says, "Ye also, as lively [living] stones, are built up a spiritual house, an holy priesthood, to offer up spiritual sacrifices, acceptable to God by Jesus Christ" (I Peter 2:5).

I doubt whether there is a Christian but at one moment in his or her life has pictured himself as a great and successful servant of God—a missionary, a Christian leader, a Bible teacher, a powerful preacher, an evangelist much used by God—but somewhere along the line God has said "No." He says it in different ways: perhaps by putting you on a sickbed for the rest of your life, perhaps by choosing a different sphere altogether for you.

If you are living with such a frustrated desire, an ambition which God has cut right across, what have you done about it? When your great dreams of accomplishment lie shattered around you, have you allowed your appetite for the service of the Lord to turn sour, or can you truly say that you are doing your part to build the church of Jesus Christ?

I have always found in my life—and I have had to learn this again and again—that one of the hardest things is to give up some cherished ambition of my own. To die to one's own desire and to accept God's will is most cruel to the flesh. There is something in every one of us that the Bible calls self, which always wants to initiate something. But God says, "I don't want you to initiate anything. I want you to be a channel through which I am going to do everything. If I choose not to put you into the bay window of the church, as it were, to give you work in that popular place where you are in full view, and instead I send you to work in the basement where you will never be seen, how will you react?"

The simple question is, whose glory do you want, yours or God's? How do you react when you are banished from the place of publicity and put in the place of obscurity? How do you react when you are taken from the place of success and reckoned a failure? How do you react when your early dreams of doing great things for God are shattered? Do you leave the work of the Lord, or can you, like David, do your best at whatever God has given you to do, thankful that you are privileged to share in His work?

I am reminded of the words of the Apostle Paul: "I have planted, Apollos watered; but God gave the increase. So then neither is he that planteth any thing, neither he that watereth; but God that giveth the increase. Now he that planteth and he that watereth are one: and every man shall receive his own reward according to his own labour. For we are labourers together with God: ye are God's husbandry, ye are God's building" (I Corinthians 3:6-9).

Have you accepted the blessing of a frustrated desire? So many people, I am afraid, never do anything to help to build the spiritual temple of the Lord. In fact, they love to pull it apart and throw away the stones.

Sometimes they even hide their own particular little talent in case the great Builder, the Lord Jesus, should lay hold of it and use it.

Though you may not reap, yet you can sow. Though you may not water, you can plant. We can take some of the stones and begin to knock off the rough edges, not only in the lives of others, but in our own. We can clear the ground for the temple, or we can fight the battles and bring in the precious material, for without these things the job will never be completed.

Are you really doing your part for the Lord in His church today? Remember what David said, "In my trouble I have prepared for the house of the Lord" (I Chronicles 22:14). I like that! "In my trouble. . . ." There must have been much opposition to make him feel it wasn't worth while and many setbacks to make him feel he couldn't go on any longer, but he didn't allow trouble to depress him and make him quit.

Am I speaking to one of God's troubled servants today? Do not let that trouble turn you sour, my dear Christian, or let His "No" make you give up. Remind your heart of the great trouble through which the Lord Jesus went to lay the foundation of His church. "Be strong and of good courage, and do it: fear not, nor be dismayed" (I Chronicles 28:20). Learn to enter into the blessing of a frustrated desire, and gladly accept your part in God's plan.

Let me show you some of the riches that come to the life which accepts disappointment with full dedication—no complaining, no withdrawal, no souring of disposition.

What reward did David reap for his dedication to God's will, for his acceptance of God's denial? "All this," he said as he was describing the wealth of gold and silver designated for particular uses in the temple, "the Lord made me understand in writing by his hand upon me, even all the works of this pattern" (I Chronicles 28:19).

The temple of God was to be built in minute detail according to the pattern in the mind and will of God. David received these details from the Lord, who wrote them on his heart by His own hand. In other words, the reward of David's full dedication was a personal revelation from heaven. It wasn't secondhand, but something David received from the Lord Himself, the plan of God's temple which one day He would fill with His glory.

When we learn with David that difficult lesson of accepting gladly before God His refusal of some great ambition, and taking our share in the great task of evangelism and testimony in the building of His church, do you know what Jesus Christ does? I'll tell you the secret—

perhaps some of you know already! To such a life He will begin to unfold His plan for the temple of your body which He desires to fill with His glory on that great day when you are presented in the measure of the stature of the fullness of Christ before God's throne.

David became a man who understood the mind of God, and it was accomplished in writing by the hand of God upon him. Does God do that today? Yes, He does. Every detail of His will for each individual life and for His church is in His Book. There is nothing you need to know apart from what is in the Bible. He has written it, but sometimes we fail to understand it, because spiritual things are not naturally understood.

A man may be interested in parts of his Bible; he likes the third chapter of John's Gospel, and First John, and some of the epistles of Paul, and sections of the Gospels, but he is not quite sure what else he can believe. The Word doesn't sink into his life; it doesn't grip him. The Bible is a book which he studies to get his degree, of course; he knows something of the Scriptures along with a bit of theology and doctrine. I have seen men go through right into old age without ever showing evidence of the pressure of the hand of God upon their lives. God writes His Word upon our hearts by the pressure of His hand upon the life; then His child begins to understand God's Word written in the Book.

At times the pressure is so heavy we are almost crushed by it. I find in my Christian experience that there is no pen in all the world that cuts and burns like the one God uses when He begins to write His Word upon my heart. It cuts deep into my soul as He tears away all my own selfish ambitions and writes there in the fleshy table of my heart, "This is My will for you, My child." That is what God wants to do with each of us today.

How does God write upon the heart? There is a closing word in this book summing up the reign of David: "With all his reign and his might, and the times that went over him" (I Chronicles 29:30). I want to stop there because we have our clue. How does God write His Word upon our hearts, and make His Book live in our lives? How does He use the steel to cut into the self-will of a man's heart and make him tender and yielded to whatever God's will may be? How does He deal with the stony heart, breaking it of stubbornness and selfishness?

With David, it was "the times that went over him." What times? He was a shepherd, a soldier, an outlaw, a king, a fugitive, a sinner, a saint, a poet. As he said, "All thy waves and thy billows are gone over me" (Psalm 42:7), and "My times are in thy hand" (Psalm 31:15). His experiences were the writing of God upon his life, making him into a man after God's own heart. Because they were God's times, the waves never overwhelmed him, the hurricane never uprooted him, the floods never drowned him. They were God's times, and by them He wrote upon David's soul all the pattern of His will and purpose.

That was heaven's reward for the acceptance of a frustrated desire; that was the benefit of it in David's life. It wasn't always easy to take, but it was what the Lord desired to do.

I find that when I begin to talk like this (or when other people do), the reaction of many is, "We're too busy to bother. We must produce results, you know. We must get going quickly!" In these times people don't dwell much at depth with God, but that is what the Lord desires us to do by the pressure of His hand upon us as the waves of time go over us.

The people of Issachar were "men that had understanding of the times" (I Chronicles 12:32). That is a good thing to have. I'm glad to have an understanding of what is going on in the world, for I know the Lord is on the throne, no matter what the situation is. But above all I want an understanding of God's times in my life: times of bereavement, times of temptation, times when His billows go over me until I feel I can take it no more. I want to be able to say, "Lord Jesus, my times are in Thy hand," when I suffer pain, affliction, loneliness, misunderstanding, persecution, joy, blessing, victory. They are all God's times; let them all come because they come from His hand. But the waves will never overwhelm, the hurricane will never uproot, the floods will never drown, because my times are in His hand.

When I accept before the throne of God the blessing of a frustrated ambition, when I give up my egotistic desire to be the big shot, when I allow the Lord to take the knife and cut His will deep into the fleshy table of my heart, when I am prepared to let Him break down my stubbornness, pride and intolerance—it is only then I begin to have an understanding of His times.

What sort of times are you going through just now? Most of us like to look back on times that were wonderful and anticipate those that are going to be even better, but we don't do much about the times that we are in right now. This is God's time in your life, and what is happening? Is it pain or affliction? Is it something that makes you cry out, "Oh, if it were only tomorrow! If I could only get through this next week! If only I could start over ten years ago! If only I could move out of here and go there!"

Why, bless your heart, this is God's time! What is He teaching you now? Mother, father, brokenhearted friend, even if you are living in the midst of frustration, it is God's time. May He give you an understanding of it!

Let us see, finally, the benediction of a final departure. As David charged his son Solomon and handed on to him the torch he said, "Know thou the God of thy father" (I Chronicles 28:9). He did not say, "Solomon, know the God of Abraham, Isaac, and Jacob."

One day you also will have to say goodbye to your children for the last time until you meet in heaven. I wonder if you will be able to say to them when that day comes, "Son, daughter, I want above everything else that you may know the God of your father, my God."

Yes, that mattered most to David. In the midst of all the storm and turmoil he had learned to know God, to understand His times and His way with him. What a benediction it was to look back! I love to think about how David got to know God so intimately, as reflected in these words: "Then David gave to Solomon his son the pattern of the porch, and of the houses thereof, and of the treasuries thereof, and of the upper chambers thereof, and of the inner parlours thereof, and of the place of the mercy seat" (I Chronicles 28:11).

It may be only a little while until you will pass on the torch to someone else. Can you speak to your dear ones and say to them, "I can tell you all about the pattern of the porch of God's house; I can tell you the way to get in: 'knock, and it shall be opened unto you'" (Matthew 7:7). Have you preached a Lord Jesus who is completely adequate for an empty life, telling your friends that all the fitness they need to qualify for heaven is to cry to God for mercy? Do you know the pattern of the porch of the temple, and have you made the way clear to another?

What can you tell about "the houses thereof," the places of joy in which you have lived from time to time in the presence of the Lord? There are beautiful houses of His presence and His comfort, mansions that we may inhabit and enjoy even this side of heaven.

"And of the treasuries thereof"—have you something to pass on about the riches of God's way with you? The all-sufficiency of His grace, the fullness of His Holy Spirit in your heart and life, the great stores of blessing He bestows every day to fill you up with Himself—do you know anything about these treasuries?

"And of the upper chambers"—have you been there? Have you walked upstairs in the temple of the Lord? In your soul have you come so near to heaven you felt as if you could step right in? Have you been consciously near to God in the upper chamber?

Then there are "the inner parlours" of fellowship and communion, the secret joys which none but His loved ones know. And "the place of the mercy seat," inside the veil and above the ark, under the wings of the cherubim, the place where God met with Moses. Does He meet with you there every day, at the mercy seat in your own soul?

What do we have to pass on? Is there anything worth while, or have we just spent our lives in busyness and activity as Christian workers? In the days that remain to us, let us do our part in the building of His house in our lives and characters, that together we may enhance the temple of the Lord, which is His body, the church.